'Mirror, Mirror On The Wall ...'

My Journey Of Grace!

An autobiography by

Victor Coert

Dedicated to
Julie
&
our sons Calum, Caleb and Joel

'Mirror, Mirror On The Wall ...'

My Journey Of Grace!

An autobiography by

Victor Coert

ISBN: 978-1-913232-17-7

Victor Coert
42 Mullaghbrack Road
Hamiltonsbawn, Co. Armagh
BT60 1JT
Northern Ireland, UK
Vichere215@aol.com

Edition 2020

Printed in Poland

Table of contents

Forward

But God demonstrates his own love for us in this:
while we were still sinners, Christ died for us."
Romans (5 vs 8)

But God...

"When hard times come, be a student, not a victim" (Jim Graham). This had a tremendous effect on me when I first heard it and still challenges me to this day.

It is so easy in a fallen and sinful world to play the self-centred and miserable role of a victim, when God would have us be His students learning to react faithfully in the light of His sovereign will and gracious providential care.

Behind a smiling face there is often a tale of hurt, pain, disappointment and unanswered questions. We can pretend the pain of the past is not really a problem at all, as we present a stiff upper lip attitude and a 'grin and bear it' posture to those around us. Furthermore, we can play the blame game, so evident in the Garden of Eden where bitterness against people and even God becomes our normal reaction. On the other hand — as Jim Graham points out, we can be a student of God's gracious ways in hard times.

In *Mirror, Mirror on the Wall...*, we have the story of a man who grew up in difficult and often painful times. While Victor often struggled to see the hand of God at the time in those situations, it is clear that now, looking back, he sees that it was all a journey of grace. He is really describing the sovereignty of God worked out in his life on many an occasion. A constant refrain in the book, in the midst of sin and depravity, is — *But God ...!*

He describes how God provided for his and his family's needs in South Africa. For example, the often miraculous provision of money for education, protection from a descent into political violence, knife gangs and even depression, the kindness of so many people, the call of God into ministry situations, the provision of jobs at key moments and God's great gift of Julie, Calum, Caleb and Joel. Ultimately, we see the provision of God in salvation to Victor and his family: *But God ...!*

Life is often described as the 'groaning' and the 'glory' — **Groaning**, because we live in a suffering world that is full of evil things like apartheid, murder, injustice, violence, hatred, poverty, death, grief, addictions, depression, doubt.... Victor honestly reveals the ups and downs of his faith in the midst of so much brokenness. *But God ...!*

Glory, because we live under the grace of God and receive more than we could ever deserve. Victor describes how God intervened so many times in his life and revealed that He is real and also a God of grace, sovereign power and providential care. *But God ...!*

So easily Victor could have become a victim in the hard times he faced. However, we see him become a student of God and His gracious will. He honestly describes his struggles and sin — the chip on his shoulder, his rebel heart, his arrogance and pride, his anger, his struggle with the Church, his complex character, his wrestling with faith in the midst of grief and guilt. *But God ...!*

The journey of grace is not over for Victor nor for us. We all must continue to be students in God's school, saved by His grace, learning among His people ... for the Church of Jesus Christ continues to be fed by His Word and led by His Spirit.

I commend this book by my friend to you and may we all be encouraged to look in the mirror and see Jesus and His grace.

Rev Alastair McNeely
Minister and Pastor
Richhill Presbyterian Church
Northern Ireland

What counts in life is not
the mere fact that we have lived.
It is what difference we have made
to the lives of others that will determine
the significance of the life we lead!

(Nelson Mandela)

Introduction

*And no creature is hidden from His sight, but all are naked and
exposed to the eyes of Him to whom we must give account.*

(*Hebrews 4 vs 13*)

The Scriptures inform us that it is destined for a human
being to live once and thereafter face the judgement of
God (Hebrews 9 vs 27) — one life given to make an impact
upon one's world and thereafter a reckoning of sorts. It
seems that at some stage it is appointed for humanity to
find themselves at a point of judgement — having to give
account of two things; firstly, as to whether or not they have
rejected God's saving initiative to the world in the person of
Jesus and secondly, to account for how they lived in the years
allocated. One life, one opportunity to create impact — one
opportunity to prepare for eternity! Whichever religious or
non-religious belief system or philosophical thought you
may personally align yourself with at this stage in your life,
it is evident that there seems to be a generic understanding
that judgement and accountability is very much part of our
human destiny — an understanding perpetuated in particular by those in Ancient Greece. It's just the form and nature of

this event that scholars and academics seem to bicker over. Holding one another to account, seems to be part of our human nature; as kids we are accountable to our parents, as pupils we are accountable to our teachers, as spouses we are accountable to each other, as employees we are accountable to our employers and so on. We live daily within a hierarchy of sorts, for by our very nature it seems that we are not masters, however hard we try, of our own destiny!

What a sobering thought! The idea of being accountable to a divinity of sorts for one's actions over a lifetime, is pretty scary. When contemplating this, one is either driven to utter fear or to the other extreme of welcoming death, so as to move beyond a world filled with hurt to one of eternal bliss! I guess for most of us, we find ourselves somewhere in between! However, it is the possibility of judgement that we dread most — the fear that shameful acts and experiences over the years will be exposed — not only to the Judge but also to others we know! We dread the exposure of things we have said or done ... people we have hurt, comments we made and could not retract, thoughts we entertain about someone other than our spouse, the many times we cheated on our taxes or failed to declare something on a form which we know would lead to personal financial advantage! I'm sure that if you and I had a chance, we would do things very differently. The reality is that we cannot! It's done and we can only but deal with the consequences of those experiences — the apologies, the rebuilding of relationships broken during these experiences and so on. However, the toughest repair jobs are the moments of self-reflection and personal honesty — those moments when we confront ourselves in the mirror, when we see glaring eyes looking back at us, eyes which look beyond the cornea, iris and every blood vessel within one's eye-ball — the eyes which reach into the very core of who we are and sees the entity within! It seems that this inner self lies well beyond our physical make-up, a 'being' which we don't often like to encounter for by its very nature it brings out the worst in us and seems to glory in wrong. It is a presence we fight every day, that which the Bible chooses to call 'sinner'!

Like you, I've seen it in myself — the worst of me! I have often surprised myself at how intensely overpowering sin can be. Sometimes the phrase 'to err is human' sounds more like a 'get out of jail free' card than anything else — a sort of excuse for letting me get away with wrong acts I deliberately implement out of self-will and pure negative decision-making. Yes, I know — I see sin in others too and some so caught up in their own self-righteousness that it becomes sickening. However, I have long learnt that I am responsible to God for my own actions, for own wrong-doings, for my own sin! So like you, I look into the mirror of my own heart and many times I don't like what I see. During those times of personal reflection and identification of negative attitudes and behaviour, shame and guilt attacks my being like a sharp double-edged sword intent on one thing only — a reminder of failure! Yet, it is during moments like these that two words flood my conscience like a tsunami, like an anti-biotic flooding through my spiritual bloodstream to bring healing to a sinful heart, those two words of hope, life and expectation ... 'but God'!

Then there's the other side of me — the side ignited and alive, energised and powered by God's Spirit, the 'good' side as it were, the part of me which pursues global mission, which rejoices in fellowship, that desires for people to come to know Jesus — that part of me which feels content with who I am and so on. I encounter that entity time and again — driving to school, working hard to provide a pupil a means of study at a renowned university, the part that buys a pupil lunch in the canteen simply as an act of kindness, the part which looks at family and cries out to God in thankfulness for His goodness to us, the part of me that feels content with life, the internal blueprint which reflects the heart of God ... a life of thankfulness for the salvation which brings a changed life!

Contentment, spiritually and physically ... what does that really look like? Is it the realisation that one is happy with that which has been pursued through life — money, work, goals, family, house, faith, spouse, career? Why is it that even though we realise potential within ourselves, we remain focused on the pursuit of trying to be better tomorrow than we are today? Is this the nature of God's grace within us or simply a generic hunger to constantly pursue life goals? Why are we constantly dreaming of the 'what ifs', the possibilities, the opportunities, the next best thing, the next challenge? Are we ever content or is our pursuit of contentment directly linked to who we are as individuals? Does our desire to achieve — personally and professionally stem from the difficulties of life, the 'hard knocks' taken along the journey of life; the fear of living the mundane, the fear of struggling the way our parents did? Is contentment therefore a state of mind which is unachievable — a dream or an utopia of sorts?

Surely my contentment should be in God, should it not? It is often suggested from the pulpit that faith in Jesus Christ leads to inner contentment and that He has this ability to redefine who we are as people. It is suggested that Jesus has the capacity to make us look at life from a very different angle — allowing us insight therefore into God's view of contentment — bringing us reassurance that nothing we do or pursue or the accolades we collect along life's journey can ever compare to the reality of God's love for us — expressed in the historical event of the sacrifice of His Son two thousand years ago. Therefore, if God cannot love us more than

He already does — if nothing I do in this life can ever earn his love — why am I therefore constantly searching for contentment? Is it a spiritual deficiency, a character flaw, a 'disturbance in the force' or simply a lack of true spiritual faith? Is it that I am somehow an individual so lacking in positive self-image that my life's journey is not so much about finding contentment, but more the pursuit of coming to terms with who I really am as a human being — that I am in reality lacking in self-worth, weak, in need, troubled, flawed, scarred by life and ultimately sinful?

The mirror has this capacity to never lie! It is evident that when we evaluate who we are as individuals, we look into the mirror which God Himself holds before us. We cannot escape what we see within it — for this mirror reflects who we are every single moment of our lives. It tells us when we are at our worst and also at our very best and it will remain with us till God calls 'time' on our earthly life.

This book is not a 'spiritual' or 'religious' piece of work … it is just a life story of which Jesus is very much a part. As you read it, you will discover that at various stages He plays a big part and at other times He doesn't feature at all. The reality however is that He is there, like a piece of cotton holding the threads of my life together! You cannot separate me the individual, from His influence on my life over the years, so when I talk about Jesus in this book I'm not trying to be spiritual or religious, for those of you who know me well will testify that the word 'rebel' seems to be more apt to describe my personality, as opposed to 'religious'. Many of you know that I'm not into wearing a suit on a Sunday and given the opportunity, I would prefer to play football on any given Sunday rather than 'observe the Sabbath' — if my knees allowed me that is! I love the Church (God's people), but I have had my fill with church politics and legalism over the years. Therefore, if you encounter Jesus within these pages, I am simply referring to my relationship with Him and not church as such!

I was advised many years ago to tell my life's story. Initially I pondered the idea but never really considered it to be something I could do. If I were to put pen to paper, what would I say? How honest could I be? Would I say things which would offend those I love? Would I embarrass myself with honesty or have people sneer when they realise my struggles over the years? What would their reaction be? Would some suggest that this exercise would simply be arrogance on my part, that is, expecting others to learn from mistakes I made over the years? Then there were self-doubts! How could I honestly expect others to be interested in my life's journey and would they really care?

I started experimenting with simple 'diary writing' after dad's death, as a means of dealing with my anger — but more about that later! The motivation for this 'book' arrived while listening to Amy Grant (contemporary Christian singer) singing 'In a little while', one morning while driving to school. It suddenly dawned on me that life is fleeting and that all experiences had in my life to that point were simply part of a very small journey called 'life on earth,' for I am of the opinion that our ultimate destination as people is not the grave — but eternity thereafter! Compared to eternity, seventy odd years (if we are blessed to live that long) is but a movement of an eye-lid — quick, fleeting, fast!

When discussing the idea of this book with Andy van der Byl — one of my closest friends, he suggested that ...

The wild 'skollie' (boy gangster), ex-revolutionary with his raw faith and calling, who seems to stuff-up in equal proportion to doing something good for the Kingdom, who turned out into a school headmaster of a school in a first-world country – now there is a story that needs to be told in person!

At this point in my life I am a couple of months shy, of my fifty-second birthday. I am experiencing a degree of contentment — I have a lovely home and a family who loves me. I have a good job and coach football to a group of players which include my youngest son. I've given up on church politics but am relatively at peace spiritually speaking ... and yet daily I battle against my personal demons! However, I have long stopped worrying about what others think about me and I have tried to live my life before God as best as I can, knowing however that His love for me is not determined by what I do or my 'performance' as a Jesus-follower ... for His love for me was expressed years before I stepped onto the stage of history.

My life is one of grace. I view it as such! Every experience you will read in these pages is grounded in God's grace to me. Those of you who know me well are aware that I've blown it time and again ... but often I have blown it because of decisions made — not because I'm part of this cosmic race of people who have a design flaw. I have made mistakes as such, I know that — but the majority of the time I have created difficulties for myself because of my own willingness to do so. Bottom line is that I have sinned and wilfully so! Although re-building the damage with others remains a long process, I ultimately live my life in the eyes of my Father — for it is before Him alone to whom I must account for my life. I have never been interested in money, probably because for most of my life I never had any. It is a means to an end — although others pursue it as if it truly is the pot of gold at the end of the rainbow. Money doesn't interest me, but character does. In my pursuit of developing my own character, I have come to realise that life generally is pretty messy — sometimes I think Christians don't seem to understand that. However, life is also fleeting. Soon and 'in a little while' — I will be called to eternity but until then, I will take the opportunity to create change in my own life and in that of a messy world!

This document is dedicated firstly to my wife ... who chose me as her life's partner and has demonstrated her love to me through the good and difficulties in our marriage. I honour her for her patience and her wisdom as well as allowing and supporting me in the pursuit of my professional goals. Secondly to our sons Calum, Caleb and Joel. Already between them — they display more character in their young lives than their old man! This piece of writing is for them — in the hope that they avoid life's pitfalls their old man regularly stumbled into. It is my hope too that they understand their roots in South Africa and that they take pride in the family name which they bear, for they have a very rich family history. Finally, I hope that they become individuals who love Jesus, young men who develop Godly characters — better individuals than their father ... whose lives are dictated not by others, but by their heavenly Father. Like me, they live this life in preparation for eternity and it is my hope that I role-model and reflect to them but a small part of the character of God. It is my hope that they learn from me that life is all about loving and caring for people — not goals, nor money, not prestige, nor fancy homes and cars, not church programmes, not careers ... but loving people, for this is what Jesus exemplified for us when He walked our planet.

So here's to you my sons ... and many other sons and daughters like you!

Chapter 1: And so it begins — life!

Take my life and let it be consecrated, Lord, to thee.
Take my moments and my days; let them flow in endless praise,

(Francis Ridley Havergal; 1836)

How far back does one's memory go? Sometimes when thinking about one's early life there are flashes of memory, certain experiences that your mind either joyously recalls or hurriedly banks for later recall — events so destructive that your mind stores it for later use, to be re-looked at a different time or a different setting — therapy maybe! Early child-hood memories are like flashbacks, the anamnesis of bits and pieces. I'm sure that there must be some scientific or neurological wording or terminology for this recall of memory, but seeing that I'm not a scientist ... I'm not going to bore myself or you with researching this phenomenon, because I'm sure that you get the gist of what I'm talking about!

My grandparents (on mum's side) died when I was about four or so. To be honest, I can't quite remember them but I do have memory glimpses of the funeral, awaiting the arrival of the hearse and so on. My grandfather — on mum's side was a dentist, best known by his nickname 'Tanna' — meaning 'teeth'. The sad reality was that due to being black (or 'Coloured' in South African terms), government legislation dictated that he could not hold a dental license to officially practise dentistry. More about South African politics later. Furthermore, all I know about them is what I've seen on photographs. It was evident though from the photographs — and particularly mum's twenty first birthday photographs that they lived well. Their home was one of large rooms, very large bedrooms and an open-plan kitchen which contained an original Aga cooker — the one you actually make a fire in. At the end of my grandfather's life, no one had any idea what he had done with his money, let alone the large house my mum lived in. Rumour had it that his love for gambling had a financial consequence, which included losing his home. Others suggested that a relative stole the family home from him but sadly, nothing concrete is known. The stark reality was that by the time mum and dad were married, the family fortune was no more!

My earliest memory of childhood in Kensington — Cape Town that is, not the posh Kensington in London, was dad carrying my sister and I to the child-minders at the break of dawn. As mum and dad never owned a car till years later, we were hurried off to the child-minder in order for dad to make the early morning commute to work via public transport, while mum had but a few hundred yards to walk to the local factory in which she was employed as a machinist. Sharon and I had a child-minder called Mrs Lantry. She reminded me of Clint Eastwood's character in Heartbreak Ridge — they don't make sergeant majors like that no more! However, the fun memories of child-minders and nursery school was a far cry from the early childhood memories, which are painful to think about and include choking on a fish bone as a toddler, having my grandfather throw his cane at my cousin Ian while we were little, eating pudding at nursery school which even a dog would refuse — mundane stuff like that. However, there are a few difficult memories about early life which haunt me still — images I cannot get out of my mind — images that harm, images that shape character!

Mum and dad did the best they could in their first years of being married. They worked hard to provide a roof over my head — even if this roof was a tiny single-car garage! We lived in a car garage for the first six years of my life. Small, cramped — but home! Mr and Mrs Parents were kind people — allowing mum and dad to rent their garage and 'servants' annex as living accommodation for us — thereby becoming our home! Other children my age lived in houses — I lived in a single car garage! Mr Parents was an entrepreneur and he ran two little businesses from his premises. Firstly, he had a huge workshop from which he repaired and re-covered sofas and secondly, he bred racing pigeons. A workshop and pigeons were major attractions to one of life's most hated creatures — rats! The cages filled with pigeons were on our tinned garage roof! Many a night I awoke listening to the flutter and squeals of these birds, the sounds of scratching claws on the tin roof — sounds which told me that the rats were looking to feed! Often I looked forward with anticipation to the silence which meant an end to the ordeal and a few less pigeons in the morning. To this day I hate rats! I have no problem dealing with mice — but rats bring back bitter memories!

Six months before dad's passing, I raised a very difficult childhood memory with him! I explained to him that I often had visions of an incident in my childhood, where dad and I were standing awaiting public transport and where suddenly I was in danger — afraid and fearful. I explained to him that in my 'vision' he held me tightly while I cried, but that was it — I couldn't remember any more than that. That morning on the 'stoep' (porch) my father looked at me with an expression I very rarely encountered. His voice was soft as he inquired as to how I remembered that?' I told him that I had no memory of whatever happened but that I had these regular flashes which ever so often popped around in my mind! Dad went on to explain that one evening, after spending time in the 'flats' (a Capetonian word for apartment blocks generally inhabited by 'Coloured folk') with my grandparents and after being involved in a fight that afternoon, dad was confronted by the fellas of the rival gang while on his way to the bus depot — while carrying me in his arms. Knives were traded — not in a bartering type of way as such. Soon blood was shed, just before dad jumped onto the awaiting bus which brought safety for both of us! Memories — they hide away and ever-so-often they remind us of days gone by — like flashes of light in a dark world! They bide their time waiting patiently for many a year but pierce our thoughts at the most inappropriate of times, like tiny pieces of broken glass under one's finger nails, they have but one purpose — pain!

Another painful childhood memory concerns my sister Sharon. Many a night I held her as she cried herself to sleep. I stated earlier that our little garage became our home. However, due to schooling age, mum and dad shipped-off my sister and I to live with my Aunt Francis and Uncle Andrew — a woman whom I still regard as my second mum! It was here where I was to learn the importance of certain things in life. Aunty Frances loved us very much — I knew that but that did not mean she was soft on us. Chores and discipline were implemented when and where required. Schoolwork and cleaning tasks came first! Don't even think about going to play outside before your homework and chores were complete — your backside will know about it later! It was here I learnt how to 'earn my keep' and although I hated it at the time, there were major life-skills I learnt to develop during my time with my aunt and uncle.

It was the late-seventies and my aunt was lucky enough to have a television set. While evening television was now a highlight for the few in our community, my sister Sharon and I however, were sent to bed at eight each evening during the school week. It was at this time that often I cuddled my sister to sleep as she sobbed away, missing mum and dad. This was not ideal, was it? Children at this age are supposed to experience the safety and security provided by their parents, correct? A three-year old is to have her mum and dad to cuddle, not her six-year old brother but this was us, brother and sister, being there for one another ... while the tears of separation from parents told the story of a messy life! My job as a six-year old was to look after my sister, to parent her, to be there for her. *No time for feeling sorry for yourself. Be tough Vic. Build barriers. Be resilient! Life is painful. Deal with it!*

It was under my aunt's tutorage I learnt the basics about life — chores, study, respect, love! Aunty Francis took no nonsense from me — but it was clear that she loved me ... and I her! It was also in her home where I displayed the worst of my character. I discovered something at school called 'money' and it was evident that I had none. Stealing became my hobby as a six-year old — steal things, sell it and money would be available. I stole and sold a necklace belonging to my cousin and used the proceeds to purchase a packet of cigarettes, which my friend Gary and I inhaled away over a few days ... 'becoming a man', rites of passage and all that, at seven years of age! Of course, it was only a matter a time before I was caught out. A simple phone call from school to inquire about those 'value for money necklaces Victor was selling' soon put a stop to my trade, as well as my three-week smoking addiction! Not only did I face the wrath of my Aunt Frances but things got a lot worse when mum and dad visited that Friday night to collect us for the weekend. Due to possible embarrassment, or sheer frustration that she was not in a position to truly mother us ... my mum was outraged at my behaviour. After a severe telling-off, discipline was implemented in the form of a hot stove! Mum was to teach me not to steal again, by placing my hands on the cooker! The cooker was to become a teaching tool, a permanent reminder that one should not steal — but thanks to the physical intervention and rescue by my gracious aunt, nearly-burnt hands gave way to a severe beating. I was seven years old! Already I developed a built-in mechanism for survival — steal if you must and do what you must, for life is all about survival! Memories — like the light of an on-coming train in a dark tunnel ... painful!

While living in Silvertown at Aunty Francis' house, I started attending Norma Road Primary School. It was possibly the best primary school in the Athlone area! Mr Cloete was our school principal, a lovely gentleman who truly loved teaching. It was in this institution where I realised that I was 'a little bright', as I ended up being placed first in my class five years in succession. I loved school — it was my second home and the staff were amazing. Bottom line — the staff cared about us and we knew that! I'm sure they worked on a tight budget, but the staff truly gave us a well-rounded and balanced education. It was at this school however, where my desire and hunger for living life to the full, was ignited!

My best friend, who was also my neighbour in Silvertown, was Gary Scholtz. We got on very well and we were always together. In Primary 6, we developed a huge crush for Lushane Abrahams, but unlike Gary, my crush further developed into 'feelings' ... my first experience therefore of the 'love emotion'. My emotions for Lushane were so strong that I ended-up in an after-school fight to decide as to who would date her, for I was not the only suitor. Needless to say, I lost the fight and therefore had to adhere to the protocol of the other guy winning the lady's hand! However, this 'love-emotion' would raise its head again many more times in the future.

School was fun, but in every class and on every playground there is always a 'Mr X' ... let's call him such — individuals who 'lord it over' us normal folks ... the pupil displaying bullying behaviour! For Gary and I, our Mr X arrived in the form of the class jock, who was sporty and most of the times, brash! He became the focus of our thoughts each morning we arrived in school. Gary and I often had our arms punched first thing in the morning on a daily basis, as a show of his dominance over us! No such thing as 'anti-bullying' or 'pastoral care' back then. Life was about taking the bullying behaviour and getting on with it! Gary and I would do all we could to avoid the morning beatings, but it was simply an inevitability of our school day. Irrespective of what we did to avoid seeing him in the morning, we knew the punches would come at some stage during the school day! *Pupils displaying bullying behaviour ... they don't realise the mental scars they leave!*

Norma Road also provided us with various extra-curricular activities. I was involved in Speech and Drama and really enjoyed it. Mr Sampson was our drama teacher and he ignited within me the desire for the arts. Soon I was getting lead roles in school musicals alongside a classmate called Jeremy Hendricks. Auditioning for my first lead role, Jeremy beat me to it. I got to play a black southern slave and had to speak in a southern American accent. For the life of me I cannot remember what that darn musical was called but Jeremy and I would soon become rivals in a good way ... not just jostling for lead roles in future musicals but more importantly jostling for first place academically! I'm pleased to say that he won most of the lead roles, but I always seemed to beat him with regard to academics. In my final year at Norma Road, I auditioned for the lead in 'Oliver', alongside Jeremy. It was my last year of primary school and I longed to get the lead just once. I had my fair share of eisteddfods and public speaking and excelled in those, but a lead role in my final primary year would be awesome. My voice was starting to break as it were and I knew that getting it was therefore a long-shot. However, I landed the role! Mrs Cloete, the principal's wife and the staff member who looked after the school musicals, decided that Edward Harn, a fellow pupil, would sing most of the songs sung by 'Oliver', but she insisted that I sing 'Where is Love'. I gave it my very best for the three performing nights and for each of those nights I encountered that which is called a standing ovation! Months prior, Mrs Cloete suggested that because I was achieving in Speech and Drama, I should attempt ballet — to improve my performing skills! I tried it for a week but got so much stick from the likes of Gary that I never returned! The highlight of my year however, was attending and participating in Mr Sampson's wedding. He entrusted me with the reading of a poem and I therefore got to spend the weekend with the principal and his family, as they too received an invitation. I also enjoyed playing various codes of sport which included football, table-tennis and so on. I excelled however in school rugby, but more about that later! Speed was not my thing and I can hear some of you agreeing with me right now but I often stood in awe of my peers who had the ability to run and compete in the sprints. Due to my love for athletics, I would soon meet someone who truly excelled on the track and Jo-Ann Woolf was a joy to watch!

Jo-Ann was the daughter of my History teacher Mr Woolf — a teaching practitioner I would come to respect, alongside my new principal called Mr Slingers! On a school tour to the Eastern Cape one year, I had the opportunity to meet Jo-

Ann — who was a pupil at Silverlea Primary, one of the finest schools in the area. Having met Jo-Ann, we initially kept in touch, saying 'hello' to each other whenever we bumped into one another. Jo-Ann and I became friends — more so because I visited her parents who were extremely good to me. We started writing to one another in our teens but remained friends — nothing more! Many times I would arrive at their family home and although on reflection I'm sure I was a major inconvenience ... I never felt as such. Although my History teacher, Mr Woolf would later become a lot more than that after a domestic incident. Mum woke me very late one Wednesday night, to inform me that dad had not arrived home. She was worried and I ended up sitting with mum until dawn, awaiting dad's return. Eventually dad arrived home with some friends — after a night in jail! As it was after nine in the morning already, mum encouraged me to get to school — a forty-five- minute walk from Greenhaven to Silvertown. I arrived to school in the middle of Mr Woolf's History class. When asked why I was late, I refused to say anything. Mr Woolf continued to enquire as to where I had been. I swore at him, ran out of class and headed for the nearest exit I could find, tears streaming down my face. Alongside the principal, Mr Woolf eventually found me after a short search. I told him what happened at home and due to the fact that he resided a half-hour walk from where I lived, he invited me to visit him and his family whenever I desired. He became a father-figure to me! I owe much to him and thank God for their goodness as a family, shown to me over the years! Never underestimate the role of an effective teacher in the life of a young person!

'I want to be a pilot' I shouted in Mrs Naidoo's Primary 3 classroom one year. There was no doubt in my mind that I would be anything else. Of course, it would be simple — all I had to do was finish school and then train to be a pilot! The idea of combat and shooting down other pilots was a little boy's dream — well, at least that's how one thought in Primary 3. How does one know what life is going to throw at you in the years that lay ahead? It was soon hereafter that the lights about being a pilot would go out for good, for I lived in South Africa and a career in aviation was a profession for Whites only — separate schools, separate beaches, separate train carriages, whites, blacks, anger, boycotts, riots, violence, prisoner named 'Mandela', 'gutter education', learning Afrikaans in schools, ... Apartheid! Welcome to my world! The reality then occurred to me in Mrs Naidoo's class — I had never seen a coloured or black pilot. Those sort of professions were reserved for Whites! There was no way on this earth that I would become a pilot while the National Party governed South Africa. *Change of plan Vic! Think again! What other career prospects did you have in mind? You will never be a pilot — you have a different skin colour! Welcome to your reality!*

Getting back to domestic matters, I would have loved a normal childhood in those early years ... with mum, dad and sisters. It would have been lovely too to maybe even have a very small house. Only seeing mum and dad on the weekends and constantly having to be strong for Sharon's sake, I developed coping mechanisms, which I should only have learnt much later on in life. I learnt to cope with mum and dad saying 'good bye' each Sunday evening and then having to pretend to Sharon that all is well. I started to 'man-up', build barriers, develop walls, incorporate protection mechanisms as part and parcel of my character development. *Be strong for your sister! Do not let her see you cry! Be a man! Cope!*

At age seven, I encountered something within me that has become a character trait to this very day. I discovered that I had a rebellious nature and thanks to the South African police at the time, it raised its head in 1976. It was student protests and Gary and I discovered that if we made hand-held catapults, we could shoot at police vans as they drove by. It was our 'mini-protest' against the 'system'. We carried those 'ketties' everywhere and we became quite accurate at hitting our targets! Later that year our family hit the jackpot ... mum and dad got us a new home in a different part of Cape Town. We now moved from a garage, to a double garage! This garage had a small building attached to it and once the walls were broken through, it was small, but homely, allowing us a small living room, small kitchen and a bathroom. Yes, we lived in someone else's garage, again! That garage at Aunty Dinah's, was to be my home until I was fifteen. Even at that age, I longed to have a house like many other people in Cape Town. Adding to the tightness of accommodation, my Aunt Elaine and cousin Cecelia lived with us too — a family of seven — sharing a double garage! Though I longed for normality, I understood that mum and dad worked hard to support us and that we all had to play our part within the home. I learnt to wash and hang clothes, tidy and polish and ensure that my sisters had a bath by the time mum and dad got home from work. Many an early morning was spent with a bucket filled with hot water — a quick wash in order to get ready for school, then a forty-five-minute walk to school. Although we struggled financially, many a happy memory was had in Aunty Dinah's garage. Many a visitor and extended family member came and went. No use worrying about wanting a house. At least we were not living in tin-shack accommodation like many others in Cape Town. *This was it Vic! Make the most of it! No use wanting a house! At least you are better off than many others in the townships! Keep perspective!*

As mum and dad worked during the day, my sisters and I were introduced to another child-minder, who cared for us after school. The Howard family were to become my 'second family'. Mr and Mrs Howard were Christians. They had six kids of their own and had another five whom they fostered and whom they would eventually adopt. Take on board my sisters and I, we are talking fourteen kids. The Howards were not the wealthiest family in our neighbourhood, in fact quite the opposite. Black tea and brown bread with jam and no butter, was what you received on most days when returning from school, for nothing else could be afforded. However, even living in my double garage, I never really struggled as the Howards did. We at least had a small car at this stage, where they had none. However, it was Mr and Mrs Howard's faith that would become the one thing I would aspire to.

In September 1977, Mrs Howard invited me along to a Holiday Bible Club. I jumped at the opportunity, for two main reasons. Firstly, they were giving away free food and secondly, there was another seven-year old called Catherine who had planned to attend too, so making sure that I was going seemed like a good idea at the time. It was my first experience of 'Bible things'. Although mum had done a good job taking me to church and Boys Brigade as a kid while being raised as an Anglican, this new experience at the Howards' church was different for some reason. The Holiday Club was run by a couple of strange people who I had never seen before. Apparently they were called 'missionaries' and they came from a place called 'America'. Furthermore, they were white and in my neighbourhood that was a very rare thing! That very Monday morning in 'Bible hour', one of the leaders told us a story about Jesus and how He referred to Himself as a 'Shepherd' (John 10). She went on to explain who the sheep represented in the story and how the Shepherd eventually died for the benefit of the sheep. I remember being impressed by the way the Shepherd was willing to sacrifice Himself for the sheep.

Now, let's clear the air here. I was seven-years old and generally knew nothing much about the Bible, in fact, I was clueless. Besides my limited Anglican experience as a toddler and being a junior in the Boys Brigade, I had no biblical knowledge as such. All I knew that particular morning was that somehow I identified myself as being one of the sheep and I appreciated the Shepherd sacrificing Himself for me. Jacqui, my team leader that morning, explained to me what the story really meant, and on that particular Monday in September, I responded to Jesus' call and claim on my life. I guess my life changed — not in any sort of magical way, but Jesus seemed to initiate a contract with me where He promised to be faithful to me ... to do whatever was necessary in my future to educate me as to who He is, His purpose for my life and the person He wanted to develop within me. I was a boy, but that Monday morning something happened to me which would affect the remainder of my life — I was now in a relationship with a Divinity and although I had no idea what that was or would look like, I knew somehow that the core of who I was had been affected. I have no other way to explain it. The Scriptures and the universal Church use phrases like 'salvation', 'coming into faith' and so on. Fair enough, but those sort of phrases were alien to me on that particular morning. All I knew was that I had encountered something which my rational mind could not quite comprehend — I had encountered God and He was about to lay claim on every aspect of my life ... every aspect!

The Evangelical Bible Church — which hosted that Bible Holiday Club, was to become the teaching foundation of my newly acquired faith. Sure, like all churches, they were flawed. It was evident that the elders ruled with a rod of iron. Playing a football match on a Sunday would result in church discipline and the Sabbath would be observed by wearing the best you had in your clothing cupboard! Things like questioning the elders and in particular the theology and dogma of the church, would not be tolerated! When 'engaging in error', you would soon be informed that you had overstepped the mark! Church would be great if it did not have people inside it — but that's not what churches are for! Ever so often I would disagree in my thinking with what was happening in church and yes, I hear you ... that has not changed forty years later. Although that particular church and I had issues now and then, that church provided me with a tremendous foundation to my newly acquired Christian faith. Simply speaking ... I learnt about the Bible in that little church. It was a Bible-teaching church, emphasis on 'Bible'. I remember attending a week-long study on the Book of Daniel and was amazed at the apocalyptic nature of that book. The preachers who spoke from that pulpit were gifted — not just with regard to oratory but also with regard to making the Bible relevant and meaningful to young people like myself. I was not forced to attend that church, but I never missed a Sunday! That church was my home and I loved every minute of being there. It was here where I learnt the meaning of words like sin, holiness, commitment, etc. I attended everything I could, the highlight being the Friday night youth events. It was here where my passion for Youth Ministry slowly began to ignite. I remember being impressed by the youth leaders who organised events week after week, with very little resources, which included week-long 'coffee-bar' ministry and outreach events. Yes, 'coffee bar' ministry ... all the rage in the late seventies and early eighties! This church also introduced me to the annual six in the morning Easter sunrise service, which came with coffee and hot-cross buns. Truth be told, this church was tremendous in developing firm foundations for the building of my faith, preparation ground for the turbulent years to come.

What I learnt all those years ago from many within that little church, was that the Gospel of Jesus was simply about presenting a different lifestyle to young people like myself. Christianity, I came to realise, is not just about programmes and attending church — you know that and I know that. However, it is all about lifestyle, impact, learning, modelling, laughter, tears, hurt, blessing and joy. It is about sharing, trips away, mountain walks, talking, witnessing, camping, athletics, football, church, friendship and so on. Discipleship is what Christianity is all about — men and women teaching and learning, modelling lifestyle, one to one, one leading and the other learning! In Northern Ireland, we seem to make such a big deal about the role of the minister that we often fail to see the ministry potential within ourselves. We become like the disciples — who were so dependent upon Jesus, to a point where they failed to see the instruments they could become in God's hands. Being 'Jesus-followers' is simply that ... we follow Him, not the institution of Church! So many Christians are so caught-up in that trap of 'Church-life' that they forget that Jesus himself challenged the religious institutions of His day. The Christian life is about modelling Jesus to one another, full stop. The local church is simply the mechanism through which we partner and support one another on a weekly basis, the instrument through which we fellowship together and are taught from the Scriptures. Yes, Jesus initiated the Church through His Spirit at Pentecost. It is His, He drives it forward and no one on this planet will stop its advance in our modern world. Believe me, many have tried. We are to love the Church, but it must never become the centre of our faith, for it is Jesus Himself to whom we owe allegiance!

Though I loved the Howards' many sons, I found a role-model and brother in Donovan! He was bright, articulate, athletic, an immense footballer and my friend! Being a few years older, he looked out for me. Donovan was a natural athlete and swimming was about the only sport where I had an edge over him. Besides being a footballer, Donovan was also an athlete and the four hundred metres would become his speciality. One Saturday morning I travelled with him to the regional athletics final at Athlone stadium, where he would compete in the four hundred metre final, the last eight athletes from the thousands of non-white schools across the Western Cape. He finished third and alongside his girlfriend, I remember feeling immense pride at his achievement. Donovan, alongside his sisters and brothers were born athletes, but they excelled at football. My love for football therefore started while watching Donovan and his siblings play. Donovan, very much like his eldest brother Randall — was a phenomenal striker. Vincent, Donovan's older brother — nicknamed 'boots' — named so for being a no-nonsense defender, was a joy to watch too — strong, determined, a lion! Then there was Afrika, one of the foster siblings who played alongside Donovan. 'Affies' was the midfield maestro and could run forever, fit as anything! These gentlemen were my heroes, my brothers, my second family! I loved them as if they were my own blood!

Many a Friday night we would meet at the Howards, make our way to the back corner of the yard and get a fire going. It was here where we often chatted way into the night — friends, brothers ... talking about life as if we were running the world! Conversations centred upon the important things in life — football, table-tennis and girls, for now we were starting to learn about them and the kisses we could receive from them! Stories and tons of laughter often interjected our conversations. We were simply young men who enjoyed being together, masters of own destinies, kings of our own castles, rulers of our own worlds but inevitably something horrible happened to each of us which would see us part company in the future ... we grew up!

If only life allowed us to remain children ...

Chapter 2: Foundations of Faith

The Church shall never perish! Her dear Lord to defend,
to guide, sustain, and cherish, is with Her to the end;
though there be those that hate Her, and false sons in Her pale,
against both foe and traitor She ever shall prevail.

(S.J. Stone; 1839)

The Evangelical Bible Church was to be my spiritual home
for a while. The more I got into the life of the 'going-
ons' at EBC, the more that little church became central to
my faith. It was here where I had the opportunity to attend
the AWANA club ... an American Christian-based children's
club where one learnt memory verses, played games, earned
badges etc., very much an evangelical version of the Scouts.
The name AWANA had its roots in a verse from the Scriptures
... Approved Workmen Are Not Ashamed (of the Gospel that
is — 2nd Timothy 2 vs 15). I therefore not only attended this
club but also made my way through the ranks, eventually
becoming a leader. I became skilled at memorising verses
from the Bible, but as much as I enjoyed it, AWANA club
could not quite top my love for Sunday School.

'Teacher Christine' and Mrs Howard (as in the previous chapter) were the Sunday School directors. My love for Sunday School developed out of watching these two ladies lead with enthusiasm in the singing of old Christian songs. I learnt songs like 'There is Victory for Me', 'Did you ever talk to God Above' and many more. This Sunday School had its foundations built around memorisation of Bible verses as well and man, did I learn verses. I loved Sunday School but I loved it even more when we did a years' study on the life of David ... as outlined in 1st and 2nd Samuel. Ruth, my Sunday School teacher for that year was amazing. Each Sunday you could tell that she was so well prepared because she seemed to know the life of David inside out and was able to make connections between his life and ours. When she taught us about the friendship David had with Jonathan and how Jonathan did everything in his power to protect David, I was taken aback at this story of true friendship, for now I too was at a stage in my life when I was beginning to forge strong friendships of my own. Sunday School mornings were brilliant, but later on Sunday School camp would become the highlight of my year.

Canvas-tent camping is very much part of the South African way of life and our Sunday School camps were no different. It was here where I was to encounter my most fond memories about Sunday School days. As this was a church denominational Sunday School camp, I got to meet teenagers from different areas of Cape Town. I was placed into a tent group with about eight boys and a tent leader who, for a few years just happened to be one of my AWANA club leaders and one of my role-models ... Alrick Steyn. He was a great guy and someone I came to respect highly. I loved my first camp and quickly learnt that breaking of rules meant washing pots after the evening meal — while everyone else was enjoying a movie. Needless to say, I ended up washing many a pot over the five years of attending camp. One of these pot-washing scenarios occurred at the time when a young lady and I discovered young love. The young lady concerned had a very strict leader who slept alongside a hockey stick, at the entrance of her tent! I needed to get into that tent but I was not going to get smacked with a hockey stick! Having engaged in 'intelligence' in order to discover where exactly this young lady slept, I pretended to be ill one afternoon while everyone else made their way to the beach for sport. I arose from my 'ill' feeling and made my way to the girls' quarters. Finding the tent and the exact spot where this young lady slept, I proceeded to dig a hole just outside the place she slept, filling the hole with a large boulder. That night I snuck out of my tent and made my way to hers, knowing full-well that I would be slaughtered if caught! I removed the boulder and slid inside her tent. Having awakened her, I lay there for a few minutes and had myself a good few kisses, before making my way back. Sadly, I had not realised that Alrick had noticed that I was not where I was supposed to be and when eventually caught, I spent two days scrubbing pots. Needless to say ... it was worth a few kisses!

What I loved about Sunday School camps were the evening 'testimonies', where kids my own age were openly sharing what they learnt during that day and how Christ was working in their lives. We ranged from eight to sixteen years of age, but kids of all ages were sharing about the influence of Jesus on their personal lives. As peers, we paid attention to what each and every one of us shared because we generally knew each other and knew if someone was 'spoofing' or not. These were moments of learning, spiritual journeys and life-faith matters ... no wonder we all listened attentively what others were sharing during these occasions.

The morning Bible-hour and memorisation times were superb and I got to learn so much about the Bible during these moments of biblical teaching. I was fascinated about stories of biblical characters and modern missionaries and how they often did spectacular things in their pursuit of sharing the message of Jesus with others. From the Apostle Paul to Hudson Taylor, one of the first missionaries to China, I sapped-up knowledge of these amazing people who did special things for God. I imagined myself one day doing the very same thing — going to other countries to tell other people about Jesus, but in the socio-economic climate of my community, being a missionary would simply be a dream — nothing more! However, what I failed to realise back then was that those stories of missionaries were simple embers which God would use to ignite a flame of ministry within me, which would see its fulfilment much later on in life.

As the morning session cared for our spiritual needs, the afternoon session cared for our physical and sport was a big deal. Every camper was placed into a 'house' at the start of the camping week. House competition was fierce — whether sport or learning Scripture and trying to earn every available point for one's team, was our daily goal. As we queued for tea that evening, we watched the colours being hoisted up the flagpole, resulting in cheers and banter as to the position of one's house. Thereafter, competition was all forgotten until the next day. We were no longer competitors but mates and the evening centred around relaxing and sharing as to what God was doing in our hearts while at camp. It was the highlight of my day. Let no one say to you that children are too young to understand the impact God can have on a human life even at that age. Maybe as adults we simply complicate spiritual matters too much. No wonder Jesus encouraged his listeners to be like children — dependent upon Him alone for all they would require from life! (Matthew 18)

I loved that church, but that church had problems too. We were not allowed to visit the cinema; a football should not be kicked on the Sabbath and you were to be well-attired on that day ... for the Sabbath was simply that, holy! However, I was now slowly beginning to meet people at school who challenged those standards and ideas. I found myself beginning to question as to why I could not kick a football on a Sunday! I remember Donovan and I attending a Baptist youth camp one year where the hottest day of that week was the Sunday — and we were not allowed to swim. We had to wait until midnight until we could! I began to question as to whether my local church and others like it were really the types of churches I wanted to attend for the remainder of my life. Was I honestly expected to be a Sabbatarian and adhere to conservative views with regard to the fourth commandment in Exodus 20? What did 'keeping the Sabbath holy' actually mean within the twentieth century? Did God mean "no football" long before football was ever invented or did elders throughout the decades simply interpret it that way?

I get the idea that we are to implement imperatives stated within the Scriptures. I get that! I am all for also applying principles found within the Scriptures, but not being able to swim because it was the Sabbath? Did Jesus himself not challenge the Pharisees as to their approach regarding the Sabbath? Do not get me wrong, EBC was a sound church theologically, but was its leadership truly expecting us not to kick a ball on a Sunday? The Scriptures are filled with imperatives and I have no issue with that, but there are many a statute which Jesus himself had to fulfil and redefine for 'modern-man' in the fifth chapter of Matthew's gospel, now commonly known as the 'Sermon on the Mount'. I started to ask questions which challenged the leadership, which seems to be the story of my life — but in my arrogance as a young man I wanted to know 'why' these church laws were being applied. If we are to observe the 'Sabbath', should we not be doing so "on a Saturday, the day of Jewish worship?" I argued that if the fourth commandment was steeped within the context of resting from one's work or labour — that is, that we have six days in which to work followed by a day of rest on the Sabbath, then surely any 'relaxed' or 'rest' activity can be pursued on the Sabbath, for surely swimming is a relaxing activity, correct? Surely one can swim and give allegiance and thought to God at the very same time, right?

What did Jesus really mean when he stated that the Sabbath was made for man and not man for the Sabbath (Mark 2)? I understand that God Himself took time to rest and reflect. I have no problem with that! The New Testament suggests that this day should be one where we focus on corporate worship. I have no problem with that either! However, I have an issue with those who think we simply cannot do things like — play or watch a football match because it would be deemed to be 'law-breaking'. Really? If the Sabbath is considered to be the day we remember the Resurrected Christ — for this is why Christians worship on a Sunday and not the Saturday and if we keep in mind that Jesus often despised those who sought to impose the Law of Moses at all costs and the legalism which came along with that, are we not in danger of therefore becoming legalists ourselves? What would be more beneficial to my spiritual life … occasionally taking my family to the beach on a Sunday and just enjoy being with them or worrying about the fact that the elders in my church would wonder why I was at the beach and not in church? Am I living my life to please Jesus or the leaders within my church? Which is it?

Reading the Gospels as a young man, I remember being so impressed at the way Jesus lived His life — how He was not bound to social or religious convention. He observed the

Sabbath to identify with His people in their worship of God, but He constantly challenged social and religious custom, particularly when the Pharisees engaged Him in conversation. His issues with them always seemed to centre around their reasons, motivation and purpose for their strict observance to the Law ... and not the Law itself. They always seemed to make the Law say more than it really did! Are our church leaders today doing the very same? It's like our modern-day equivalent of Bible translations, where some churches would only preach from the King James Version and discard every other modern piece of Bible translation. Now, if we were to be stranded on an island and the only copy of the Scriptures available to us just happened to be a Good News translation for example, we would read it, wouldn't we? Though we may long to read our Authorised, New International Version or any other modern translation, the Good News version would suffice in a situation like this wouldn't it? Is it not the overall message of the Scriptures that is of prime importance and not necessarily the translation itself? If this is the case, why do Christians become so hung-up about issues like this? Why do we become so legalistic about issues that are peripheral to the heart of Christianity, namely personal faith in Christ?

We forget that Jesus was so radical in what He said and did that it would eventually be the reason for His death — but not the sole reason! The Pharisees wanted Him to conform to religious and cultural convention but they had no idea that He came to redefine what a spiritual heart really looked like, for it had nothing to do with 'observance and conformity'! Have you noticed how quickly the Church, expect people to conform to 'the way we do things here in OUR church?' Is it not interesting to see that our expectation of 'new converts' is often to sign on the dotted line and do as we do? Is this what the church in general have become — an avenue for conformity? Would Jesus feel comfortable bringing along a leper or an adulterer to the Sunday morning service next week or would He apologise to His guests for the fact that they were made to feel most unwelcome because they didn't quite fit the bill of what a parishioner should look like? You see, Jesus often challenged the Pharisees with regard to their sense of entitlement and realm of self-importance. You ever wonder why the church loses so many young people between fourteen and eighteen? Is it because we are so hung-up about the do's and don'ts of church rather than guiding and allowing young people to self-discover what discipleship is all about?

I once knew a thirteen-year-old boy who was fed-up with going to Sunday School. He felt that the questions he asked his teacher resulted in fairly simplistic answers. I encouraged the boy therefore to stay home and not attend, which his mother clearly objected to. I was adamant that he should stay home from Sunday School for a period of time. He did so. I honestly felt that this young man was at a stage where he needed to personalise his faith. He needed guidance, not instruction. He needed an opportunity to chat through things, not to be spoken down to and he needed time to develop respect and love for the Scriptures and not to view it as something that he could not spiritually or morally attain to. It was the best thing that could have happened to that young man at that stage of his life. I should know, for he just happens to be my eldest son — but more about him later on! You see, our role as the Church is not to impose religious convention — but to tell people about God's plan of rescue in the person of Jesus, challenge lifestyle and allow God's Spirit to do His thing ... for is that not what Jesus did when He graced our planet?

Sometimes I do think that our interpretation of Sunday observance is very much culturally-based. In South Africa, we often headed from church on a given Sunday to watch cricket in the Summer. Many of us often had a surf as well before church. Many a marathon or cycle event was held on a Sunday and so on. Did that make the Christian family in South Africa less spiritual? What about those Christians in Muslim countries where Sunday is generally a work day, including countries like Israel, Nepal, Malaysia and so on? Should those Christians be looked down upon for not 'observing the Sabbath?' Do you honestly think that Jesus would lose sleep because a member of a church who happens to be a nurse by profession, has to work on a Sunday? Here in Northern Ireland we seem to have a much more conservative approach to Sunday observance, particularly within rural areas. With the relaxed atmosphere of Sunday observance within cities across the world, the onslaught of the possibility of national football on Sunday afternoon and the now regular opening of retail, are we approaching a time when Sunday as we know it, will look very different in future generations?

What about dress code? Should we be well attired? If you are of the opinion that being well dressed to church enhances your attitude of worship, then I support you one hundred percent. If you feel that the attitude of your heart has nothing to do with whether you are well dressed for church or not, then I support you too! I guess what I'm getting at is that the Christian life is not one of legality, which results in guilt ... but one of freedom in discipleship! Did the apostle Paul not write to the Galatian Church dealing with this very issue? Your attitude of worship is simply that ... your attitude! Why is it therefore that we are still seeking to impose upon others, the very attitude the Apostle wanted the Galatians to rid themselves of? Do you honestly think that God's ultimate aim is to impose guilt upon us with regard to issues like Sabbath observance? Of course not! He is interested in the daily welfare of our hearts and our personal attitude to Him. Church history would tell us that hundreds of years ago, the universal church built huge and fancy church buildings, thinking that this was the way to enhance worship and honour a holy God. Sadly, many of these churches are now empty all across Europe or have been turned into coffee shops. Were the Reformers right therefore to worship in simple 'Gospel-hall' like buildings? What truly enhances our attitude of worship ... buildings, dress-code, carrying large Bibles, or is it the realisation that as a people we are living daily in the presence of a holy God who really couldn't care less about things we spend our time pontificating about?

Of course every church has laws, processes, procedures, disciplinary measures etc. Churches are organisations and therefore by its very nature its members must comply to certain standards and policies. However, churches often seem to come full circle with regard to their politics. Let me explain. Churches often split because certain members want to experience a sense of 'freedom' in their thinking, in their worship, etc. They break from established churches because they view the hierarchy as being archaic in their thinking and so on. Soon these 'free-thinking leaders' establish their own churches and twenty years later they become the very thing they despised twenty years earlier — an established church! Bottom line ... there are no perfect churches and you would be a fool if you were looking for one! Irrespective of denomination, size, minister, etc., the church is not just home for Jesus followers and seekers of truth but also a political entity ... and due to the fact that it has people at its very core, it cannot but be a socio-political-theological being! Churches are filled with messy people, not saints — so don't view churches as places filled with 'goodie goodies'. Church people may look like they good, but they not! Churches are filled with sinful people who have discovered God's grace and seek to now live in the way Jesus wants them to. No wonder the New Testament writers worked aimlessly at instructing Christians in their day as to how they were to live as people of faith alongside each other in this new community called 'church'. Christians know one thing the rest of the world does not and it is this ... they know that they do not deserve to be recipients of the goodness of God.

I am happy to concede that I may be wrong on matters that I have raised here, but having spent forty-five years of my life within a church context and having seen how Christians look down upon one another because of differing views with regard to Sabbath observance and so on, sometimes I wonder if we are really missing the point here! Allow me to stretch your thinking for a minute. Fifty or sixty years ago, it would have been unthinkable for noisy electric guitars and drum kits to be part of Sunday worship, or to walk into a church in a t-shirt or a pair of long shorts, for shops to open at two on a Sunday afternoon or to go sailing on a family yacht after Sunday service ... but these things are now part and parcel of the 'Sabbath' in our modern world! Is our faith therefore shaken by these 'worldly' initiatives? Of course not! Is observing the Sabbath not about our attitude to God and the importance of corporate Sunday worship, rather than whether or not we play a game of chess with our twelve-year old, push our kid on a swing or mow the lawn on a Sunday?

Let me ask you to name the key reason why you attend the local church you currently do ... if you do that is? If the preaching of the Bible is not your key reason, then I suggest you start thinking about finding a church where the preaching of the Scriptures is paramount! The Bible as we know it, is a fantastic work of history. It provides us with a historical record as to the origin of man and the birth and development of a historical group of people, namely the Jewish race. Yet behind the history lie God's initiating work of relationship,

His communication with humanity and the future He has planned for the human race. In order to communicate this plan to our twenty first century world, God uses the Church — which exists to enlighten it about Jesus! The church's main medium of doing so is the preaching of the Scriptures and the sharing about the person of Jesus — His Life, death and His resurrection ... and let me warn you, the message of Jesus comes with a health risk — yours and mine, for the emphasis of the Bible is life-change!

I have listened to many young people and adults over many a year who often suggest that Christianity is simply 'a crutch needed by some to get through life!' When hearing this, I often have a quiet giggle, for they have no idea! Reality and in-your-face television productions, 'follow me' links on Facebook, Twitter, Instagram and so on are quite the rage these days. We like to have an in-depth look at how people live their lives and for some it makes good television. However, the one thing television and the internet do not reveal, is one's thoughts and feelings. Now imagine someone watching you every minute of every day, but coupled with that, this someone also has access to your thoughts and feelings! Not just that, but this someone also sees your motivation and reasons why you do as you do! That's intrusive! That's what it's like being a Jesus follower! Jesus has this ability to not only see and know everything about us, but also to challenge every single reason as to why we do as we do! Christianity is therefore not about having a crutch for daily survival — for no individual would generally choose to be a Jesus follower. Christianity is not a 'self-help' idea or something we purchase to get us through a crisis, for humanity ... as we can well observe within our modern society, has generally turned its back on Jesus! That's the beauty of this whole Christian-deal. We don't choose Jesus — He chooses us! Due to His love for us, Jesus desires for us to be more than we are and that's why He is so intrusive! That's the reason we often feel so uncomfortable when reading the Bible. Jesus wants us to undergo a transfusion of sorts — our self-centred nature replaced for His selfless one ... and that's painful. So next time you view a Jesus follower with disdain or ridicule, consider the courage it takes to have a new standard to attain to, the courage required to change your character and the determination to follow down a path which is socially unpopular!

The Evangelical Bible Church back then, like some churches today, was hung-up on aspects of legalism but their focus on the Bible has been of life-long benefit to me. My advice to you, whether you are a teenager, an adult, a church-goer or someone simply at a stage in your life where you need some answers ... find a church that will teach you about Jesus. There is no such thing as an ideal church so don't look for that but do find one that makes the Bible alive and relevant to you. The EBC did that for me and I will be eternally thankful to God for their investment in my life through the preaching of the Bible.

Anyway, dad was about to drop a bomb-shell that would change my life and my loyalty to EBC forever! Dad bought a house ... a real one!

Chapter 3: Reading the signs!

Follow the signs; Open your eyes
Read between the lines of what you see
Look into the soul of reality ...

(Michael W Smith; 2010)

'Semeion' ... I love this word! It's an ancient Greek word meaning 'miracle' but used exclusively within the New Testament. This word has but one purpose — used within the context of miracles performed by Jesus; the idea that although people stood in awe of the miracle, the miracle itself was simply but a sign-post, pointing the onlooker to the miracle-worker ... Jesus himself! In the same way, life has warning signs for us too, signs which allow us opportunities to learn, to take stock and to undergo personal change! The problem is ... do we choose to learn from them?

It was the happiest day of my life!! We eventually got a house in a place called Strandfontein Village. It was a new development on the coast, miles from everything I knew but it was to be my new home. I was fifteen years old when we moved into our very first house. Uncle Ivan and Aunty Mary Paulsen (not blood relatives but very good friends) were neighbours of ours in Greenhaven, the town in which we had the double-garage dwelling. Not only did they encourage mum and dad to get a house, but they also dipped into their own pockets in order to assist my parents whenever it was required. I will forever be grateful to both of them for their goodness to us as a family.

I was not to know that as one of the first families to move into this new development, our family would become over-night celebrities ... well, my youngest sister. Glenda accompanied me to the shop one afternoon when a gentleman and lady stopped us and enquired as to where we lived and so on. 'Stranger danger' yes, but not quite in this case. It transpired that these people were from a marketing company and they were given the contract to now market Strandfontein Village. Soon Glenda's face and the new development were splattered in newspapers all across Cape Town. My sister therefore brought the family a little bit of celebrity, but more importantly a little bit of extra income for mum and dad.

For the past eight years I had shared a tiny space with my family in Aunty Dinah's garage but now I was about to have my very own bedroom! Wow! Moving day was an exciting affair, with many an extended family member assisting with the move. It was like a dream come true and although it was a tiny house in comparison to most, it felt like a palace after fifteen years in a single and then double garage. It had a small garden and some space toward the back of the house and more importantly, it was homely! However, there was a snag — Strandfontein Village (at the sea) was a forty-five-minute drive from the Howards, my home church and the school I was currently attending.

Having completed my time at Primary school, I later attended Crystal High School in a community known as Hanover Park, a community blighted by gang activity. The school building itself was in need of major repair, not to mention the general internal upkeep! I don't think the worst school building in Northern Ireland would come close to the neglected academic institution which was Crystal High School. However, it was here where I met Jarret Dalton. As we had just moved to Strandfontein, I spent the afternoons with Jarret and his family until mum collected me for the long drive back home. Jarret was streetwise and pretty soon I was introduced to the 'ways of the world'. Jarret seemed to know much about girls and my education with regard to the female body was about to begin. Here I was, a young Jesus follower now being introduced to the realities of life! It was also here at Crystal High, where I had my first major teenage crush. Her name was Brenda Beppo and we were in the same class. Brenda had a black belt in karate, and so did her boyfriend ... who later became her husband! I was not about to lose my teeth over a crush, but this crush eventually led to a good friendship. However, as we both represented our school at middle-distance running that year, we often arrived at school early in the morning to train together, both achieving success in the fifteen and eight hundred metres at the inter-school competition. It was during times of training that Brenda and I connected and got to know one another very well, but that was simply that!

Due to the long journey to and fro Crystal High School, I soon moved to a school closer to home, a school known as Strandfontein High. I moved at the start of my GCSE years and it was to be a school I really enjoyed being at. Having excelled at Primary school, I now discovered that I had difficulties in one or two subjects, while still excelling in others. My love for English Literature was simply due to Mrs Chatre, our English teacher, who was more of a mother to us than a teacher. It was at this school where I would witness firsthand, the use of marijuana ... for some fellas in school were regular users, part and parcel of the gang culture which permeated schools across the Western Cape. In a class of about eleven boys, there were three or four of us not involved in anything resembling gang affiliation. Co-ordinating the Scripture Union at my school, meant that I was labelled and affectionately known as 'the preacher'. However, one Friday afternoon at school I found myself caught up in a fight between two rival gangs. Not only that, but I would witness the stabbing of two of my class mates.

It was Friday morning and a non-uniform day. We had a double period of Biology first thing in the morning and as usual, our teacher sat in his store room nursing a migraine, or possibly a hang-over. He decided at one stage to leave the classroom while we were working. Soon two of my classmates approached another and furiously laid into him. It was obvious that this altercation was the consequence of something which happened outside of school. Having had his face punched, the pupil concerned left the classroom just prior to the teacher returning to class. The teacher had not even realised that a pupil was missing from his class. Soon it was the end of the lesson and we made our way to the Geography classroom. While awaiting the teacher outside the classroom, the pupil who had his face punched, arrived with his fellow gang members who were also pupils and a fight occurred outside the Geography room. At the teacher's arrival, things quietened down as we were about to enter the classroom. Things later seem to escalate and in a space of a few hours, two sets of gang members were squaring off during the lunch break ... while the teaching staff made their way to the administration block for their own safety. I witnessed gang activity as a boy, for it seemed to be part of the culture within the Western Cape but this was something else — this was my own generation, my peers, my friends! This squaring off between the two sides was like something out of a movie scene. As we had balconies as part of our school building, pupils made their way upstairs looking down onto the open quad area, awaiting the fighting ... as if it were pay per view! This was supposed to be school, not a theatre to view gang activity.

Months later it was athletics day, meaning that our school competed alongside ten or twelve other post-primary schools at a sports arena about thirty or so miles from our school. As this event was open to all pupils and not just the athletes, many of us boarded buses that morning to enjoy a day of competition. Athletics or 'Sports Day' is a big deal in Cape Town, unlike here in Northern Ireland where only the athletes travel to the athletics event. In South Africa, the entire school is involved. The day before the event, you are learning various songs that you would sing the next day. If you don't compete, well then you sing and cheer your athletes! In Cape Town in particular, school athletes are like heroes to the various local communities. The sports arena was in an area called 'Athlone'. I knew it well, for it was a stone's throw from Aunty Francis' house. I knew the surrounding area too, for I spent my early childhood there. I attended Norma Road Primary in the same area, swam in the community swimming pool right next to the stadium and knew many a face in the wider community. It was also at that very stadium years earlier, that dad was involved in a gang fight at the conclusion of a 'Coon Carnival' competition ... an annual event enjoyed by the 'Coloured' community for many a decade in Cape Town. Behind the stadium was the little community of 'Kewtown' — apartment blocks which were home to the poverty-stricken, many of whom were unemployed, home as well to the gangs. Growing up around the area, I knew that when you travel around in Kewtown, what you wore made a big statement, as certain shirts and trousers aligned you with gang affiliation. Due to the fact that I ran the fifteen hundred and eight hundred that year, I was attired in my school tracksuit, unlike some of my classmates whose clothing that day, brought some attention from watching eyes.

I grew up in that area — so I knew the score! Little boys were sent over the stadium wall to scan for rival gang members in the various schools attending the athletics meeting. Sadly, my class mates were sighted, and therefore targeted. As the sports event finished and everyone headed for the exits, the main gang in Kewtown suddenly attacked my classmates. It was pandemonium. You can imagine the scene ... a few thousand pupils running in all directions as this gang now attacked indiscriminately. My main concern was Sharon, my sister — where was she? Last I had seen her she was with her friends heading to the exits too. It was her very first year in secondary school and I had to ensure that she was safe! Teachers from different schools tried to protect any pupil they could, whether that pupil was from their school or not. It was chaos! Pupils were screaming — teachers who tried to intervene were smacked and punched, students ran in all directions. In all the mayhem I had but one objective ... I had to find my sister!

I ran back into what was now one to one fighting among gang members. I ran past a gang member who had a sword in his hand. As I passed him, I recognised him! It was person Y, one of my Norma Road Primary school friends who was one of our cast members when we starred in the production of 'Oliver'. I could not believe it. We recognised one another and after exchanging pleasantries in this hostile atmosphere, he encouraged me to get into a bus and get out of the way. I informed him that I was looking for Sharon and due to the fact that he knew Sharon or possibly because of his historical friendship with me, he walked alongside me, protecting me from his fellow gang members until we spotted my sister. She was safe — in a school bus and looked after by Lance, one of Cecelia's class mates (my cousin Cecelia who now lived with us). Once I knew my sister was safe, I said my farewells to person Y and ran as quickly as I could toward an awaiting school bus. It was the last time I would ever see him! However, his gang was responsible for the near fatal stabbing of two of my classmates. Another classmate had a gash in his hand, a result of trying to protect his face from a slashing knife. Other pupils — some from other schools who were trying to protect themselves, friends, etc., were stabbed in arms, shoulders etc. I was concerned for one classmate who was stabbed in the back and thanks to the quick thinking of some of our teachers, my friend was rushed to hospital. Needless to say, what started as teenage bravado of wanting to be the 'hard lad' or 'being in a gang', soon went by the wayside. It was clear that gang affiliation also meant possible termination of life. It was a lesson we all learnt that day. A warning sign of life ... one which seeks to encourage you to change your life and literally walk the other way.

Arriving home that evening, Sharon wept uncontrollably in mum's arms, as she tried to explain what had happened that day. It was an experience she should not have had. I had seen this sort of violence before and learning to read the signs was important for personal preservation — never ask another guy's girl for a dance in a disco — it could cost you your life; if you see loads of guys arrive in a community event or disco and you don't quite recognise them, get out and go home, for there's a strong possibility that the evening would end up in a fight; don't bad mouth anyone — someone could be listening and pass on the information to someone else and soon you could find a knife in your back; etc. Most of the time I read the signs correctly! One Saturday evening, having played football in Mitchell's Plain, I took a long walk to my uncle Johnny's house. I noticed a little kiosk across a field with some guys standing at it. I also noticed two fellas heading towards the kiosk, but it was their body language I noticed more. They both walked with straight right arms. It could only mean that they had something up those arms — swords, a very long knife etc. I was right. In a flash, the two fellas who were standing and chatting at the kiosk, lay dead a minute later! Being able to read the signs of violence was one way of ensuring safety at all costs.

It was great in Strandfontein Village and I loved living there! The difficulty was that I could no longer travel to the Evangelical Bible Church, as it was simply too far. My time at EBC therefore soon came to a very natural end. I stopped attending church due to the distance and my mother saw an opportunity which she grabbed with open arms. Being an Anglican, mum felt it her obligation to have us confirmed in the Anglican faith and many an argument was had between mum and son about the spiritual significance or not that Confirmation would have on my life. I was raised in a 'Gospel hall' type of church and thought I knew all the answers with regard to theology. I was soon to learn that I was clueless and that I had a lot more to learn about this thing called 'Christianity'!

I enrolled in my confirmation class! It was all brand new to me. I was now worshipping in mum's church, so different to what I had been used to. I struggled with the fact that they sang everything! Let's not mention the incense which had me choking on every occasion! However, I believe that God has a way of bringing strategic people into one's life at certain stages of one's life. Previously I had Mrs Howard, Ruth — my Sunday School teacher, Alrick — my AWANA club leader and now I had an elderly gentlemen called Mr October. Truth be told I was an arrogant so and so and Mr October was as gentle as he was wise. Even now as I write this, I shudder to think how disrespectful I was to him as I argued about the validity of Confirmation and about sections of the Apostle's Creed I disagreed with, yet never taking time to quite understand this document in its entirety. He made it all so clear. My education about the historical matters of the Christian Church was enlightening as I came to understand what words like 'catholic' meant. I encountered something I had not experienced at my previous church ... an education about the early history of the Christian Church. I soaked it all up. What started out as a major dislike for the established church, now developed into an appreciation of not just the universal church and its origins, but a love for this Anglican congregation. Soon Mr October got me involved in speaking at the Youth Fellowship and pretty soon I embraced Anglicanism with enthusiasm, for I had promised my mother that I would obey her and would have myself confirmed.

I made good friends at St Francis of Assissi in Strandfontein. Mr October's son Cecil was soon to be a mentor as we openly discussed matters of theology. Cecil was responsible for getting me involved in teaching Sunday School at St Francis and I enjoyed every minute of it. I got to know mum's friends and developed a deep love for that church, an affection I have to this very day. Not only did I learn much about myself but I was also given the opportunity to learn about the theology of the Anglican Church in South Africa, which was an invaluable experience.

I came to understand that every experience one encounters are opportunities to learn! Each time one is confronted with difficulties or a lack of knowledge about an issue, there is the potential to broaden one's mind about areas one is generally ignorant about. As a teenager I was now learning about life ... educated with the knowledge that life is messy, that it could mean the possible demise of a friend, that it contains pitfalls and so on. In all these scenarios, one has the opportunity to ensure that you do not end-up within the same context. God has this ability to allow us to encounter difficulties to teach us, but in order to do so, we must however maintain a teachable spirit — and I was about to learn a lot more about something I generally knew very little about but which encompassed my life on a daily basis. I had encountered signs while growing up, not figurative signs which would help prevent me from certain situations but literal signs which I encountered everywhere ... signs which read 'Whites Only'!

There was something wrong in South Africa and 'Apartheid' was its name ...

Chapter 4: 'Rise of the fearless'

'There is a growing awareness of the role the black student may be called upon to play in the emancipation of their community ...'

(Steve Biko: 1977)

I now attended Strandfontein Senior Secondary School, a state-funded school made up solely of 'Coloureds', as opposed to 'Blacks', as opposed to 'Whites', as opposed to 'Indians' ... welcome to the racial mix which is South Africa! I was in year twelve and rose to prominence as Chairperson of the Scripture Union in my school, which meant running from class to class each Thursday morning inviting students to attend our Christian group during the lunch break. I worked hard at preparing short talks which would inspire and encourage other Christian young people in my school to live out their faith within the school environment. I enjoyed it and was encouraged at the many who came on a weekly basis. With the external help of Daryl Henning, the Scripture Union regional officer ... our little group of witnesses were thriving and many a young person sought to introduce other young people to a way of life initiated by Jesus Himself.

Mrs Chatre was my English Teacher and one of the very few so-called 'white' teachers in our school. I often wondered why she chose to travel for about an hour to teach in our school when we knew she could quite easily get a post in a 'white' school. Anyway, she faithfully helped me each week with our SU group, but often took a back seat before the rest of the pupils. She was a smoker and felt a sense of guilt I guess! She knew that there were some Christian students who judged her for her habit, but God had helped me to look beyond that, for I was convinced of the fact that she loved Jesus — and that was good enough for me. Time however had come for another regional SU meeting and the next one was to be at Muizenberg High School, a 'white' school about half an hour down the coast. On arrival there, I was totally amazed at what I saw and I think Mrs Chartre could see it in my face! These students had a very smart school uniform and immediately I started to compare it to mine! Although we had an official school tie — it was only worn by those of us who could afford one! This school had several rugby and hockey pitches, while we had what looked like a little field! As I walked into their school hall, my eyes gazed at the various display boards ... names of past rugby captains, trophy cabinets filled with accolades, and so on. This school was so clean and when meeting the pupils, I could not but notice how smart they looked in their uniforms. To say that I was impressed at what I saw is an understatement. As we left that school later that afternoon, I could not help but feel a certain sense of injustice. There was something not quite right about all this. How was it that schools could be so different? I had never been in a 'white' school before. I had not had the opportunity of being invited to one, other than at this occasion for a Scripture Union regional meeting. Did these 'white' pupils realise how lucky they were? Had they any notion what my school actually looked like? More importantly, did they really care?

It was mid-1985 and a few months later, at the start of the new school year in January 1985 — all hell would break loose in non-white schools across the country. Another year and another non-white generation in protest, internal national voices crying alongside voices around the world seeking for the end to inequality, injustice and state-sanctioned murder in South Africa ... voices seeking the termination of laws which supported this racist regime, voices echoing over loud speakers from individuals standing on platforms and voices too of comfort from mothers whispering to children of imprisoned fathers — all with one message saying "down with segregation; down with the enforcement of racist laws; down with Apartheid!"

As the second world war came to an end, Germany saw it-self divided between two key stakeholders, namely Russia and the USA. The British crown now 'owed' countries within the Commonwealth who had forwarded manpower to aid the war effort against Hitler. As part of the Commonwealth, South Africa was now ready to benefit from the loyalty it showed to the Crown and the leading Nationalist Party in South Africa, was ready to collect. Born in Amsterdam in 1901, Hendrick Fredresch Verwoerd instituted the policy of racial separation in South Africa in 1948 — a policy that would last until 1994. A year earlier, he referred to himself as 'an extreme Afrikaner', drawing a line between himself and the British in South Africa. Having initially arrived in South Africa in 1903 with his father — a father who sympa-thised with the Afrikaners during the war against the British (known as the Boer War), Verwoerd returned to South Africa in 1928, having resided in Germany. As a social scientist, he already had separatist views when returning to South Africa and in 1948 he was instrumental in helping the National Party come to power. He rose to leadership in 1958, succeeding DF Malan and in 1966 was assassinated by stab wounds to the body and a fatal wound to the neck.

The National Party under Malan and Verwoerd enforced the idea that residents of the country were not South Africans as such, but four complete separate racial groups — White, Black, Coloured and Indian. This idea of separateness found its way into legislation — the National Party now legally enforcing the policy of apart-hood, or Apartheid! Various organisations in the 1960's and 70's rose in opposition of these laws, but the Nationalist Party had the might of the police and army to enforce legislation. Robben Island — a picturesque island just off the coast of Cape Town, became the home of the 'agitators' against the state, the most famous of these being Nelson Mandela. Organisations like the African National Congress — as well as the tireless work of Winnie Mandela, kept the international community informed as to what was happening politically in South Africa. The international community by large were powerless to improve the plight of non-white South Africans, for its vast mineral wealth allowed South Africa to function independently of the world. Apartheid had massive economic benefits for Whites and allowed them to develop business and the economy, while non-whites simply became ... the work force!

The Apartheid regime used its powers of legislation to now forcibly remove all non-whites from land owned within racially mixed communities, which the regime now wanted to acquire. District Six was one such area! Being named the 'Sixth Municipal District of Cape Town' in 1867 after slavery was eradicated in 1833 in the colony, this district flourished. Being ethnically mixed, the district became a hub of activity — due to its easy access to the city of Cape Town. Its growth over the years meant that District Six became a 'mini city' within a city, encompassing a tenth of the population of Cape Town at its height.

After the conclusion of the war in 1945, this 'city' was ethnically cosmopolitan but due to the concessions given to people like Malan and Verwoerd by the Crown, the Sixth District was earmarked by the Apartheid government for change! In 1966, the Group Areas Act allowed District Six to be 'cleansed' of non-whites, as legislation now declared it an area for 'whites only'! In the years which followed, thousands of Coloureds, Blacks and Indians were forcibly removed from the area. The majority now settled in areas twenty to forty miles away from the city centre — now commonly known as the Cape Flats. Houses in the Sixth District were demolished, although a minority were left untouched. As my grandparents lived in 'Bloumeul Flats', I was a regular visitor to District Six as a child, until they too were moved on!

Like all parts of South Africa at this time, the claws of the Apartheid regime laid siege to many areas which were home to non-whites ... District Six in Cape Town, Sophiatown in Johannesburg, etc. What the regime wanted from these communities was simply the land for redevelopment. The greed of the regime was a far-cry from the cosmopolitan and all-embracing heart of the people within these districts. No wonder my generation — who were but toddlers and children during the years of forcible removal, feel so strongly about the wrongs done back then. Having returned to District Six to share with my own sons the ruins of the Sixth District — now consumed by its new owners, the Cape Technikon — they remain as such ... ruins! Unless one has been touched by its atmosphere at the time, District Six is nothing more than a regional area for redevelopment. However, for the past and present generations of those who once lived there, the

Sixth District will forever remain that which was taken from its people ... our home!

The Apartheid regime enforced its rule of separate-ness throughout the sixties and seventies and early into the eighties. The Rivonia trials of the nineteen sixties — so named because of the area of Johannesburg the leaders of the African National Congress and others lived in at the time of their arrest, had come and gone and names like Mandela, Sisulu and the rest imprisoned on Robben Island for acts of terrorism against the state ... were now names never to be forgotten. Organisations like the United Democratic Front, founded by the Reverend Alan Boesak and who represented us Coloureds — called for a united front of churches, civic associations, sports organisations etc., in its opposition of Apartheid. If truth be told, we were slightly better off economically than our black brothers and sisters. The Sharpeville massacre of residents in 1960 due to 'pass laws' and the Soweto massacre in 1976 of school pupils by the police, were testament to the fact that the National Party had no problem ordering the deaths of many in order to uphold its policies and laws, even if the many included teenagers and children. South Africa was at war with itself and the international community either looked the other way or were powerless to do anything. Many a country bought their gold and diamonds from South Africa and objecting to the overt abuse of legislative power within the country could possibly mean termination of purchase. The international community therefore remained silent while the Apartheid government did as they saw fit!

In February 1985, Black and Coloured schools across the Western Cape and in many other areas in South Africa, decided that we had had enough of the poor standard of education we were receiving. There was now a strong consensus that non-white pupils deserved better. Parity in education was required, urgently! This was not a new request, for nine years earlier pupils in a township called Soweto objected to the enforcement of the Afrikaans language as a medium of teaching within schools. Afrikaans was the language of the Afrikaner, a people who years earlier emigrated from Holland and settled as farmers. The Afrikaners were now in government and were not accepting of black school pupils objecting to Afrikaans. The Soweto uprising culminated in the killing of an estimated number of seven hundred school pupils — although the government totalled it as one hundred and seventy-six pupils only ... young people who stood as one to protest an education system which they could not agree to. The brutality of the Apartheid regime was nothing new. Sixteen years before, non-whites all across South Africa protested at the new 'pass laws' — the internal documentation which now had to be carried by blacks as a means of ethnic classification. In a place called Sharpeville, thousands of black people objected outside a police station to the carrying of this documentation. Soon sixty-nine people lay dead, including children, with many more sustaining gunshot wounds. The Sharpeville and Soweto massacres, not to mention the plight of individuals like Steve Biko — a young activist who spear-headed the Black Consciousness Movement in South Africa, beaten to death by the police and left on the side of a country road ... were reminders to my generation in 1985, that protesting the South African regime could cost you your life!

In order to give you some idea as to what the Afrikaner community thought about people like me, let me enlighten you. Racism in South Africa was steeped in theology! The Dutch Reformed Church — the theological wing of the Afrikaner Apartheid system, declared on the 23rd October 1986, that Apartheid was morally wrong. The Synod declared that Apartheid could not be 'scripturally justified' (October 1986).

However, for many a decade prior, this church was happy to both support the regime theologically and look the other way when state-sanctioned atrocities against non-whites occurred. Before this period of 'enlightenment' by the Synod in 1986, the implication was that non-whites or 'natives' were lesser and therefore this denomination implemented a whites-only policy with regard to membership and formal worship. This mentality and understanding held and communicated by the leadership of the Dutch Reformed Church, underpinned Apartheid for decades and therefore to many Afrikaners sitting within a local church, Apartheid was justified!

The regime had robbed us of equality, particularly with regards to education. It seemed that a very small part of the education budget was earmarked for non-white education. Textbooks were scarce; we had no school hall; broken windows permeated the school building; no heating in the winter; school assembly was held in the school quad and if it rained, well then Assembly was short and you simply got wet. I remember one morning in our English class — after a rainy winter's morning, my fellow class mates and I ended up congregating to the far side of the classroom, as rain poured through the broken windows! We had one little oil heater which Mrs Chatre had organised, mostly used to dry our wet clothing. There were just three classroom blocks, no closed corridors and no place to find shelter at all. If the weather was against you … well then just too bad!

Standard Nine — or year thirteen equivalent within the UK, was very much a blur. School started in January of that year and a few weeks later, student boycotts in South Africa began. What were the reasons for this student uprising? Simple … Coloured, Black and Indian students were dissatisfied with the unfairness of the education system, which included the teaching of Afrikaans as a compulsory subject on the curriculum. That year I was elected as class captain and represented my class on the Student Representative Council or 'Prefect' system, which meant that I was very much involved in political discussion and later ... political action. Soon I was assisting in addressing the student body on issues political, as I too now felt the injustice of the Apartheid regime. The more the students protested, the more the government affirmed their position that the curriculum will not change! As pupil protests continued, we soon saw the introduction of the police in our neighbourhood and on our streets, accompanied by the military ... there to 'maintain the peace'. Their presence did one thing only — it fuelled the tension which existed between police personnel and pupils and pretty soon, peaceful protests became violent.

The heart of man is a very sensitive entity — for it has tremendous capacity to love, but so too capacity to hate! My reasons for being part of the 'Struggle' were reasonable and justified, but student violence was now leading me down a path I had not known before. My anger at the South Africa government was slowly developing into hatred for all whites. I had previously not experienced this phenomena — how one's heart, consumed by hatred, could now turn to stone. Student violence in our area was spiralling out of control and I found myself now engaged in all that. One morning we stopped a meat truck on its way to make a delivery at a local butcher. We handed meat to as many pupils as we could and torched the truck! On another occasion I stopped a car who had two occupants, a woman and her baby. I instructed her to drive two pupils and myself about ten miles up the carriage way, where I knew a large student protest was underway. I informed her that in no way was she coming to harm and that we simply needed a lift. While sitting in the passenger seat and seeing how terrified this woman was, it dawned on me what I had now become over the past few months. I was no longer a protesting student — but simply a hoodlum! The longer these student riots continued, the colder my heart became, for I could no longer tell the difference between right and wrong. I had turned into someone I never wanted to be! A cause which was initially justified had now turned me into something I was not. I could no longer recognise myself. While I externally displayed the role of 'freedom fighter' to my peers, I could no longer look at myself in the mirror, for all I saw looking back at me were eyes of hatred. It did not take very long before I realised ... I was lost!

When writing to the churches, the Apostle Paul often describes the sinful heart and nature of man. He paints an accurate picture of depravity and the potential humanity has to display evil. He reminds us that we are born with the blue print for evil — that it's in our DNA and part of who we are! The Apostle reminds us too that we have no cure for the evil within us and that we are powerless to rid ourselves of it. In painting this dark picture of sin and depravity, Paul often uses the two most beautiful words in the Scriptures ... 'but God'! This wise man often reminded us that in the state of our depravity when all seems lost, when we are at the lowest moments in our lives, God reaches out to us and sets our feet on a new path, if we are but willing to reach out and grab His offer of help!

As I was encountering the depravity within my being in the mayhem of student violence, the voice of God appeared in the form of my English teacher. Mrs Chartre kept reminding me that the Apostle Paul commanded us to pray for and obey those in authority over us — as outlined in Romans 13. How could I possibly do so when this authority — the South African Nationalist Party, were clearly depriving all non-whites of equality in South Africa? In my opinion, non-whites were set-up to remain subservient to whites, indefinitely. How does one ... educated within a biased education system, aspire to university study when you are expected to write the same external examination as white students who had every opportunity afforded to them at school, while you had none? Even if you did manage to make the grade, how could you afford to attend university? The majority of our parents were part of the 'work force' and even if our parents had some sort of management role in their areas of employment, they were not paid the equivalent salary as whites. Apartheid therefore was designed to ensure that the majority within the country were simply the 'workers' and not decision-makers or game changers. In reality, non-whites were simply ... slaves!

God had an action plan for dealing with the hatred in my own heart. The 'Struggle' was a just cause, but my way of dealing with that had harmed me deep inside. I was in need of re-pentance and more importantly, in need of healing. God was about to heal my heart in the most unexpected of ways. He was about to burn upon my heart a statement that was going to stay there and impact every relationship I would have from that day to this ... a simple statement spoken by the mouth of Jesus himself ... 'Vic, you are to love Me and love your neighbour'! What I did not expect, was that God was going to use a 'white kid' to teach this 'coloured kid' what reconciliation, love and grace were all about. God was about to teach me a lesson and this lesson was called ... Donald Graham.

We met on a Scripture Union camp. SU were running a camp solely for boys, aptly called Camp HAV-A-GO. It was a rough and tumble sort of camp and from the stories of years gone by, I was slightly apprehensive but pretty keen to attend nonetheless. Mum had dropped me at the SU office in Rondebosch fairly early that morning while on her way to work. Being the first to arrive, I observed the arrival of each of the campers being dropped off by family members. Donald Graham arrived! He got out of this lovely Mercedes Benz and made his way to the back of the car to collect his bags. As he removed his belongings, I noticed that he had a guitar with him. Soon his mum gave him a big hug and he finally made his way toward the rest of us! If this camp was to be a rough and tumble kind of one, Donald was heading for trouble. There was nothing athletic about him. If he was in my community and we were picking players for a team, Donald would be the last player standing — and I'm sure the two team captains would be fighting over who would have him in their team! As I contemplated the issue of tent groups, I thought that this fella was the last person I would want to share a tent with. Lo and behold, that is exactly what happened. Donald ended up in my tent and better still, he slept right next to me. As it were, Donald and I became the best of friends. We could not have been more different. He was white, I was Coloured. He was wealthy and I came from a working class community. He was very bright and I struggled to make my way through post-primary. Yet, we got on very well and became friends.

Donald and I learnt much about the problems within our country and we chose to work through it together. The troubled political years in my life were resolved, not through political expediency and communication but through simple friendship. We learnt together about what South Africa could be like if people embraced one another and looked beyond their difficulties. Relationships overcame political turmoil and in 1994 South Africa became an example to the world because individual people learnt to take risks and trust one another.

One particular year, Don invited me to spend a few weeks on the road! It was one of those random things and we had a great time travelling together in his newly acquired car. We travelled up to the Eastern Cape and ended up in a little place called 'Hogsback'. We spent a night there and travelled further, making our way into the Transkie. We had a good time — hanging out as mates. However, there was an occasion too when we nearly lost him. One year while at Camp Havago, Donald spent some time out on the lake getting to grips with a windsurfer. He must have struggled to turn the sail and for those of you who ever attempted windsurfing, you know how key turning a sail is. In his failure to do so, Donald could not make his way back to the shore and back to the campsite. I don't know how long he spent lying on the board in the cold water. By the time we got hold of him, Donald was hypothermic. We got him out of his wetsuit and for the next hour or so Donald and I were cuddled up naked in a sleeping bag trying to warm his body with mine. It was a scary moment and one we both would not forget. He had come close to no longer being with us. Donald was my friend! Many times however, I let him down ... possibly due to my own selfishness, but I loved him as if he were my brother! Having met at Havago, we later attended a gig at St James Church. Andy and his band were playing and due to it being a rock concert kind of thing, the hall was obviously dark etc. Donald had brought his girlfriend along and it was the first time I met her. As she stood between the two of us, Donald was unaware that I had started holding her hand in the darkened atmosphere. It took a few years before I told him and I was happy enough to take a punch to the jaw, if that were his intention. However, he got his own back when I asked him to make a speech at my twenty first birthday! On that night, many soon learnt about my bad antics in my youth! Needless to say, we all had a good laugh!

As a child I once witnessed my father address a young white policeman as 'baas' (boss) — and that would not be the only time. My father was a grown man, addressing a possible twenty-year old as 'boss' and the authority he wielded over my father was uncanny, so much so that it plagues my memory to this day! My birth certificate classed me as being a 'Cape Coloured', which brought with it many legislative restrictions. From the time I could read, one sign dominated various areas in Cape Town — the sign which read "Slegs Blankes" or "Whites Only"! When travelling by train I had to observe that sign as 'third class' was reserved for people like me! Certain beaches in Cape Town were out of bounds to non-whites and don't even bother looking for a clean public toilet in the 'non-white' section because you would be hard-pressed to find one, for very little public money was allocated to non-white usage. As a family, we often spent a week in Kommetjie, a campsite right at the ocean on the other side of Cape Town where tourists hardly ventured to in those days. It was a far-cry from the many 'posh' campsites in France my family and I now annually frequent. The public toilet block for the Coloureds was simply a cement building with a toilet inside — no plumbing but a 'long drop'. There was no floor — simply the beach sand under your feet. There were no locks on the doors and no loo paper. This toilet block was as basic an ablution as you could imagine! It had about five actual toilets to thousands of people. In the morning you would join the queue and await your turn. This was how it was! We were non-whites and the government did everything they could to remind us of that fact. As a non-white, one could also be stopped, questioned and arrested if found in a 'whites only' community after dark without the necessary documentation on your person ... and so on. Apartheid was an evil and the non-white majority in South Africa suffered under its whip. The government's expectation of people like myself was that I should accept my lot and get on with it. However, I have a character flaw — I have a rebellious streak inside me and I am not good at maintaining the status quo!

It was evident that being white meant privilege and white pupils had no idea how privileged they were. Apartheid was designed to not only keep non-whites in their place, but to also make progression in life as difficult as possible. The system of Apartheid funnelled the non-white communities down one pathway only, that of servitude. Education — which was meant to provide all pupils with opportunity, became a stumbling block to many non-whites! Why attend school when there was no hope of becoming a decision-maker in the country? That chip of injustice on my shoulder was growing and the thinking machine within my head was transferring what I saw with my eyes, into emotions ... which was now slowly having an impact on my world-view. Something was not right in my country and the arrogance inside me and the chip on my shoulder were sending messages to my brain — *"I was nobody's slave, nobody's monkey, nobody's 'kaffer (nigger)'!"*

Why aspire to anything? There was no fair playing field in South Africa! The odds were stacked against you from the word go. So how was I supposed to play this? Do I become the angry anti-Apartheid campaigner — alongside millions of other pupils? Do I do my bit for 'The Struggle' and grow out of it later on? Do I become cynical and look for other experiences which may include gang activity or do I aspire to get out of South Africa at some stage in my life and reside in a place where the colour of my skin does not matter?

Like many an angry student, I found myself shouting 'Aluta Continua' on many an occasion– the idea that the cry for freedom continues — the words translated into English simply meaning 'the struggle continues'. A new generation of pupils would now raise the flag of freedom and remember those who initiated the Struggle and who were now incarcerated for their efforts! *"Mandela Mandela ..."* we would sing *"Mandela says freedom now ..."* Although the struggle contin-ued in the mid-eighties, there was a major mood swing in South Africa which the National Party wasn't quite expect-ing. People within general society were now engaging more and more across the colour line. Organisations, churches, colleges, etc., were taking brave steps as they opened their doors to all colours. Some suggested at the time that God Himself was initiating something new within South Africa — a movement that even the mighty National Party, could not stop — a biblical watershed that the police and army could not stamp out, a movement known as 'Koinonia' (the Greek word for 'fellowship').

South Africa was engaging in Koinonia more and more in key geographical areas around the country. At that stage of my life my world centred around two things — the Bible College I studied at and the church I fellowshipped at! It was at St James Church where I saw people of all colour, mix on a weekly basis. It was a white majority church with few col-oured people and even fewer blacks in attendance. I liked the fact that it was, racially-speaking a progressive church — al-though I saw no non-whites on its leadership team. What I despised most were some Coloureds who acted as if they were white and this chip on my shoulder harboured major resentment towards these my 'Coloured-brethren'! I was a nineteen-year-old Coloured young man, proud of my her-itage and culture but evidently scarred by the hatred in my own country. At St James, I had the opportunity to now en-gage within a 'racial-mix', which also included church mem-bers who were Afrikaners. Needless to say, I distanced my-self from many of those brothers and sisters of the faith and was cautious as to who I befriended within my new church. However, God was about to initiate a work of healing at the very centre of my being. I was so proud to refer to myself as a 'Coloured', that I often forgot what it meant to be ... a human being!

It was a Friday evening and our youth ministries had just finished. As always, there was time for chit-chat as everyone waited for the pick-ups by parents. A young lady with a German accent was being introduced to us and it was then that I had the pleasure of meeting Martina Sackmann — an exchange student residing with a local white Afrikaner family. She was at St James on the invitation of friends from school and it was evident that she was somewhat different. In the weeks which followed, Martina and I would spend many a Friday evening having a chat and pretty soon, we became friends. I had arranged to visit her one afternoon at the house she was staying at and soon found myself in a white area at a fancy house. Obviously I was very nervous. I made my way up the driveway and rang the doorbell. Unbeknown to me, the wife of the owner had her Bridge club round that very afternoon. As the door opened the lady looked at me and said "Die baas is nie hier nie" (in Afrikaans) — "the boss isn't here" — and told me to come back and clean the garden when the owner returns! Clean the garden? Wait a minute — she thinks I'm the gardener? Now let me explain that within South Africa at the time, all menial and labour-intensive work was generally done by non-whites. Just as I felt all self-respect drain from my soul as I stood there in embarrassment, I heard footsteps running to the front door. It was Martina! I could read the shame in her face as she tried to explain to her 'house-mum' that I was not the 'gardener' but the guy she was waiting for. Many years later, while meeting Martina alongside her family in Dublin, she recalled that moment with embarrassment and shame — and my reply to her simply was ... "it wasn't your fault!"

Martina never made it to my twenty first birthday party — as her host family informed her that their decision not to let her attend, was due to 'security reasons'. Security my ass! This was good old bigotry and hatred wrapped up in nice language and concern. I wonder what that family would say if they realised that Martina and I have remained friends to this very day! Maybe I'm being harsh on that family. Maybe they felt a major sense of responsibility to her and therefore having her attend a twenty first birthday party in a Coloured area was a bridge too far. Well, all I know is that my white friends, coloured friends and black friends all had a crazy night at my birthday party — but to this very day Martina struggles to forgive that couple for not allowing her to attend.

Apartheid at present has ended — but the struggle to overcome bigotry on all sides remain. "Aluta Continua!" ... the historical struggle for freedom in South Africa may have ended at Mr Mandela's appointment as President, but the struggle to see one another as equals still remains in South Africa, in Northern Ireland and in many other countries around the world! Having spent my penultimate school year involved in student boycotts, I now had to focus on my final year. Thanks to Mrs Chatre, I concentrated on doing the best I could in the year ahead. Needless to say, it was a tough year, having to do two years in one ... as we had just lost an entire academic year due to student boycotts. However, under Mrs Chatre's personal tutelage, I made it through. I passed my matric exam and my schooling was now officially over. Now what? John Lennon once said that life is what happens when one is busy making plans! He was right of course, but in my case I had no plans! Life was happening and I had absolutely no clue as to what I was going to do with my future! I simply had to make my way through the quagmire of a troubled world, but I had no understanding as to how I was going to do so!

I was now just one of many, trying to find *'my place in this world!' (Michael W Smith: 1991)*

Chapter 5: 'What do I do after school'?

'I know the plans I have for you' says the Lord 'plans to prosper you and not to harm you, plans to give you hope and a future'

(Jeremiah 29 vs 11)

My time at school was over and my journey to future employment had begun. Dad enrolled me as a student of Information Technology into Peninsula Technikon — a further education college created for and attended predominantly by Coloured and black students. 'Pen Tech' was a popular option for us due to the fact that it prepared one for the world of work, as it centred predominantly on skills development for employment. The question as to what I would do after school was often a topic of heated debate within our family, for it was my aspiration to attend Bible College and study Theology. However, dad saw no future in that and due to the fact that computers were the craze in the eighties, Computer Programming became my daily bread at Pen Tech. Although I was not as bright as my sisters when it came to Mathematics, I made the grade to get in. Needless to say, I hated the course and spent more time in the college gym and on the squash courts than I did in the classroom.

This was now my very first experience of campus life and I was making the most of it.

It was here however, where I developed a friendship with a third year student whom I initially met months earlier. He just happened to be a student leader of the Computing Department. Andy van der Byl was as cool as they come. He had striking long hair which ran to his shoulders and drove a scrambler as his mode of transport. He was not just the coolest person I knew but also a Jesus follower. Needless to say we became friends — never realising that we would remain so for life! Andy attended a church called St James, a non-racial church in Kenilworth. While chatting to him about the difficulties I was having with life generally, Andy invited me to attend a national Youth for Christ camp which he was about to attend that Summer. The camp would cost me the current equivalent of twenty pounds or so and in 1987 in my community — that sort of surplus cash was pretty hard to come by. I paid what I could and Andy took care of the rest. So, Boxing Day morning in 1987, I got onto a bus filled with white young people and very few persons of colour and headed for the outskirts of Johannesburg. I was off to a Youth Camp, never knowing that this event would literally ... change my life!

These teenagers were pretty trendy and the leaders were loads of fun. I got to know some of Andy's mates and by the time we made our first stop at Beaufort West, I was just one of the crowd. The bus journey was long — Cape Town to Johannesburg by coach ... a nineteen-hour journey, one way! Soon we arrived and stopped in a place called Welkom, in the Orange Free State and enjoyed some much needed lunch and a swim with a white family, who hosted two bus loads of us! As Welkom was in the heart of the Afrikaner 'heartland' I was sceptical about this family to say the least. As one of the few non-white faces in the group and due to my own personal prejudice, I was unsure as to what to make of this family. The Lewis family and I would not just become life-long friends but they were a family I grew to love as if they were my own. Janine was the second eldest of four kids and for some unknown reason, we just hit it off. She had a tremendous zest for life and although we chatted a little while visiting, I discovered she was coming to Youth Week too!

Youth Week was a blast! I had never attended a camp like it before — two and a half thousand teenagers from every corner of South Africa having a brilliant time for a week ... then a break for a few days and another load of teenagers arrived for week two — white and black worshipping and hanging-out together. I was so impressed with this camp that the following two years I worked in the kitchens for the first week of camp, as a means of payment for the second — allowing me therefore to be a camper in week two, as there was no way I could afford to attend. One year I could not afford the bus payment from Cape Town and decided to hike from Cape Town to Johannesburg with my friend Tony Figaji, now one of South Africa's leading paediatric neuro surgeons. We made it to Port Elizabeth and jumped onto a postal train on its way to Johannesburg, having spent a night sleeping on the side of the motorway.

The morning and evening sessions at Youth Week were dedicated to spiritual development, while the afternoon was geared toward sport and relaxation. Many an evening Janine and I were hanging out together. We became inseparable and even engaged in the odd kiss now and again. I also met so many people, particularly guys I competed against playing football that week. I was meeting all these people and making so many friends but something else was happening to me ... I was encountering God on a major scale and although I seemed to be pretty cool on the outside, I was in total turmoil within. In all that I was learning and experiencing at Youth Week, I kept thinking about having to start my second year at tech, doing a course I simply did not enjoy. It was uncanny; amidst all these young people, I still desperately needed time to myself. One evening while at camp, I made my way to a hilltop overlooking the vast landscape which made up the Magaliesberg mountains. I started to speak to God and pretty soon I was in tears. What was I going to do with my life? What was my future to be? I could not see myself sitting behind a computer screen for the remainder of my life. I did not want to return to tech — I knew that in my heart, but how was I to share that news with my father? What else was I going to do even if I did leave tech?

The majority of these youth leaders from St James were at university. They seemed to know what they wanted from life and what they needed to do in order to get there. I on the other hand was lost, unsure and in desperate need of direction. I knew that I wanted to do something of value with my life. I come from a community whose lives seem so mundane — school, marriage, kids, work, drive home, sleep etc., the same treadmill-like existence every single day. My community were not decision-makers — we lived in the grip of Apartheid and racial segregation where we were funnelled down a path not of our own making, the path of being the 'work force'! South Africa however was slowly changing politically and I wanted to have a future where I would not be caught in this mundane lifestyle of servitude, where some had and others did not — where rules are made by the few and labour done by the many! Maybe I just wanted too much from life! Why did I constantly have this rebellious streak within me that would simply not bend to the fate of so many non-white South Africans? Maybe I was at a stage where I wanted my life to count for a lot more than what I was seeing in my community. I also knew that there was more to life than the simple acquisition of money and therefore pursuing wealth was useless too. I wanted to make my life count for something long-term. I wanted my life to be of use to others so that when my time came to leave the planet, I would be satisfied in the knowledge that the world was a better place because of me! I had this vision for my life but had no idea how to get there! I needed God to intervene and in a miraculous way and inevitably, He did!

Do you believe that God speaks to us individually? Ministers tell us that we encounter God when reading the Scriptures. It is evident that the Holy Spirit often assists us in understanding what we are reading, challenging us to physically apply the words on the page to our very lives. It is generally accepted that God speaks to us through His Word and not necessarily in an audible fashion ... or does He? Well, whatever your thoughts on that issue, it seemed that God spoke to me in the depths of my being while sitting on that hill. In talking to Him about the uncertainty of my future and the fear of going back home, God told me to trust Him and although I had no idea as to the implications of those words, I decided to do so. Here I was, having a conversation with someone I could not see and entrusting my future to Him, still having no clue as to what my future was really going to look like. I arrived at the top of that hill unsure of the future and I left it in the same way. However, something happened on that hill between God and I!

Stories about missionaries at Sunday School and church camps left a large impression on me, so much so that I desired to be a missionary too! While hanging-out with Andy at Youth Week, I happened to ask him as to what he was planning on doing now that he finished tech. Andy informed me that he had applied to a Bible College. He shared with me his desire to work for Scripture Union and studying theology would be the key to achieving this goal. I suddenly contemplated the thought of Bible College! If I wanted to be a missionary, what better place to be! However, my parents would blow their top at this idea and sitting in the coach returning to Cape Town I could think of nothing else but the major row we were going to have about my future when I got home. There was this expectation within our community that when leaving school, one would find employment and hand over your salary to your parents. You would then be given some money by your parents for personal use until you were ready to be married, in which case your salary became your own. I observed this cultural norm every single day. Young people in my community seemed to have no ambition, no desire to do something out of the ordinary with their lives and the expectation was that once they get married, they would build a small accommodation for their parents in the back yard of their home and they would move into the family home — all living together! Is this really what I wanted for my life? What I did know was that my life was my own — and I don't get to have another. Was I going to spend the remainder of it in front of a computer screen and follow the cultural norm? Yes, this sort of lifestyle may come with a regular pay cheque, but is this what I wanted for my life or was I really going to trust God with my future, the way He asked me to up on that hill? Either way there was a fight coming! I knew my father and I expected the worst!

I was right! On arriving home from Johannesburg, I tried to tell mum and dad about this new idea I had ... the possibility of going to Bible College. It didn't go down well. Words were said and phrases like move out, not with my money, a disgrace to the family and so on, were very quickly thrown in my direction. This 'trust me' thing God had spoken about was coming at a cost and being disowned by my father became unbearable. My father made a decision that night that I was now lost to him; it would be another six months before he uttered another word to me. I now felt totally alone! I had nothing else left but to trust God as He had asked me to. I was now going to learn first-hand what real and practical faith was all about! I made up my mind, I was going to Bible College!

One January afternoon, Mrs Howard (my child-minder and Sunday School teacher years before) and I made our way to the Cape Evangelical Bible Institute, not too far from where she lived. As we arrived late that afternoon, we met a gentleman who was busy locking the premises. I knew he was not the caretaker, for he was white and I asked him if the Principal was still on site. He introduced himself and I quickly realised that I was in fact speaking to the Dean of the school, Dr Donald Aeschliman himself. He invited me in and inquired as to who I was looking for. I responded and informed him that I wanted to see him as I now sought to make CEBI my place of study. He politely informed me that applications had to be made months ago and that the in-coming first year students were starting the very next day. I was too late to make application! As I stood there in tears, I started to tell 'Dr A' the story about the hill in Johannesburg and how I had made a decision to trust God with my future and how this trust had now led me to the doors of this insti-tution. Dr A smiled and invited me to his office. We chatted about what I wanted to do with my life and I informed him of the dream I had of being a missionary. I let him know that I had nothing else to do with my life and that I could not be-lieve that having told me to trust Him, God would now fail at the very first hurdle. He then inquired of me as to how I was to finance myself over the three years of study, should there be a place for me. I told him that that too was problematic, as I knew that there was no way dad would be paying for me to study at a Bible College. Dr A then agreed to let me attend the registration event the next day alongside the rest of the first year students, but enforced the fact that I had until the end of that week to find the fee to at least register with the college. It was clear in my own head — I had four days to find money in order to pay the registration fee. If not, I had to walk away. Dr A and I left it at that. I now needed to find myself a little money ... fast!

What could I do to raise money? For the next few days I washed cars and mowed lawns. I jumped the trains up and down the white suburbs and opened up people's garbage bins as they awaited collection and took out as many 'empties' as I could find — empty coke and soft-drink bottles that I could sell back to the shops for a few pennies ... but come Thursday night, I was still well short. I did not have the necessary money required to pay the registration fee. There it was ... I now saw the writing on the wall — this 'faith and trust in God' thing, simply was not for me! It was very evident, that God's promise on a hill just a few weeks before was literally — pie in the sky!

I arrived at the college early that Friday morning, way before the other pupils as I was too embarrassed to have to clear-out my locker in front of everyone else. I simply wanted to get in and get out as quick as I could. I was embarrassed — what would my fellow first year students think of me — I couldn't even afford the registration costs, let alone study fees for three years. I was the first to arrive that morning and I made my way to the corridor to empty my locker. When opening my locker, there it was ... a white envelope with my name on it. I opened it and looked at the few notes of cash which totalled to the exact amount required for my registration fees. Needless to say, I was in floods of tears. I slipped to the floor, sat on my bum and wept! It was only five minutes prior that

I honestly thought that God had forsaken me. Five minutes ago my faith was shattered — now it soared to the One who told me to trust Him. I made my way into the toilets and sobbed! *Lesson one learnt Vic — God makes the impossible possible!* Later that morning, I made my way up to the admin office and registered to commence my pursuit in attaining a Diploma in Theology. What I did not know at that stage was that I would receive a scholarship from the faculty for the next three years as well -as long as I maintained a good academic average, cleaned toilets each week and developed a character which was acceptable. The first two was dead easy — the whole Christian character thing was another story!

My three years at the Cape Evangelical Bible Institute was possibly the foundation stone for my professional life. The opportunity to study, clearly provided me the building block for future employment. Many a life-long friendship was formed here. Andy became a close friend and mentor, someone I looked up to and someone I wish I could be like. He was independent, well-respected and a true spiritual leader. However, he was always up for a laugh ... a fellow 'coloured' who understood me and the culture I came from and someone who also encountered his fair share of personal problems too. Maybe Andy tolerated me for three years, but we became best of friends then and remain so to this very day.

My interest in Theology was awakened by excellent lecturers and a dynamic pastoral staff. I guess it was obvious that I was not the easiest person to get along with, for now I encountered some classmates with whom I had nothing in common. I was one of the proverbial rough diamonds that needed shaping. It is fair to say that I had a massive chip on my shoulder at this stage of my life — not that I thought that I was 'all that' — but more in the sense that I felt that life owed me something. I was under no illusions — I clearly did not belong and neither did I fit into the ethos of this Christian institution. I was out of place! My life's background was so different to that of my fellow students. My life up to that stage was all about protecting self — and if it meant lying and stealing when I needed to, being harsh in manner and in my usage of words ... well then I did as I needed to. Mum and dad raised us well within our home but I was a city kid who learnt to survive out there. It was clear that I had severe design flaws and my behaviour was not conducive to someone seeking to be a missionary. I therefore awaited the moment when the faculty would call me in order to show me the door.

By providing me a scholarship, the faculty secured my academic future but they also had plans to develop my character. It seemed however, that my negative behaviour was not just of concern to the faculty but so too the senior class. Philip Frost — a final year student, made it his business of pointing out my design flaws. Philip was a pain initially, but in but a few weeks I had grown to love this white Zimbabwean farmer as if he were my own brother. Alongside the 'Golden Girls' — Luisa, Jenni, Caroline and Sandi ... Andy and Philip took me under their wing. Gift Zokufa — a tremendous footballer, was another individual who was wise beyond his years and often offered a word or two to aid my development of character. I had all these people investing in my life — sharing their lives with me every day, encouraging me to be better than what I was. I had a choice, I could reject their goodness or I could allow God to transform me through them. South Africa was in trouble politically, but in college we were encountering something very different — we were building community — white, coloured, black — church-people and rough diamonds like myself ... we became a family — a family of young Christians learning from one another ... a family doing Koinonia (fellowship) and slowly developing into Jesus people!

The faculty had a profound impact on me! Dr Aeschlimann was a man we all respected. As principal, we not only admired him for his leadership and for giving people like myself an opportunity to study, but he truly was a Godly man who led by example. Alan Jansen — as the coloured member of staff, was an individual people like myself could aspire to. He understood people like me and knew our cultural background. He was a very astute and impressive lecturer as well as a dynamic preacher. I often listened intently to many a sermon under this inspirational leader and I thank God for him! Margie Gustafson was the college music director as well as one my lecturers. Due to my 'rough-diamond nature', I was extremely surprised when Margie asked me to be on the college deputation team. This was a small music team who would visit churches, sing a few tunes and be the public image of the college as a means of public relations and marketing of the college in the city. I loved this group. Musically we gelled very well. Margie was excellent in bringing out the best in us vocally but unbeknown to us, she mentored us. I only realised that much later on. You see alongside the other lecturers, this was not just an academic institution — the Cape Evangelical Bible Institute was a family — people nurturing and mentoring one another, serving each other as Jesus served His community.

My first and second year flew by. I was doing well academically but as far as my character development was concerned, I often took two steps forward and one step back. I was getting there, slowly but surely. However, at the start of my third year, things changed slightly. I had just celebrated my twenty-first birthday and was determined to work on my character and implement within my life key spiritual concepts I was now learning about. As a third year student starting my final year, I was determined to keep my nose clean and do the best I possibly could academically. There was now no time for silliness, laziness or girls. However, it was then when I met Lisa!

About three weeks into the start of the academic year, pupils and staff went away for a weekend, more as a welcome for the incoming first year pupils. Andy and I happened to find ourselves in the library that Friday afternoon prior to the weekend, when Lisa walked in. Andy however had no interest in Lisa as his attention was already captured by another first year pupil working in the library, who would later become his life's partner and wife — Shan. As Lisa walked past us, it suddenly dawned on me that I had met this young lady before — quite recently, for her face was familiar. Andy and I discussed as to where we had seen her and we realised that we had met her recently at a Scripture Union 'Swimathon' fundraising event. Lisa got out of the pool and walked past the table where Andy and I were playing music and doing a bit of 'DJ-ing'. I had made a cheeky comment to her and as she passed she in-turn smiled and replied with an even cheekier comment! We nodded at each other and kept our gaze on one another but that was it. I thought to myself — *no use looking any further Vic — the girl you are looking at is white! No need to entertain any thoughts!* Andy and I carried on studying in the library that morning, but every now and then I looked up at her; I was distracted — I was interested; I was hooked!

As everyone made their way down to the "Fresher's" weekend that Friday afternoon, I could only look forward to joining them the next day. I was competing in a pre-season football tournament on the Saturday and therefore only joined everyone on the Saturday evening. I guess I felt a little out of place as everyone seemed to be having a good time. That evening, I got my dinner and made my way outside. While eating, I was joined by a young lady. Lisa formerly introduced herself and for the very first time, we had a conversation. Later that evening, we took a long stroll on the beach along with the rest of the students and members of the faculty. We sat down in the sand and chatted. The next morning, I overslept and was awakened by my friend Stafford Petersen ... an individual who would later rise within the ranks of the Full Gospel denomination in South Africa. Lisa was apparently looking for me. It seemed that our closeness on the beach the night before meant quite a lot to her. If truth be told, I couldn't wait to see her either. Something was happening that I hadn't encountered before — I was pining to see her!

Although I developed friendships with people like Martina and Janine, I had never seriously dated before. I knew nothing of the 'dating protocol' ... what to say and what to do. Lisa and I got to know each other very well that year. Her mum and sister provided me with employment in one of their businesses. It was good seeing Lisa at college every day, but I regret to say that I often took her for granted too. On reflection, I'm amazed that she stuck with me as long as she did. The end of that academic year, I got the opportunity to go to Namibia as a missionary and the relationship came to a very natural end. If truth be told, I think Lisa was planning to end things anyway. Yes, I loved her very much. Yes, she was an amazing friend but I must admit that I was very selfish in that relationship too. The one positive aspect of that relationship is that Lisa and I have remained friends to this day.

Graduation day came and went. It was possibly one of the proudest and most memorable days of my life. Three years had come and gone and besides the many 'first-place' certificates achieved at primary school, this Diploma in Biblical Studies was the greatest achievement in my life to date. Along with my family, Lisa was there to share that moment with me. Later at home, mum and dad provided me with a graduation evening tea for the extended family. Reuben, my

New Testament and Greek lecturer shared some words in preparation for my move three weeks later to Namibia. He spoke from Jeremiah 29vs11 ... emphasising that God knew the plans He had for me, plans to prosper and not to harm me ... plans to give me a future and a hope. I was not to know then, that these words would echo in my mind for the remainder of my life, for I would ponder those words in the good and bad days ahead. Three weeks later those words rang true as I got on a plane, waved my family goodbye and took my first step in the next chapter of my life ... being a missionary.

CEBI had a profound impact upon my life. I never got to thank Dr Aeschliman for providing me an opportunity — not just to study but also to learn about what being a human being was all about! I was never a 'bad boy' as such, but I had issues — personal attitudes that needed challenged and CEBI did that — it not only challenged me spiritually but more importantly it challenged me with regard to my character. I have come to understand that very few people get an opportunity to study at an institution where the development of character means considerably more than academic achievement. Of course we had to meet an academic standard, but life-long friendships were made because we were all travellers on the same journey, passionate about Jesus but trying also to find our way in the world as flawed people. In my spiritual journey prior to my three years of study, I had burnt bridges and had destroyed relationships ... but by the time of graduation, I was a better man than I was when I started at that institution. However, I now had so much more to learn about life and being a missionary was going to be a steep learning curve!

One man gave me an opportunity to study and because of that opportunity, I was about to embark on my first job in full-time employment. Needless to say ... *I owe you Dr A!*

Chapter 6: Thirty nine steps to glory!

Do you know what my favourite part of the game is?
The opportunity to play!

(Mike Singletary, NFL ex-player and current coach: Chicago Bears)

I was a fairly late arrival to the world of competitive sport. While we were afforded every opportunity to play sport at primary school, my ability to compete at sport arrived much later on. Yes, I was a late developer and due to the fact that I enjoyed and excelled at the arts, the world of sport was a new phenomenon, except for swimming of course which allowed me to shine from a young age. Sport would have remained but a pipe-dream had it not been for the generosity of the school staff who gave of their time freely before and after school for our benefit. My love for sport was therefore honed because others volunteered and gave of their time for my enjoyment.

While at primary school, it was obvious that I was not built to partake in the sprints and therefore summer athletics always remained a challenge to me. For an hour a few mornings a week — and for a period of about three weeks or so, staff and pupils of Norma Road Primary would make their way down to the local playing fields to train for inter-house athletics.

My goal was to get into my House relay team and many a year I never even made that, let alone receive colours to compete against other schools. I loved watching athletics and looked forward to our inter-house athletics competition day as well as the inter-schools. As a school, we would compete against twelve or so other schools and the competition even at primary level, was fierce. Years later in my early teens, playing football meant that I was often running in order to keep fit. As we lived on the coast, I would run down to the beach and then run as long as I could up and down the sand dunes. I had done so much running for football that pretty soon I had the physical capacity and opportunity to compete at middle distance running, making the eight hundred and fifteen hundred metres my specialty. Although I never excelled as such, it was great to just compete. Finishing second in the fifteen hundred at an inter-school's competition one year, was as good as it got, for though this result got me through to the next round of the competition, I finished in seventh from eight competitors at the regional semi-finals, or second last in layman's terms!

While at primary school, my love for playing rugby was ignited not at school as such, but through watching the Springboks on television with my father. Dad was an avid fan of the Springboks and having played on the wing for many years for his club 'Wanderers', we never missed an international on television. Due to Apartheid, the Springboks could not officially compete at international level but were often invited to Australia and New Zealand on 'rebel' tours. Those internationals were often preceded by major anti-Apartheid demonstrations and it was obvious to me at the time that the international community too disagreed with Apartheid. However, the Springboks were our team and we supported them — well, dad and I.

Watching these matches early in the morning, was a great way to bond with him. Dad and I got up, made some coffee and sat with our duvets ... rugby supporters, father and son!

My love for rugby later ignited into a passion due to the influence of my primary school coach. Mr Summers played himself and seemed to know what he was doing as a coach. Many a training session was had on that sandy school pitch and I loved every minute of it. Representing my school at rugby was a tremendous honour and under Mr Summers' leadership we excelled as a team and were one of the better school sides in our region, culminating in a regional school's final one year! That particular year, the last game of the season would determine whether or not we would end up being the top primary school in our district. We were trailing by six points in a very tight game. As scrumhalf, I remember collecting the ball from the base of the scrum and as time was running out, I opted for a 'grubba' kick to the right-hand-side of the opposition try-line, rather than run the ball to the out-half. The ball crossed the side-line a yard from the goal line! We were one yard from the try line but never quite made it there in the final five or so minutes. Our opponents were a good team and they deserved it, but the loss was a tough pill to swallow and for those of you who know me well, you will agree that I hate losing! Many years later, after 'hanging up the footi boots', I would yet again have the pleasure of playing rugby, but this time on another continent!

Competitive football began not at a club as such, but in the church grounds. As the Howard brothers and I attended the same church, many a football game was had on the grassy pitch at the side of the church building. Mr Howard later decided to start an official team, allowing many of us to then compete at football within a local league. As newcomers we had a fairly average team, but we were blessed with a class striker in the person of Leon Livesy — strong, athletic, quick and an eye for goal! Many a game was won because of his ability but inevitably, Leon left us as other teams too were now keen on his services. However, one year we progressed in a cup competition and got into a semi-final. It was a big match and I injured my ankle in the quarter-final of that competition. I had a very bad sprain and the likelihood of missing the semi-final was quite high. However, I had other ideas. I was not going to miss that match. I discovered later that I had a fracture but I was determined to play. For the next week I went to school with cabbage leaves wrapped around my ankle — for it was well-known in our culture that cabbage leaves had powerful anti-inflammatory properties which reduced and relieved swelling. At night I slept with bandages soaked in vinegar, which did the very same thing — reduce swelling. Between the cabbage leaves, vinegar bandages and a medical ankle guard strapped tightly around my ankle, I made it to the game ... which we lost by one goal. It rained during the entire match and for most of the second half we were defending — but at the end of the game we were beaten. We were underdogs, but we worked our socks off and even though we lost, we were proud that we gave a good account of ourselves.

As a teenager, my love for football further developed not at school as such — but also in the streets! My neighbours, the Lewin family were athletes and footballers and we organised a 'street' team — sometimes a team of six, sometimes more ... it didn't really matter. Adding to the fact that the Thompson family a few houses away had four boys who were very athletic too, we had a formidable team. Many a match was organised after school and soon we were playing street football at least three or four times a week. It was during one of those matches when one of the opposition players disappeared from the game and returned with a bread knife, seeking to plunge it into my body. Having kicked the legs off each other, it seemed he had had enough and decided upon a different plan of action! The bread knife itself looked menacing and I had no intention of having it plunged somewhere into my body. It was the first time that I would be confronted with someone wielding a knife at me, but it would not be the last. It was just one of those things!

A few years later I ended up playing football for St James. It was during one of these games that competitive football would come to a sobering end! It was May-day long weekend and we were involved in a pre-season tournament. We got to the final, playing Observatory — our nemesis. Mum had arrived from work in time to watch the final. It was a tight game — scoreless until the very last minute. 'Obs' got a corner and playing striker meant that I took-up a position close to the half-way line, with two defenders for company. One of these defenders was unfortunate to lose a hand earlier in life but used his stump to work away at my ribs each time we tussled. He was a great player! Anyway, our goal keeper caught the ball from the corner and threw it up-field in my general direction. As the ball rolled toward me, I was very aware of the one defender at my back. It was instinct — I had done it before; step over the ball while running toward it — clip the ball to your left with your back foot and turn immediately, taking the ball away from the defender. Having turned all in one motion, I progressed toward the opposition goal! One defender taken care of and now the other! He was back-peddling. Brilliant! I turned one side then the other — all the time heading closer to the goal! It was clear that the other defender was catching up. As I got to the edge of the box I took an extra step to the right — opening up my body to curl the ball into the goal with my right foot. The goal keeper came running out to close the space and make the save. The ball was in the inside of my right foot. I was just outside the penalty box and had a clear view of the goal-keeper and the net! Just as the goal-keeper went to ground, I slid the ball between his legs. Both defenders then tackled me a split second later — one having 'scissored' my right-ankle. Having hit the ground, the goal-keeper kept sliding on the rain-soaked pitch and could not stop. As his right foot was high, he caught me on the inside of my right knee, pushing it back with force. As the defender had my right ankle between his legs, both he and I heard a tear, for he immediately called for medical attention. I had torn the cruciate ligament in my right knee! I watched the ball roll into the empty net and I heard the joyful shouts of my team mates, but it was when they got to me that they realised what had happened. My days of competitive football were over — I was twenty-one years old! Awaking from the operation, it was possibly the worst pain I had experienced. What followed was months of using crutches. I started to gain weight and got really depressed about not playing again. Somehow God would do what He always does — intervene ... even in a footballing incident!

My second cousin Alan, attended a lively 'happy clappy' church and he had informed me of a visiting American preacher who was on tour in South Africa. Alan explained to me that this gentleman was gifted in the area of healing and immediately I thought about my knee. Would it be possible that this preacher could bring healing to my knee? Is it possible that I could commence playing competitively after a 'miracle'? In further discussion with Alan, I decided that I had nothing to lose and intended on attending the crusade. So off we went one Sunday evening ... Alan, my crutches and I.

I sat through it all — anxiously awaiting the 'healing' part of the service. Eventually the time had come and the invitation was made for those wanting a miracle, to progress to the front stage. My crutches and I very slowly made our way onto the platform. I stood at the end of what seemed like a very long line and I could see the preacher — with helpers, make his way down the line toward me. One by one I saw people fall down in the line. It seemed the preacher had a 'modus operandi' — he prayed for them, hit them on the forehead and down they went. I presumed they had been overcome by God's Spirit and some sort of healing was taking place — or so I believed. Now it was my turn. The preacher asked me what my healing request was. I informed him about my knee and requested prayer in order that my knee would heal well. As I had ripped all the cartilage around the knee joint in the tackle as well, I knew therefore that stability would be an issue if I was ever to play competitive football again. I asked him to pray that my knee would heal well. Then he took over.

He asked me to close my eyes. Now, I seldom pray with my eyes closed. To this very day, whether in church or doing school assemblies — I would very rarely shut my eyes when praying. So, I simply looked down as the preacher began by praying in tongues. Now, I'm not a 'speaking in tongues' guy. Let me clarify that I have not received that gift from the Holy Spirit. Other brothers and sisters whom I know well have that gift but I don't. However, I'm fairly relaxed about all that so it was no issue when the preacher started to speak in tongues. What bothered me was the first shot of his open palm against my head! Then another — then another! It was clear that I was not going to fall and the two guys behind me in the 'catching position' were going to be disappointed. The problem was that I was not for falling! Eventually the preacher told me that God had decided not to heal me due to the immaturity of my faith. Then he moved on!

Fair enough — he was a preacher who knew about all this stuff and maybe my faith was immature. However, as I made my way back to my seat I couldn't help but wonder if all that falling down stuff had more to do with being hit against the forehead while having your eyes closed. I don't know. A few years later I attended a national Youth for Christ camp where, during a prayer time after worship, a teenager ended up barking like a dog. When I inquired as to this chaos I was encountering, I was told she was barking 'in the Spirit'. Now, I have no issue with God affording the Church His gifts; the Apostle Paul spends quite a bit a time explaining and listing these gifts in his correspondence with the Corinthian church — but smacks on the head and barking like a dog never made it into Paul's list of gifts! Reading the Scriptures, I am also aware that God is a God of order. Although I firmly believe in God's ability to heal and let me add that I align myself to the fact that God has given his Church a variety of gifts to be used within the Church for its edification. I struggle however with some modern interpretation of its implementation. Maybe I'm too conservative in my thinking ... for which I'm happy to concede that this may be the case! Anyway, my relationship with these 'modern gifts' was now at an end! My knee was not healed and that one tackle would physically bother me for the rest of my life!

While rugby and football were my passion, I was introduced to baseball while at high school. As baseball was a fairly new sport to the 'Coloured community', it pretty soon became extremely popular. I joined and played for one season only due to the fact that I could never get to the matches — with mum and dad both working Saturday mornings. A few years later while in Namibia, I ended up playing men's softball for Sparta. Two years later we switched over to baseball. We ended up winning the Namibian Men's League, being runners-up the previous year. Initially I played short-stop but then was asked to catch (the fella sitting behind the diamond plate and behind the player seeking to hit the ball). I loved playing catcher. It was a fairly important fielding position and one could call the play from there. There was no let-up playing in that position, for it required concentration throughout the game and a good arm to peg (throw) the ball to any base when required. An instinctive catch while playing short-stop one year, led to our very first championship. It was a very proud moment for all of us, for we were a very young team going up against a seasoned group of players who had dominated the sport for years. We were now the young lions — up and coming and hungry and under the tutorage of Dion our coach, we excelled! However, the up and down movement required while playing catcher, coupled with my love for playing football, would have a negative impact on my knees for many a year.

When arriving in Northern Ireland in 1996, I commenced playing football for our church 'old Boys Brigade' team. While playing one Saturday, I tore the clip holding my cruciate to my thigh muscle. Another operation — more time on crutches. While recuperating, I received a call from Musgrave hospital asking me if I would like to be involved in a trial operation, as a certain physician was experimenting with a grafting procedure — grafting a piece of one's hamstring into the cruciate and allowing the two to grow as one muscle. I agreed and what a success that was! Three operations in total to repair one tackle! However, I now had to be sensible — I was getting older. I had a bad knee and competitive football was now no longer an option, but playing rugby was!

Moving to Armagh, I was invited by Johnny Nesbitt — a friend, to come and play rugby at Armagh Rugby Club. One game to 'help out' ended up in a three-year period, playing for the thirds. Calum was four at the time and started playing mini-rugby too. Watching Calum in the morning and then playing in the afternoon meant that Julie felt like a single parent each weekend and pretty soon she reminded me that I had a responsibility to be a father, as now Caleb too had come along. Soon my time of playing competitive team sport was coming to an end. If truth be told, I was getting to a stage where I could no longer hack the sore body or the odd punch to the face while awaiting the ball at the base of a ruck! My time of playing sport was over! During the years I have also played table-tennis, football, rugby and enjoyed swimming. I excelled in some and others I enjoyed. However, I would soon be introduced to one sport I simply cannot master — welcome to the world of golf!

Growing up in South Africa, golf was a sport generally played by whites, for they alone could afford it! There was no such thing as 'disposable income' in my community and money for clubs and rounds of golf were unheard of, unless you were lucky enough to have a bit of money on the side! Whilst teaching at Antrim Grammar School, I had come to learn that the staff and pupils played each other on occasion. This particular year, the staff needed an additional player and my friend Jason decided that due to the fact that I played baseball, I should be at ease with playing golf. How wrong he was! With the principal's permission, Jason and I spent a bit of time hitting a ball on the rugby pitches. Needless to say, I was hooked! Having been involved in team sport all of my life, this was now something completely different. Due to the fact that I hate spending money, I visited many a car boot sale purchasing the odd club for a 'fiver' until I had a full set. I am yet to purchase a golf-set in a shop! Over the years playing golf with close friends like Jason and Bryan (a fellow South African) has been a pleasure, for not only does time on the golf course improve our game but it also provides opportunities to catch-up on life and talk about issues as men. To date, I find playing golf with these two friends invaluable.

Jason and I often are amazed at Bryan's ability to hit a ball, for as an ex-cricketer he has a very natural swing. Jason's recovery shots on the fairway and short game are amazing and many a time he has got the better of 'Bags' and I over eighteen holes because of his skill with his short game. However, it is the conversations about real life issues that I truly enjoy — which begins at breakfast before the eighteen holes, then on the course and finishing with lunch. Good conversations yes, but more so, good friends! The joy of my life too is playing with my sons. Watching Calum, Caleb and Joel have the opportunity to play golf at such a young age gives me a tremendous sense of pride, for it's not just about learning the game — but also simply about having the opportunity to hang-out with them. They are now at a stage where they compete with one another, which often results in one being grumpy at the end of it all. I can't blame them, for they are very much like their father — coming second is not part of our DNA!

Of the many codes of sport I have played in my life, there is nothing quite like swimming. Living at Strandfontein, which is right at the sea ... I was constantly swimming in the ocean or in the huge tidal pool at the seaside facility. Coupled with surfing, I was always swimming and it is the one thing that I often could lose myself in, irrespective of how tired I was or what my day had been like. Currently I try swimming three mornings a week, for it seems to be the only way I can keep my weight under control. Doing one length after the other also allows me time to think about the day ahead, processing decisions I need to make when I get to school etc. It also allows me the opportunity to pray for others and get some great exercise at the same time.

I have come to discover that there is nothing quite like being a fan, especially when you have close mates watching a game with you. Wives, let me say something to you ... your husbands and partners need time with their mates, either playing or watching sport. In the same way that you require time with your friends, your partners need to hangout with theirs when it comes to sport. I can't quite explain the dynamic of going to watch a game of rugby or football with your mates — the pre-match beer or two, the chat, the expectation, chatting to other supporters in the pub — be they opposition supporters and so on. My most memorable moment as a fan was spending time in Cardiff with friends, when Ireland beat Wales to win the Six Nations. What a celebration! What a night of friendship and just hanging out! What a night of comradery! What a night of mutual friendship and just being a fan! As men, we require this time. It's vital for us!

Thirty-nine steps to glory ... the amount of steps it took the late Bobby Moore and his team mates to collect the Jules Rimet trophy from Queen Elizabeth in 1966. Many after him have walked those steps too, some victors and others collecting the runner's-up medals. However, glory always manifests itself when we play sport ... maybe not in the form of a medal or trophy, but in the realisation that we have given of our best and exhausted every sap of energy in pursuit of victory! That pursuit my friend is in itself, glory ... the joy of giving it all for the cause. Win or lose, sport is about giving our best and entrusting team mates to mutually strive toward the same goal, toward a shared victory. Sounds very much like the journey of life doesn't it — each of us supporting one another as we try to make sense of life, mutually seeking to find meaning and purpose.

No man is an island!

Chapter 7: Friends, parties and surfing!

A true friend is someone who realises that you are a good egg,
even though he knows that you are slightly cracked.

(Bernard Meltzer)

St James Church in Kenilworth became my home church
and many a life-long friendship was to be made here.
Andy's invitation to attend my very first Youth Week in
Johannesburg, set in motion a chain of events which brought
along with it an entirely new church family. I had spent a
week at this camp getting to know these youth leaders and
young people from this church and they, me. Although we
would attend Youth Week on a few more occasions in the
future, my first one was most memorable, for I spent a week
with peers who really couldn't care about my skin colour, but
simply viewed me as being one of them.

Like all return journeys, it was a long way back to Cape Town.
I had met Graham Vermooten for the very first time seven
days earlier. He was the Youth Pastor at St James Church.
Unbeknown to me, St James had one of the largest youth
ministries in Cape Town and Graham was the reason for that.
On our journey back to Cape Town, Andy informed me that

'Vermooten' was in the front of the bus and wanted to have a chat with me. Graham got straight to the point; he inquired of me if I had a home church. I informed him that I was kind of 'between churches' at the time, as I was seeking to move on from the Anglican church I was currently attending. As we chatted, Graham informed me that he had watched me carefully over the past week. Oh crap! That meant only one thing — he was disappointed and did not want me near his young people. Surprisingly, Graham informed me that I was the type of individual he needed on his Youth Leadership team. Graham did his homework! Having spoken to Andy, he knew I was keen to attend Bible College and being a graduate of CEBI himself, Graham saw an opportunity to assist me in my dream. There it was — "would you join us on my team?" I jumped at the opportunity! Graham had kept eyes on me for an entire week. He knew I was not the finished product as such and yet he took a chance on me. He trusted me, knowing a little bit from what he had learnt from Andy. He was now willing to give me a chance as such and I simply could not mess up this opportunity. Nervously I accepted and I was about to undergo a three-year education in youth leadership. St James became my home church and youth ministry became my thing! The problem was that Graham ran a tight ship! Monday evenings were set apart for training and development as well as planning for the coming weekend. Four Saturdays a year were planning days — which often interrupted my football. No wonder St James had a thriving Youth Ministry — there was no room for half-measures! We planned crazy programmes and also gelled as a leadership team. For three years I was in a team of young leaders who gave of themselves and their best to this ministry. Guided by Graham and a church leadership which allowed us to do our thing, we built a thriving and effective Youth Ministry. I will forever be indebted to Graham for this opportunity!

Gus Leslie and I became great mates. Gus was a Geography teacher and also one of the leaders in JAM (Jesus and Me) — the younger youth group I would later be involved in at St James. He and I simply hit it off, we just clicked and got on very well. One year at Youth Week, Gus and I encountered a couple of guys from Johannesburg who were hitting on some of our girls. We decided to teach them a lesson by turning on a nearby fire hose into their dormitory at about three in the morning. Needless to say having done that, we ran as fast as our legs could carry us. The shouting voices behind us was evidence that we were being pursued, possibly due for a beating — but I was with my friend Gus who was built like a tank! As we ran, we headed to an opening in the field. At that time of the morning, the moonlight-sky illuminated everything — except for the barb-wire across the entrance to the field. Gus and I hit that barb wire with some force, so much so that we were flung back — into the arms of the pursuing pack! Maybe they felt sorry for us — or maybe they could see what we could not at the time ... blood all over our faces and bodies! Gus and I came off second best. We were lucky not to lose an eye but our faces and bodies had been cut and those scars would remain for life! Lesson learnt! What seemed like a great idea at the time, ended up being a bad one! The next morning the story of the barb-wire filtered through-out the camp. Needless to say, we got a good telling off but Gus and I would become inseparable — white and coloured, big guy and little guy, rugby guy and football guy — friends for life!

Warren Bevan was a co-leader in JAM too. Gus, Warren and I worked under the leadership of Ingo van der Merwe, who directed JAM! It was these guys who introduced me to their special past-time ... surfing! Now what did I know about surfing? That would require a board and a wetsuit and to get that you needed money, which I clearly did not have! As the three of us spent most of our weekends together, it was inevitable that they would get me to try this very cool sport. Warren gave me an old wetsuit and board and soon there I was no longer in the water just watching these guys surf but now lying on the board trying to surf myself! It was not easy, especially as I had a dodgy right now which was a hindrance when it came to balancing myself on a surfboard! Soon we had an idea to use surfing as an outreach and take some un-churched kids in our youth group who were surfers and those who wanted to learn to surf ... for a 'session' each Sunday morning. The plan was to later bring them along to church after the early morning surf. An outreach it became! Leaders and teens from 'Street-Level' (the Senior Youth group) joined us too. Each Sunday morning at about five thirty, we met in the church car park — leaders and teenagers and convoyed in search of good waves. Pretty soon I learnt terminologies like 'off-shore', 'on-shore' and so on. Surfing was hard work but these guys made it look so easy. Some of the young people and leaders were into boogie-boarding and I watched them ride waves as they used their Waps (shortened flippers) to major effect. Maybe I should have tried boogie boarding too but the challenge was to get standing on the surfboard and I loved a challenge! Enjoying the water so much, we often forgot the time and raced back to church, rinsing off in Ingo and Suann's garden or at the hose pipe in the church garden, while the congregation were making their way in. Then it was straight into 'teen church' with shorts, t-shirt and wet feet. The outreach was phenomenal and it became a welcomed ingredient in our ministry to un-churched young people.

Sometimes it was lovely just lying on the board in the ocean and feeling a real sense of belonging and being blessed — good friends, beautiful mornings and enjoying God's creation. While surfing off the point in Scarborough one morning, we encountered one of nature's greatest gifts! A school of dolphins suddenly made an appearance — literally among us! I had never experienced anything like that before. I watched in awe as these dolphins bopped between our surfboards before riding the breaking waves. It truly was an awesome encounter to behold! I had grown to love the experience of trying to surf — early mornings, nature, physical exercise and friendships. Surfing became a major thrill, which would nearly cost me my life!

As surfing spots go, there was none more dangerous than the 'Cemetery'. It was close to a tiny island, inhabited by seals and the feeding ground for great white sharks. It was here where you kept one eye on the waves and the other at what lies just beneath it. That coastline had seen many a shark attack but it was a great place to surf and the Cemetery therefore, became a regular surf spot for us. Gus, Warren and I were alone one morning on the trail of another set of waves. We were up a mountain road and below we saw waves breaking into a cove! The waves were huge, neatly breaking however into what seemed like an open runway — with huge rocks on either side! Gus was tempted and we decided to get the wetsuits on! Due to the fact that these waves were huge, we had an idea — I would double-up on Gus' long board as the waves were too big for me, a learning surfer to be on a normal-sized board! I could sense that surfing into a cove was risky business and I knew trying those waves on my own would end in disaster. Somehow the idea of doubling-up on the long board eased my fear slightly — but there it was ... fear mixed with excitement mixed with silliness mixed with manhood! Let's do it!

In we went — Gus and I on one long board and Warren on the other. We paddled hard to get beyond the swell and breakwater. We waited and soon we felt a slight rise of the water! 'Paddle' came the instruction from Gus. The nose of the long board was already tilting downward as the swell grew from behind. It became obvious to Gus that we were in danger of being wiped out by this wave — so he bailed and jumped off the board. The leash was attached to his ankle and as soon as it tightened it pulled from underneath me, leaving me between water below and a ton of water about to hit me from the top! 'Dive Vic — dive' my brain screamed at me! I hit the water and kicked as hard as I could to get as deep as I possibly could. I was too late! I was carried in this barrel of water — turning over and over — aware that pretty soon I would be hitting a rock. I pulled my arms over my head and pulled my legs up! Foetal position! Bang — my body hit a rock. Thankfully I was deep enough as the wave rushed into the cove. There was a sudden pain on my right shoulder and the right side of my back, but I was ok. The problem now was I needed air ... fast!

My wet suit was cut to pieces and my back covered in scrapes from the rocks. The scratches and blood were now evident on my shoulder. However, I survived and welcomed the oxygen which flowed into my lungs as I surfaced. The first sound other than the roar of the ocean, was Warren and Gus laughing at my near demise. I broke into laughter too as they paddled toward me — now coming to my rescue. We mutually agreed — this was too dangerous and we made our way to the shore. For some unknown reason, this terrifying experience really bonded us as friends! Two white dudes and a Coloured boy — we became inseparable!

A few months later Gus introduced us to "kloofing" or wet bouldering at a place aptly known as 'Suicide Gorge' — a wet mountain trail which led to jumps into rock pools. The higher you climbed, the higher the jumps became ... the final one being a twenty-one metre jump. We decided to jump together — a group of mates! We proceeded with the count and off we went, jumping into mid-air like a bunch of idiots. Then it dawned on me — what if there was a rock or tree trunk lying just below the surface? What if I was about to hit something under the surface that would either kill me or leave me paralysed? It was too late! We were falling and then splash — we hit the water, cold and dark mountain water. My lungs ached as I now tried to reach the surface and then I felt it — the warmth of the sun on my freezing face. I scanned about and one by one my friends made their way to the surface. Exhilarating. Fun. Freedom. Rites of passage. Friends!

Our training weekends away as youth leaders were a blast. Graham Vermooten was an exceptional Youth Pastor who focused on developing our leadership skills and our development as young adults. Though at times we focused on formal training and planning, other times were spent bonding as a team with the focus on individual spiritual development. On many occasions we left directly after Friday night youth clubs, arriving late into the night at a cabin in Hermanus, a lovely coastal holiday village about an hour or so outside the city. Unbeknown to me, there was a tradition of new leaders undergoing an initiation ceremony, which was simply a story being told about the building of a tennis court — the uprooting of trees, digging of holes, the stomping of the turf as part of the levelling process and then the straightening and lining of the court, all being done on your naked chest! It was a man-thing I guess! I don't take lightly to being wrestled to the ground and having my body stretched out, but there I was ... on the ground with my fellow 'Christians' holding me down and Ingo taking the lead to tell a story about a tennis court. Oh the pain! *Go with it Vic and soon it'll all be over! The comradery is what this is all about. Bear it! Take it! This too shall pass! Done! Welcome to the club Vic!*

It was on one of these weekends that my embarrassment would know no limits. On arriving one Friday evening and chilling out, I was 'attacked' by my fellow leaders, lifted up and carried off, not into the sunset but to the bathroom! My feet were so smelly that my friends decided it needed a scrubbing and that's precisely what they did! Though it was all in gest and a bit of banter, the point was made — my feet were stinking and others could no longer bear it! My shoes were placed outside for 'refreshing' while my mind was racing! Why had they done this? Why had they humiliated me like this? Did they really care about me or was this a communal 'shaming'? How were they to know that this was possibly the cheapest pair of trainers my parents could afford? How were they to understand that besides my good shoes and my school shoes — these shoes were all I had! I was embarrassed — but the funny thing was that these guys treated me no different after the 'feet-washing' than they had prior.

The sores of Apartheid were once again beginning to ooze — my prejudice and anger against all things 'white' were once again coming to the fore. I needed to let that chip on my shoulder go! I had to get to a place in my life where I defined myself no longer by the colour of my skin and all the hurt which came along with it. I could not help being born black and into Apartheid and in the same way my friends could not help being born white and into privilege! So here we were, a bunch of white and coloured guys having a laugh at my expense! I had to either leave this race issue behind at this moment in my life or I was going to explode and cause a scene! These guys meant no harm. They were close friends who were simply being bluntly honest — in a funny way! The problem was mine — I was responsible for my own life. I had to make my own decision as to whether or not I was going to use Apartheid as an excuse for the remainder of my life. Somewhere along the way I had to move beyond that, else

I would forever be trapped by it. The time had now come — my response to this event would determine the depth of my character. I was not in control of the historical hatred of the National Party against non-whites like myself, but I was in control of my response! There was also this guy Jesus talking about forgiveness and a new community, one of equals, no longer defined by colour or creed, a community of brother and sisterhood tied by chords of mutual love for one another, a new community made-up of 'Christ-ones'! The time had now come! *Time to change Vic! Time to swop hatred and hurt for character development!* The issue was not my colour, but my feet! As embarrassing as it was to draw attention to the fact that my feet were stinking, these guys meant no harm! Had I been white, they still would have done the same thing. My feet were washed and we had a good laugh doing it! That story would be told nearly thirty years later when Gus and I visited Warren and his family. We laughed as we shared that memory with his grown teenagers — a moment of laughter between friends — between brothers!

So what did the 'feet-washing' lesson teach me about myself? I was raised within a political system that not only kept people divided but a system that unconsciously encouraged me to hate. It wasn't so much that I had set out to implement feelings of dislike for the 'other side' but it was the subconscious attitudes developed within — the bitterness about land stolen; the unfairness about education; the geographical separation from the city which our family once lived in; etc. There was a palpable feeling of being second-class and not being treated as an equal. However, I was making all these close friendships across the colour line and yet something within me kept gnawing away at my psyche. Coupled with these feelings of inferiority, I had burnt bridges too. I simply did not fit into this Christian sub-culture of which I was now very much a part — more due to my own doing. It seemed I was always blowing things — taking two steps forward and one step back. I was also getting into the habit of kissing as many girls as I could, irrespective of consequences or feelings. Truth be told, I was slowly feeding the rebellious nature within me. Ever-so-often in this new community of friendships and church, I felt lost. It became evident that I needed to find myself.

Now what does this 'finding oneself' look like? Why is it that guys in particular, do this? Why is it that at some stage in life, there is this desire for knowing who you are, the desire for honesty, this craving to get rid of the garbage in your life and look at yourself in a mirror and be honest with yourself about 'you'? Is it simply a hunger for personal transparency? A desire for re-acquaintance with self? A sort-of 'mid-life crisis' at certain stages in one's life? Why is it that people do things to 'clear their mind' in order to find new direction for their lives? I don't have a clue as to how to answer these questions I just raised, but what I did know was that I needed to get out of Cape Town, find myself and find my way in the world. I needed to have a cause I could pour my heart and soul into and find meaning in who I was and what I was doing but most of all I needed healing in my own life. Like the prophets of old I needed to spend time in the 'wilderness' — have my heart stripped bare, my life exposed to God and discover what it all meant to truly rely on Him only. I needed to isolate myself from a messy past and undergo personal transformation. If I was going to make a contribution to my world, I could not do it by remaining the scarred individual I was. I needed healing, time to myself, a wilderness experience of sorts ... and God was very much in agreement!

'Therefore behold, I (God) will allure her (Israel) and bring her into the wilderness and speak tenderly to her.' (Hosea 2 vs 14)

Chapter 8: Namibia—what on earth am I doing here?

*What makes the desert beautiful is that
somewhere it hides a well.*

(Antoine de Saint Exupery)

It was my final few months at Bible College! While many of my classmates were finalising future employment with their churches or para-church organisations post-graduation, no one was rushing to seek my services! Although I had pulled myself together in my final year at college, it was quite sobering knowing that I had possibly burnt bridges with too many people who would now think twice before offering me a job. I understood that! Lesson learnt! It wasn't that I was argumentative as such — I just hated aligning myself to the status quo. I thought very differently about things, had a mind of my own and often rebelled against the expectation of how we are to live within a Christian culture. I just hated conforming to what others expected me to be. To some however, this was not an attractive trait within my character, as I often spoke my mind. I was young and intent on finding my own way in life. If truth be told, I hated being told what to do!

I had previously worked with Ingo van der Merwe while at St James' Church. He ran our junior youth group called JAM (Jesus and Me) and alongside others in our leadership team, we had worked well together. Moving on from St James, Ingo had left for Namibia to work for Youth for Christ. He offered me the opportunity to come and work alongside him in Swakopmund, a coastal town at the edge of the Namib desert. It seemed a good opportunity at the time as I had nothing else to do after college and it did allow me the chance of getting out of Cape Town. I also wanted to be involved in mission and it now seemed that at this stage in my life, God was now providing me with an opportunity. What I did not realise at the time was that this literal wilderness was going to shape the future direction of my life.

I arrived in Swakopmund Namibia in October 1990 for an interview, having just spent six hours on a postal flight from Cape Town to Swakopmund which stopped at every little town in the Namib desert. I felt sick and had been when the plane landed in a little place called Oranjemund. It was the cheapest flight I could find. I had no money and the little I scraped together allowed me passage on this postal flight, arranged by dad through his work. Sitting on the back of the plane were loads of postage bags and boxes which kept me company. It was a long day but finally the plane eased its way onto a sandy stretch of runway surrounded by sand dunes. As the little mode of transportation came to a halt, it stopped next a little hut — the terminal building, as I soon discovered. It was like going back in time. I left a huge airport and now arrived next to a little hut! Welcome to Swakopmund! Ingo and Suann welcomed me and were good enough to host me for the week. I met the Chairman of the Trustees of Youth for Christ Swakopmund, the very day his daughter was born and my introduction to him was seeing him pull out and light a Cuban cigar — obviously kept especially for the occasion of his first born. Having made my introductions and seeing his joy at becoming a dad, I knew right then ... if I were to get through the interview, I would fit right in! I would return four months later and commence my role as a missionary!

My official title was 'Development Officer' and my remit was to now develop work in the 'Coloured' area of Tamariskia — developing ministry in the coloured and black high school through teaching Religious Education and coaching sport. The school was on the edge of the town and my 'company car' (my beloved bicycle) and I covered many a mile from the office to the school. I met and worked alongside Jules Frost — a missionary from the USA, who later went on to work for the United Nations. I very much took my lead from her, as her work within the German High School was already well established. Louise Williams — a local from the town, whose family had emigrated from Wales, looked after the admin at the office. Her family were very good to me, allowing me to pop in whenever I so desired. Her younger brother Daniel shared a passion of mine for 'Rocky' and many a movie was watched during my visits there. Over the years, our staff compliment grew, as international volunteers arrived from countries like Germany, the USA and also from Northern Ireland ... but more about that later.

I now unofficially entered the teaching profession. As Religious Education was a non-examined subject on the curriculum, it was viewed as either a period of moral guidance or a free period. I was allowed therefore to develop my own curriculum for the few junior classes for which I was responsible. I had only taught for a few weeks when the principal informed me that the school would be receiving a few bus-loads of new pupils from the north of the country. The 'pupils' soon arrived and were part of the year eight cohort — first year pupils. The problem was that these 'first year pupils' were in fact older than I. Being twenty-two at the time, I found myself teaching 'boys and girls' who were in their mid-twenties. I soon discovered that these 'pupils' had spent many a year as soldiers, fighting in the war for independence against South Africa. It was now their right to be educated and literally overnight had replaced their AK47 rifles for school notebooks. I also discovered that nearly all of these pupils could not speak English and when chatting to the principal, my RE class soon turned into an English class. As I did not speak Oshiwambo, the principal thought it prudent to provide me with a translator. *Welcome to the teaching profession Vic. Make it up as you go!*

My work in Tamariskia High School also allowed me the opportunity to get to know the footballing fraternity in the town, which soon led to the opportunity to coach football — in another school. I was asked to coach a team at the English High School, a school established within the English community. Let me explain — about fifty miles outside of the town, a very successful uranium mine known as 'Rossing', employed many international workers, alongside Namibians as its workforce. The trade-off for moving from places like the UK was a house and a good salary, comparatively speaking. Due to the fact that Rossing had its own golf club, many families spent their time here over the weekend — where mine employees could enjoy meals which were heavily subsidised. As a large part of the work force were from the UK and Ireland, the school very naturally developed and grew — providing education for British kids and English-speaking families. Due to the fact that the war in Namibia had now ceased, the school took on a very multi-cultural aspect — with more and more non-white pupils enrolling in this school, to now reflect the political change which had just happened within the country.

My coaching role became permanent. When after coaching this team for two weeks and having re-structured the team positions, the boys won their very first competitive fixture, overcoming a school who had previously beaten them on many occasions. Due to my new-found success as a football coach, I was offered the opportunity to also teach Religious Education in that school. The English High School very much became my home. I was given a little store room which was converted into an office. Having taught myself to play guitar a few months earlier, I started teaching pupils to play, not for grades — as I could not read music as such, but simply for the pleasure of learning to play the instrument. This was a brilliant opportunity to get to know the pupils, especially those who were not involved in our youth programmes. The school was very good to me and I soon became accepted by the staff — not as the 'Youth for Christ guy', but as a teacher at the English High School.

My company car and I were now clocking up the miles as I made my way between the two schools on a daily basis. As my role increased within the English High School, my teaching role at Tamariskia diminished. The reason for this was that the Principal and Governors at the English High School decided to remunerate me for my services. I therefore felt an obligation to spend more of my time there. The Principal at Tamariskia understood that and my time among the staff contingent there soon came to a very natural end. Obviously I maintained my very positive relationship with the school and its community, as I was in and out doing ministry with young people.

As part of his role as Director, Ingo had organised a basement premises in the town where young people could gather at night. It was known as the 'Subway Café'. This facility allowed us to meet so many young people — one of which was

Ombilie. He was a stunning young black Namibian who was at Tamariskia High School and also involved in our youth programmes. Having just arrived in Swakopmund, Ombilie took it upon himself to show me around the town. His love for Michael Jackson music meant that we often walked the streets late at night singing tunes, which also gave him the opportunity to introduce me to young people we often bumped into. Through our contacts, Ombilie transferred to the English High School and later auditioned for a role as 'Pharaoh' in the musical production of 'Joseph and his Technicolour Dreamcoat'. He excelled at the role. After one of the performances, Ombilie was approached by a member of the Namibian Broadcasting Corporation — a contact we had made while doing Christian epilogues on television. She was so impressed with Ombilie that she offered him a job as soon as he finished school. Having later moved to Windhoek, the capital city to pursue his life in television, I hadn't seen Ombilie for a few years. One day he arrived at my door. He looked withdrawn and had lost a lot of weight, but the smile remained. While we enjoyed a bite to eat, Ombilie told me that he was not well, that he was quite sick and that's why he had decided to visit his home town. Ombilie died a few months later! His impact upon my life was immense. I will never forget him.

Camping became one of our success stories within our ministry. The local Rotarian group had a fishing cabin up the coast which slept about twenty people. They availed it to us as part of our outreach to young people. It was a tremendous facility which allowed us to take young people away for a weekend to fish and then develop mutual respect in order to earn the right to share the message of Christ on a personal basis. Many a young person took stock of their own life on those weekends away. We also of course had our end of term camps, which ran for a week, modelled on the many camps I attended with Scripture Union as well as at St James Church while in Cape Town. Camps provided young people the opportunity of getting away for a week and doing something fun — out of the ordinary as such. The difficult part of any camp is trying to get young people interested to attend, especially those young people not affiliated to your youth programmes or church. The spiritual part to these camps were very rewarding — young people were given opportunities to see what a difference Jesus could make in their lives. Parents too were so good in many ways — some paying a camp fee for those young people who could not afford to attend; others like Mr Boegendorffer — a German butcher in the town, who gave us free meat whenever he heard we were running a camp. Our camping programmes and general ministry were going well, but we would soon embark on a journey quite foreign to 'YFC Ministry' and attempt something quite out of the ordinary!

I really loved getting to know the young people in Swakopmund and camping was an amazing way of doing this. However, Ingo had this idea about doing a youth musical — the same musical I was involved in a few years earlier at St James in Cape Town, called 'Friends' — a musical which looked at the many friendships teenagers could encounter, which included relationships with parents and ultimately introducing Jesus as the real friend. While at St James, I got chosen from among the cast to sing the song which spoke about Jesus as the ultimate friend, entitled 'I never had a friend like you'. It was a great song and I loved singing it. The song simply said ...

There's no greater love, than laying down your life
For a friend and You called me 'friend'
Those were only words, until You chose to die
For your friends, you died for your friends

You spoke of the Father's love
Then you showed us still it's hard to understand
How my life could mean so much to You
That You would give your life to be my friend!

(Chorus) I've never had a friend like you
Never knew what love could do
You had everything and laid it down for me
I've never had a friend like you
And I pray that I will be
The kind of friend You have been to me!

Those lyrics were immense and so too the lyrics of the entire musical and now we were seeking to re-do this musical in Namibia with a different bunch of young people. Due to the fact that the sound track was very punchy with potential for major dance movements, we were therefore in need of a choreographer who could work alongside and train our cast. Ingo and I met with a German dancer who had agreed to assist us with the choreography. Working together on this project, it was obvious that there was a slight chemistry between us. At this stage I was doing a lot of preaching in our church and I was so pleased that she too made it to church on the odd occasion. A few ladies in our church took her under their wing and brought her along to the women's fellowship and I knew that it took a lot for her to do so. At thirty-one, she was eight years older than I and a lot more mature. She loved life, which was a major attraction to me. We started to hang out and laughed when we both discovered that we were both plucking up the courage to ask the other for a date. Later on I took her to Cape Town to meet mum and dad. As she was an ex-international ballroom dancer, mum and dad took to her immediately, for mum and dad loved to ballroom too. They loved her — she was all they spoke of when we returned to Namibia. It was evident however, that she and I came from very different backgrounds and the likelihood of us having a future was very slim. Pretty soon the relationship came to a natural conclusion. Another failed attempt at a relationship ... I was doing well!

The young people we worked with came from a variety of different backgrounds — some had church backgrounds but for most of them the entire concept of church was a strange phenomenon to say the least. Some were rough and ready — ready for fights and for some that included knives. Some were just too cool and others simply enjoyed being involved in our school and weekend programmes. All night indoor hockey and basketball events which we organised were very popular and it was simply just another way of keeping boys off the street at night. Those who had an interest in line fishing spent many a weekend with us in a cabin further up the coast. Our annual school holiday camps were brilliant and many a young people considered Jesus as an option for their lives during these events. As a ministry team, our responsibility was to plant seeds in their lives and encourage them to think about matters with regard to eternity. Our role was not to make spiritual decisions for them, but to point the way to the true Answer in life, should they acknowledge His call on their lives. The parents of these young people were so good to us and appreciated everything we organised for them in the community. The ministry grew to such an extent that the time had come to start a ministry among children too. It was a tremendous time of growth in our office. We had a great team of missionaries — both short and long term —

young adults who offered their time to God to be used in His service.

In 1993 I had the opportunity, alongside my colleagues to visit the USA in order to attend our International Youth for Christ Convocation (conference). It was my very first experience of leaving Africa and travelling abroad. I was very excited at the prospect and would be eternally grateful to those men and women who financially contributed to me attending. Arriving in Frankfurt we met with my friend Martina and her sister Andrea (who would later become one of our short-term staff). It was good seeing Martina again and we worked our way through a rich German breakfast — anything and everything sweet in the early morning. Later on we flew to Chicago on the night of the 3rd July with so many Americans flying home from Europe for the fourth of July celebrations. Let's just say it was a very noisy journey. As we disembarked and made our way to passport control and baggage reclaim, we were suddenly approached by an immigration officer who shouted at us and instructed us to get to one side and open our bags etc. I guess one of us had that face! Welcome to America!

Chicago was a fantastic experience, but we had no time to look about as we had an appointment with a Greyhound bus which we would take to Denver, Colorado. We were attending the Youth for Christ Summer School training week at Regis College in Denver and had no time to get acquainted with the surroundings of the 'Windy City'. Regis was a fantastic campus. The Summer school was a rewarding experience, not just with regard to spiritual development and growth but also with regard to meeting people and making friends. While there, I got to know an Italian American called Ricky, who was a student at Regis and still on campus while everyone else was on Summer break. Ricky was on an academic scholarship and had a job on campus alongside a few other pupils. He was also on the basketball team and he invited me to go along and watch him play in the city — downtown! It was an amazing experience just hanging out with him and seeing what general life in Denver was all about. Life is about meeting people and taking opportunities to very naturally talk about Jesus to others. I was thankful to God that I had the opportunity to share my spiritual journey with my friend Ricky! I will never forget him!

The day before the Youth for Christ Staff arrived for their training at the 'Summer Leadership' conference at Regis, Ingo decided that we should find a local coffee shop to have some breakfast. We found a local 'diner' right across from the college. The owner, a lovely lady invited us foreigners with open arms. After the general 'where you from' conversation, we received our breakfast. I had never seen so much food on a breakfast plate before. If this was a taste of portions in the 'States', I was going to need bigger clothes in the next few weeks!

Summer school was painful — spiritually speaking, lots of soul-searching etc. It was good for me spiritually and I appreciated the time of reflection we had after each session. At Bible College many years earlier, we were encouraged by Margi Gustafson, one of my lecturers — to keep a spiritual diary and I started to implement that discipline yet again while at Regis. It was a painful but very rewarding experience. Tony Compolo, the much acclaimed youth communicator, led the morning sessions, while in the late afternoon we had time to relax. I played many a game of basketball and we even managed to see the Colorado Rockies play baseball one evening. The staff at Youth for Christ USA were so good to us, but so too the Summer staff at Regis. Many an extra helping was received at meal times, maybe because we were from 'Africa'. It was evident that Lino and I ... my brother from Angola, often received the additional ladle of food. However, I was not for complaining!

Lino and I had bonded really well — not just on this trip, but a year or so earlier. Due to the civil war, he had escaped with his family. He was a pastor and a truly Godly man. Being of similar age and due to the fact that he played the guitar too, we spent many an evening singing and playing — me in English and he in Portuguese. It was his daughter's birthday and due to the fact that they left Angola with simply a few suitcases and having experienced the trauma of having to leave everything they owned ... I wanted to treat this brother and his family. With the little money I had, it was evident that I still had much more than Lino and his family. Being a proud man, I knew that he would not accept any money from me, so I decided to purchase a bicycle for his daughter as a birthday gift. Lino and I developed a mutual respect for one another — both of us trying to find out what God had in mind for our respective futures!

Summer School at Regis was coming to an end and we needed to make plans to return to Chicago in order to attend the YFC International Convocation. We had not booked a Greyhound to return to Chicago as yet and time was now short. However, we soon discovered that the Youth for Christ USA staff who ran the Summer School at Regis, needed to get equipment and bits and pieces to Chicago for the convocation. They asked Ingo if he wouldn't mind us driving one of the vans filled with computers and resources required for the conference. Of course we wouldn't mind! Having my turn at the wheel, it would now be my first experience of driving in the USA. However, arriving in Chicago in rush hour traffic was an experience — six lane motorways! Ingo took his time

— he had to! However, we made it to the Chicago Hilton, which was to be my home for the next two weeks.

I could get used to this 'hotel thing'. The Hilton was a fantastic experience. The reception desk rings you to wake you up in the morning. What a blast! The morning sessions at the Convocation were spiritually rewarding and because I was not a voting delegate as such, I had free time available in the afternoon while Ingo was tied up with the 'business' sides of things. The hotel 'mini-van' took me to the train station and collected me whenever I returned. I was to and fro 'downtown' Chicago on my own, seeing the sites and enjoying basking in the atmosphere of the city. This was the life and what a learning experience. I learnt never again to order a 'large' pizza for lunch, as I had no idea what that meant in American terms! Katrin, my colleague from Germany and I, got to hang out a lot more and we simply loved riding the trains, shopping and simply enjoying the opportunity we were given to be here, due to the generosity of others! What a pleasure! I was living the dream! Life was good ... or was it really? While I was coming to terms with the joys of being alive, I was soon to be reminded about the brevity of life!

It was Monday morning the 26th July 1993 and life was good in the Hilton. Lifting up the newspaper that morning while having breakfast, my eye was drawn to a column on the right hand side of the front page — 'Church massacre in South Africa'! I started to read the article and suddenly the blood drained from my face. The massacre occurred the night before in a church in Cape Town — in Kenilworth — St James Church ... Ingo's and my home church! My eyes were now darting through the column as my mind raced through the events at St James the night before. Ingo and I could not believe what we read. It seemed that some 'freedom fighters' saw our church as a 'legitimate' target to 'free' South Africa from white oppression. What a load of nonsense! They were murderers! St James Church was a non-racial church who had done so much with regard to bridging gaps across the colour line. As the names of the dead became apparent later on — they were not just names on a paper, but people we had known!

One name in particular brought me to my knees ... Mrs Ackermann — a lovely Afrikaner lady who, along with her husband had opened her home to so many young people. Her kids were part of our youth ministry and I was not to know then that Braam, her son, would end up living in Coleraine, Northern Ireland many years later. They were a lovely family and I had been personally struck by her quiet manner and attitude of servant-hood each time we visited their home. She and her husband had been working and ministering with Russian sailors and had brought a few of them with them that evening. In the mayhem of hand grenades and gunfire, Mrs Ackermann was shot and killed. That was it! I was angry! How could God allow this to happen? Our church had done so much good over the years — they even welcomed someone like me into their family! Ingo and Suann had been at St James longer than I and I'm sure they mourned doubly so. I was angry at God and that anger would linger for a bit. I had no idea what God was doing here. Young people we knew personally were now no more. The very cause that we fought for as school pupils in 1985, was now the very same cause that brought death and destruction to people I loved. I was edging for a fight. Somewhere along the way God and I were going to square-up to one another. There were a few things we needed to talk about and the massacre at St James was simply another agenda item. If people like Jacob in the Scriptures could have a one on one with God, why not I? Anyway, that pow wow happened soon enough ... six months later!

The flat I was living in was no longer available and I needed to find some other accommodation. I eventually found one — a little box room. That was it — a room about the third of the size of my current school office. You could just about fit a bed and cupboard in it. Everything else I possessed sat on top of the cupboard or under the bed. I had a toilet and shower outside and that was me ... twenty-four years old — a job I loved but no set income and now a box room! I owned nothing but the clothes I had and my tape (music) collection. It was two in the morning, very early one Saturday morning. I started thinking about my friends in Cape Town who were possibly getting ready to purchase their first house; possibly at a stage of getting married; possibly employed; possibly pursuing Masters or PhD degrees. I thought about my sisters making their way at Old Mutual (insurance company) and on a small but steady income and here I was ... no income as such — other than what the Christian community felt obliged to provide me with. Thank goodness for the little bit of income from the English High School! I was at a stage in my life where I had no prospect of moving forward. I also found myself in regular frustration — working with young people I loved but whose lives I had no power to change. I was encouraging them to a heart-change but I could not assist them with a social one.

Due to my past, I was careful whom I trusted. While working for Youth for Christ in Namibia, Ingo was one of three individuals whom I respected and gave my trust to. I loved Ingo as if he were my brother and still do this day. Ingo could have a good laugh but he was also my superior and there were many moments when he needed to be sharp with me for my own sake. However, there came a time when we had a major disagreement. Having left the office after we had words, I ended up going to the flat of a friend of mine. Nicky had a few bottles of red wine which I started to work through, one bottle after the other after the other. I detested alcohol because of its detrimental effect in my home while I was growing up. However, these bottles of wine seemed appealing and would allow me to forget my argument with Ingo. I must have fallen asleep and being Wednesday, I was expected to be at a Bible Study later that evening. I woke up the next morning with the realisation that I had been drunk for the first time in my life. I could barely lift my head off the pillow and made it to the toilet before being sick. I had a bruise and bump on my shin ... the result of being carried up to my bedroom the night before and having my shin connect with the wooden staircase one step after the other. To make matters worse, Julie ... whom I was keen to date, wondered where I was as she awaited me at the Bible Study she was attending. Having heard from our friendship circle the next day as to why I missed the Bible Study, she was obviously not impressed. I was ashamed at myself and lifted the phone, spoke to my mum and had a good cry. What scared me though, was that I dealt with this matter the same way my dad often did when he faced difficulties. I was determined from that day on that I would never be in a state of drunkenness ever again. Worse was to come. Ingo suspended me from my duties as a missionary and told me to 'wise up'! He was well in his rights to do so and although I hated the suspension, it was the right thing to do. This missionary thing clearly wasn't working for me!

Who was I really? A young man who wanted to do something for God and this is where it led me, to a small box room with nothing much and now a suspension from my duties too? What was my long-term future going to be? Was I going to end up as the forty-year old cool youth worker that everyone smiles at and feels sorry for once his back is turned? Was this going to be me ... the 'ever-reliant on others' one, 'working for God'? Maybe my trust in God was at an all-time low.

Maybe missing family and friends coupled with the St James massacre and now the box room was possibly the realisation that if God was involved in humanity as such, why is He making my life so hard? Was this all part and parcel of the 'missionary' deal? The problem is that I knew many a 'white' missionary and they weren't living like this! What's the deal here God? Was mission only for those who could afford it? It was time for a fight and I started speaking to God in my little box room and I was intent on holding nothing back!

As I started to verbalise my thoughts, I did what many a man and woman in my position would do ... remind God about things, the choices and sacrifices I had made to walk this life of 'mission'. I told God how I entrusted Him with my life in Johannesburg so many years earlier, how I was prepared to leave things behind in Cape Town and so on, as if God really needed me to remind Him. I guess among the arrogance and the hidden agenda of 'you owe me God', I simply wanted some sought of progression in my life. Was that too much to ask from God? Maybe this wasn't so much about God but more about me wanting some purpose in my life. I guess that's what I learnt that night. I simply had two choices before me — I either needed to pursue a profession and in some miraculous way get to university or pursue mission as a career. The problem was that there weren't too many 'career missionaries'. Yes, loads of full-time ministers and pastors, funded and supported by their churches but there weren't too many missionaries who made mission a life-long career ... especially black ones! In order to achieve both, I needed to raise some sort of finance. I loved being a missionary but could I honestly ask people to support me financially until I was sixty- five?

'Be a missionary' they say! 'God will provide' they say! 'Live by faith' they say! Hind-sight is a wonderful thing! I had known the provision of God while at Bible College all those many years ago. The problem now was that my context as a former student was completely different to my context as a missionary. As a student, I at least had the comfort of living in my parent's home; knowing that I would have a regular meal etc. As a missionary I was on my own; life was now somewhat different!

I was always at logger heads with this 'living by faith thing'. When 'wanna-be' missionaries avail themselves to God's service — in whatever organisation they align themselves with, there is an expectation that the individual must 'live by faith' and raise the necessary finance in order to 'work for God'. There seems to be this 'pre-requisite' that before one becomes a missionary, one must embark upon deputation and encourage people to provide for you on a monthly basis. Now let's imagine that this sort of thing is okay, where does one go to raise this sort of money? One's community obviously — people who know you and people who would be sympathetic to what it is you wanted to do for the next few years. However, people in my community back home simply could not afford to support people like me seeking to be a missionary. If truth be told, people within my community were struggling to support themselves and their families. I come from a 'working class' community — emphasis being on 'working', where 'disposable income' is a foreign concept! We had no welfare state as here in the UK. No one was going to provide us with money if we had no job! I had seen the other side of this coin while at Bible College years earlier; some of my brothers and sisters from the 'more affluent' societies in South Africa arrived at college clearly supported by their home churches and individuals in their community who were happy to support their study. However, this was not my experience. I often wondered how some 'white' students at college were able to own their own cars? How could they afford that? During my three years at Bible College, I either spent my time running everywhere, hiking cars to catch or lift or jumping the train without paying due to the fact that I had no money! How is it now that wanting to be a missionary, I end up in the same situation as I did during my days as a student?

Now, context is very important. South Africa had a hierarchy of wealth — Whites, Coloureds and Indians and then our Black brothers and sisters. Many a non-white in South Africa was simply trying to find their way through the quagmire of financial resources. Some succeeded, some did not! Many a non-white Pastor therefore had a full-time job as well as pastoring a church. Churches in non-white areas were struggling to keep their ministers and pastors in position and therefore secular employment was part of the local pastor's 'calling'. That was the situation! Most ministers in my community either had secular full-time employment or had part-time employment to supplement their income. Were they less spiritual than those ministers who 'lived by faith'? Of course not! Their community contexts were very different — some had resources to give, while others had not!

So here I was — the missionary looking to 'raise' a salary from my home community, from a community who could barely afford to look after their own needs. Needless to say, the church in Swakopmund rallied, corporate and individual and assisted in providing me with a salary. Added to the little bit of money I received from the English High School, my 'salary' allowed me the opportunity to enjoy the odd treat of a pizza ever so often. Some folk also supported me in-kind, like the Labaschagne's who owned a restaurant and often invited me for a free meal. It was people like this who contributed to my well-being. There were so many who ever so often, welcomed me into their homes for a meal and behind all their goodness toward me, was God's divine care.

Money was not an issue to me generally, reason being that I never had any! My sisters and I were clothed with the reject samples the factory shop could not sell — the factory shop where mum worked in. That was life! We made do with what we had and ever so often mum took us shopping, which was always a real treat. There was no money for additional public transport either. Each time I travelled to St James Church for youth events or Sunday services — about a twenty-mile journey, I hiked, ran or jumped a train — hopping on and off train carriages to avoid the conductor, due to not having money to purchase a ticket. How I got home often depended on the generosity of others.

It never mattered what time of night it was — straight after youth group or three in the morning after late-night snooker — I always got home! Gus, Warren or Andy always ensured I got home, often taking turns. These guys never once objected; never once did they complain. Never once was it too much to ask! Needless to say I am indebted to them for their kindness for as long as I live. God had this unique way of bringing people together — Andy, Gus, Warren and I — threads woven together — me, the recipient of their goodness! In three years, not once was I asked for 'petrol money' or a 'contribution to their inconvenience'! Needless to say ... I owe them!

So, how was I to raise money while in Namibia? The simple answer being ... with difficulty! Were it not for the generosity of the local church and individuals in Swakopmund, my time on the mission-field would have been short-lived! However, God was always at work in the hearts of these people — or were they simply feeling sorry for me? I'm still not quite sure as to which it is. I guess my personal financial context is very different currently and yet today I struggle to give to church projects I simply do not see sense in, while making a personal contribution to individuals in ministry is often what I choose to do. There are times when churches spend thousands of pounds on renovation projects and that may be good and well, but often I wonder as to the value of projects like these. Of course money must be allocated to fix leaking roofs, pipes and so on, but sometimes I wonder if investing in wide-ranging mission opportunities would be better use of money than the building of another church wing!

I guess I constantly find myself in turmoil with regard to financially giving to extension development projects because I am aware of pastors around the world who could do with financial support to sustain their families and livelihoods. I am also aware of many an African minister or pastor who work within secular employment Monday to Friday so as to ensure a regular income, for there is no way the church they shepherd has the financial capability to upkeep them. They need us to support them! I do find however the additional giving to further church builds and extension projects a concern! Sometimes I wonder if Jesus could really care about the state of our church buildings, or whether we 'break ground' on the new wing! Would He rather encourage us to use that money to put more workers into His vineyard? Please don't get me wrong — upkeep of buildings is important but the problem arises when we have so much money in the 'coffers' that we start finding projects in order to spend our money on.

What did Jesus ask of us with regard to our stewardship? Are we not to look after widows and orphans — the needy that is? When have we last heard of a church paying for a couple to attend marital counselling or paying for a member of the congregation to attend an Alcoholics Anonymous support

group? Are these not the sort of issues we should be investing our money in? What about young adults who have a heart
for mission? Should the church not be supporting them with
a monthly salary for a period of five or so years or make a lifetime commitment to a family who want to be missionaries?
What about church internships — should each church not
financially support young people who could develop leadership skills within their local church? I am thankful to God for
many church leaders who see the world through heaven's
eyes and give where they see the need. I am pleased to say
that I know of many churches, including my own, where
ministry comes first and resources are made available to priorities such as this. However, there is so much more we, as
the church universal could be doing. What a blessing it is to
know that God has the ability to take the little we give and
change the world through it.

Since moving to Northern Ireland I must confess that I have
clearly lost an element of my faith — the part of me that
relied solely on God for my income. When employed as a
Youth Pastor in Hamilton Road Presbyterian Church here
in Northern Ireland, I was suddenly getting a monthly income. I did not have to pray for it, rely on God for it, worry
about it, wonder how I was going to eat for the next month
etc., ... as I had to do the previous six years. I was now in a
position where I received a monthly cheque — I no longer
had to 'live by faith'! Sometimes I wish that every individual
looking to be involved in ministry at whatever level, should
spend at least a year without a salary as such, for the lessons
we learn about relying upon and trusting God are immense!
Sometimes if this was the case, would it change our perspective with regard to our money and give us new insight into
what it means to live by faith?

In Namibia it was go fishing on a Friday afternoon or starve and that's exactly what Andrew, Paulus (the two boys I looked after) and I did. It was simply out of necessity! I also remember one Sunday afternoon being down to my very last slice of bread with enough butter left to spread onto it. I rang home to my family in Cape Town and shared with them that my Sunday lunch was one slice of bread with some butter! Situations like these drove me to my knees! To my shame, I no longer trust God for my finances the way I once used to. Sometimes I wonder if 'living by faith' is now but a fallacy in my life. Yes, I trust God for my health and that of my family and friends. Yes, I often ask God to keep me healthy in order that I provide for my family. Yes, I pray to God for the necessities in life but I have become comfortable in the fact that my monthly salary is simply part and parcel of my life. My faith in God for my monthly living has diminished! *Maybe I need to be on the shore again with a fishing rod in my hand!*

The phrase 'What would Jesus do' often rolls off our tongues so easily but what would Jesus really do if He were here with us? Would He encourage us to ensure that our priorities should be to feed the poor rather than build another storehouse? What are we teaching our children and those who will take leadership after us, about stewardship? What example are we setting for them? Are we telling them that the Kingdom of God is all about investment in the local church building only or are we reminding them that 'the fields are ripe unto harvest'? (John 4 vs 35) It is my desire to progress and further develop my faith — to live my faith, not the church's faith or that of the minister, but mine! Yet, in order to do that I must avail my finances to the mission of the church ... namely, people!

What am I therefore to do with the disposable income I have? What am I currently doing with it? I guess my answer is pretty simple — I give where I see the need. It gives me great pleasure at school to buy pupils lunch, or give to pupils who are going on short-term mission with their churches or simply provide some money to a team leader in order to treat his or her team and so on. I also have a problem giving to organisations when I know that thirty of forty percent of that money is being swallowed up in 'administration costs'! Yes, I get the fact that administration costs money, but then inform us as to how much of my giving will go towards admin and what percent actually goes toward the recipients. It's the same issue I have with building church extensions — why do we keep making buildings bigger and bigger? Should we not be church-planting in communities rather than make our church buildings larger to accommodate more and more people? Could we not be training more pastors to spiritually care for smaller congregations with the potential for growth, rather than expecting those communities to be part of 'our' congregation? Are we getting to a point where we build more and more because people must come and listen to 'our minister' because he or she is the next best thing to sliced bread? Is it not true that often people can get 'lost' as it were in large churches? Are smaller congregations therefore not spiritually more rewarding because we can get to know individuals more at a deeper level?

I applaud churches and mission organisations who seek spiritual and social change for the children and adults they minister to by identifying and training future ministerial leaders. Yet, before us lies the danger, that we solely focus on spiritual change in the lives of others at the expense of a social one. Organisations like Compassion and Lesedi remind us that the church today has no choice but to also focus on the social transformation of people. Is this not what Jesus instructed us to do when He reminded us of our responsibility to the widows and orphans?

So what have I learnt about money from my time spent in Namibia to my current context? I guess my life's prayer is now this:

Teach me Lord to give where I see the need, to financially invest in areas of ministry which tug at my heart and to discern whether or not the decisions made by the local church are in keeping with your will! Thank You for Your goodness in providing Julie and I with employment. Help us to give because we love, not because we are obligated to. All we have belongs to You any way Father and therefore help us to give to others out of gratitude to You ... for it is You alone who remains Jehovah Jireh — our Provider, the One who sustains our very lives, the One who strengthens us each day to get up and go to work, the One who provides us with the very air we breathe! Help us therefore to do our very best to provide for others.

Chapter 9: Following one's heart

... a woman who fears the Lord is to be praised!

(Proverbs 31 vs 30)

I often bore witness to the damage done by dating too early — both the emotional and sexual pressure which comes along with that. I was determined that I would never be in that position until I was mature enough to handle the complexities that come along with relationships. For the life of me I could not understand how people could go 'steady' at fifteen and yet I also knew of individuals who started dating in their teens and eventually got married. If truth be told, I had two serious relationships in my life — one which led to heartache and the other which led me to moving hemispheres!

It was 1992 and Ingo, some teenagers and I were off to the northern regions of Namibia on a mission. We were taking some young people north to the town of Rundu — a border town with Angola, right in the Caprivi Strip. From there we would drive east toward Botswana for another one hundred and fifty kilometres (ninety-five miles) or so and visit missionaries who were working with the Umbukushu people. A couple I met while at Bible College, were working alongside this tribe, learning their language — with the aim of translating the Gospel of John from English into Humbukushu — the local language of the Umbukushu. The night before we left, Ingo received a call from head office — it seemed that a university student from Northern Ireland had just arrived in Namibia and the National Director was keen for her to join us on this trip. She was named Julie Robinson.

Julie arrived late, which meant we were late in leaving. Being a very long journey to the Caprivi, we got to know Julie a little. Her accent was pretty cool and although we had Irish people in the community who worked at Rossing mine, we were taken with our new visitor. Two days into the trip, we stopped at a camp site. I was given the responsibility of making a fire for cooking. Julie came over and we started chatting. There was something intently special about her and she seemed to possess the personal qualities I had long searched for in a 'partner'. Having known her for only two days, I told myself that I would marry her. Two days! It took another five years to get there! We got to know each other well for those two weeks and friendship soon blossomed into romance when we returned to Swakopmund. However, the time soon arrived for Julie to return home as her summer vacation came to an end. My heart was in agony. I missed her! I therefore decided to scrape some money together each Friday night to make an international call from a call box, simply to hear her voice. However, it became obvious that she wasn't really interested. Many a Friday night I rang — to be told by her father that she was not there. I mean who could blame her? She had her own life in Northern Ireland and I was but a mere complication which, if truth be told needed to go away. Having got the non-verbal message, I left it at that and moved on.

Due to the fact that we in Youth for Christ were seeking to initiate a children's ministry, Ingo had been in touch with Julie about the possibility of returning to Namibia. Having just graduated from Stranmillis (Teaching) College, Julie grabbed the opportunity with both hands. Uncanny as it was, Julie and I arrived back into Namibia a few hours apart in the Summer of 1993 — she from London and I from Frankfurt. It was a four-hour journey from the capital city to Swakopmund and we decided to share the same taxi. While travelling we had this very adult conversation as to the reasons she returned to Namibia and it was clear that those reasons did not include me! Fair enough! I had just spent two weeks in Zurich cuddling-up with a Swiss international table-tennis player whom I had met before heading to the USA. I was not in Julie's plans for her life and she wasn't in mine! Adult conversation had. We were now simply work colleagues and the 'adult' thing was to leave it at that. It didn't take too long however, for the old feelings to return on both sides and pretty soon we started talking about the possibilities of moving to Northern Ireland. This idea scared me, so much so that I got onto a bus at Christmas time and went to Cape Town without much explanation as to why I was going. If truth be told, I needed to speak to my dad!

Raising the issue of emigrating with my parents was very difficult! I'm the eldest — the only son and bearer of my family name. In my culture, my duty is to financially look after my parents and now here I was, contemplating leaving both of them! Mum's first reaction to the mention of Northern Ireland was one of horror — 'they kill people there' was the expression. As my dad and I chatted through the possibility of me leaving, it was evident that mum was not for the idea and pretty soon Julie became the target of her anger. I guess that's quite understandable — mothers and their sons share a close bond and the thought of a lady stealing their son is hard enough, but taking him to another hemisphere is simply a bridge too far. The conversation soon became heated and mum chose to remind me that our community was not in the business of marrying whites, for in her opinion it was expected of me to marry someone of my own colour! Wow, where did that come from? It was evident that mum was upset. The thought of losing her only son was hard to bear, but dad's advice was simple 'you have your own life to live — you are responsible for yourself!'

Those words spoken by my father seemed to be branded on my heart and they were words that I would verbalise over and over again in my life from that day to the present: *You are responsible for yourself Victor ... for the way you live, for the moral decisions you make and so on! Own it. Do not point the finger of blame at others. Take personal responsibility for the outcomes of the decisions you make!* If only I knew then how many times I would verbalise those very same words to pupils who find themselves in my office or to all my pupils during a school assembly. In a society where it's easier to impart blame on someone else rather than take responsibility for one's own actions ... and let's look no further than South Africa or Northern Ireland, my father's words ring true over and over and over again! We are not in control of someone else's response to a situation — we are in control of ours!

How is it possible that a lady you know for two days, captures your heart and sets your feet on a path you have never previously contemplated? How is it, that one is prepared to sacrifice all, to build a future with someone who has stolen your heart? I had nothing to offer Julie! Besides the skills that I developed being a missionary and a youth communicator, I had nothing to give her — no finance, no inheritance (as I knew very early on in life that mum and dad had nothing to leave us), no job, no possibility of an income ... nothing! I would potentially move to Northern Ireland with a suit case and a little bit of cash — that's it! What life would I give her? How would I provide for her? I had no answers, except one — I hadn't met anyone like her and I would sacrifice everything for her ... family, friends, continents and hemispheres, for letting Julie go was not an option. I am sure that she was advised to walk away. I'm sure that she was told that I had too much baggage and that most likely, the relationship would end in disaster. However, within the realms of God's creativity, did He build into Julie and I a divine need for each other? Did God create her, for me ... with all of my complexities as a human being? Did God prepare her heart for me? Did He build into her the necessary building blocks of resilience, honesty, tolerance for hurt, etc., ... the necessary ingredients to build a life with me? Why would she even love me, let alone choose to build a life with me? What was there inside of me that she was attracted to? I was generally bad news but for some unknown reason, God shaped the pathway of both our lives to bring us together as individuals, to a point now where we were contemplating a life together. Was this clearly a 'God-thing'?

I returned to Swakopmund, sat Julie down and started to put in place a 'route-map' for moving hemispheres. If I were to make the move to Northern Ireland, a couple of things needed to happen. Firstly, Julie needed to leave Namibia, head home to Northern Ireland and get a job. Teaching posts are normally advertised as of January of each academic year in preparation for the next. It was vital therefore that she was around to both apply and sit interviews if need be. Bottom line — she needed to get a job! Secondly, I needed to find employment in Northern Ireland too — for it was clear that I would be sent right back to Namibia when arriving at Heathrow without some sort of employment in the United Kingdom.

Julie left early in February 1996. If I were to say to you that it was probably the most difficult of goodbyes, I would not be exaggerating. People fall in love — yea I get that but the thought of not being able to see each other for many a month was unbearable. We had no idea if we were ever going to see each other again, let alone be with each other. We literally had no idea what the next few months would bring. A few weeks before returning to Northern Ireland, Julie lost her grandmother whom she loved very much. Due to the fact that she was close to her nanny, Julie struggled with her death while still in Namibia. It was an uncertain and emotional time for both of us. Julie and I cried our way through that afternoon until she got onto her flight. I had never known heartache like it. She flew home and all I could now do was concentrate on trusting God with my future. He was the only One who could make this happen. Julie needed to get a job in Northern Ireland — and so did I! She took along with her a copy of my CV, just in case there were opportunities for ministry in Northern Ireland. In the meantime, I made enquiries about the possibility of emigrating. I was informed that due to Namibia being a high risk country for AIDS, I needed three blood tests as part of my application to the UK. Each test had to be taken three weeks apart. I also required a medical practitioner's report stating that I was HIV negative. Blood tests done — paperwork received and banked in my 'emigration file'! I had a little moped which I then sold. Money received and banked! Soon I received a phone call from Julie — she got a job! Wow, God was doing His thing. *Now one more individual requiring employment, God. I trust you!*

It was now mid-April and I had a meeting arranged with the British High Commissioner. I left Swakopmund that Thursday at four in the morning and made the four-hour journey east to Windhoek, the capital city. My appointment was for 8.30am. I had all the necessary documentation with me — HIV tests, a note from Julie about her employment and a letter stating that she would be funding me on my arrival, her parents' address, etc.

I met with the British High Commissioner all of five minutes. Bottom line was that without any fixed offer of employment, there was no way I was getting into the UK on a permanent basis. The news was what I expected! Having left the British embassy, I stopped at a filling station for petrol, bought myself some breakfast and prepared for the four-hour journey back to Swakopmund. I arrived home at about one in the afternoon. I couldn't face heading to the Youth for Christ office so I took the afternoon off, got myself a couple of videos and went home. I was depressed! It seemed that I couldn't have the one thing I wanted — to be with Julie. I had to contemplate the fact that this was never going to happen and maybe the best thing was to call Julie and terminate the relationship for good. That would be most fair to her and it would allow her space to move on with her life. She had her own life and maybe this was God's way of saying that the future I was hoping for was not in His will. Maybe I had to accept that. *Suck it up, Vic. Maybe this is how it is!*

At about seven that very evening, the phone rang. It was Gary Millar — the assistant minister at Hamilton Road Presbyterian Church in Bangor, Northern Ireland. They had advertised for a Youth Pastor and Julie had forwarded my CV and applied on my behalf. Gary informed me that they would be keen to have me fly over for an interview. I asked him if there was any possibility of rescheduling my interview for a few weeks, which would allow me some time to raise money for a flight ticket. He informed me that they had just purchased my flight ticket and all I had to do was request my ticket at Windhoek airport. I was given the date and time of my interview and the conversation ended. How does God do that? How does He connect the dots? How does He so specifically answer the very thing Julie and I spoke about three months earlier? How does He connect me to a vacant position in a church half-way around the world? How is that at the very time I am looking for an employment opportunity in Northern Ireland, a church in Northern Ireland is looking to fill a ministerial position? Coincidence?

My visit to Northern Ireland was great. It was now my second visit — the first was a year earlier when I came to meet and visit Julie's parents. I had to now prepare for an interview. Julie took me shopping — apparently I had to get a suit. Now here was a new experience. Some of you know how I feel about wearing a suit. 'Hate' doesn't come close! I'm an African at heart. We wear suits at weddings and funerals — that's about it! The last time I owned one I was fourteen and my parents got me a brand new suit for my confirmation! Apparently this was how things worked in Northern Ireland. The last interview I had at Youth for Christ was so much more relaxed. Anyway, off we went to Marks and Spencers in Sprucefield to get a suit, shirt and tie. Julie had also forwarded my CV to two other churches who showed an interest in possibly employing me. I therefore met with those two churches first and was unsuccessful in both and now I had my final one — with the church who brought me over. I felt really funny sitting in a formal interview all 'dollied-up' in my new suit.

The interview was fine — it was probably the best 'interview' I did, for it was an entire weekend affair! The Friday evening, I was involved in playing football with guys from the church. The Saturday morning, I led a Bible Study with some of the young people and finally I had the official interview later that afternoon. Sunday morning, I visited the worship service and had lunch with Mr and Mrs Gamble — members of the church who were tremendous hosts. Julie and I returned back to her family home the Sunday evening and anxiously awaited a call from Hamilton Road Presbyterian Church. I was informed that I would hear from them on Monday morning. The phone rang the next morning at about nine thirty — I got the job!

Now people often talk about God's faithfulness but I was experiencing it in a tangible fashion! God was literally working for my good ... again! So, He arranges money for my registration to Bible College; He then organises a scholarship for me through the goodness of the faculty; He finances and looks after me while being a missionary for six years; He organises Julie a job and now He does the very same for me! I couldn't handle the emotion of His goodness ... the tears were in my eyes before I realised it! People say there is no God, that all these events were coincidences but how do you account for the timing of it all? Just at the time when I was looking to move hemispheres, a church was seeking to fill a vacant post! God did all this in a matter of four months. Ten minutes after receiving the call, I headed for the bathroom to be alone and wept like a baby. The God of this universe had my life in His hands. I was inconsolable! Why was God so good to me?

Hamilton Road Presbyterian Church was so well organised — I had all the necessary immigration paperwork I would require on my return in August, handed to me before I flew back to Namibia ... legal papers; letter of job-offer, etc. I said goodbye to Julie and flew back to Africa. I was very impressed by this church but they would surprise me even further when a year later they flew my parents and sisters over to Northern Ireland — the church's wedding present to Julie and I.

It was very hard to leave Swakopmund. I had made good friends there. I was leaving people whom I grew to love.

However, saying farewell to the young people was tough! A few of them joined us at the bus depot, as I awaited a bus for the twenty-three-hour bus journey to Cape Town. It was hard to leave young people who became like family. Well, if truth be told two of those boys were family — for I looked after Paulus and Andrew for over a year. I clothed and fed them, became a father-figure to them and therefore saying farewell to them was very difficult. Then there was the local church of St Timothy's Church of England — a small group of brothers and sisters who looked after me and who allowed me to make mistakes in the pulpit during my many Sundays of preaching there. It was hard saying farewell to people who I spent six years of my life with ... a close church congregation, people in Youth for Christ, parents of the young people, colleagues at the various schools and individual families like Johan and Leanna Cilliers ... who were not just close friends but a couple who truly mentored Julie and I. How do you walk away from people who impacted your life? This farewell was not easy! I got onto the bus and waved goodbye to the faces I grew to love and whom I would never forget. This chapter of my life was now sadly ... over!

I got to Cape Town and commenced the emotional roller coaster which I was now experiencing. I was getting ready to emigrate! I had left family and friends six years earlier for Namibia but I was still in travelling distance of Cape Town — be it a twenty-three-hour car journey which Julie and I often made. This time round I would not have that luxury of simply visiting home. Northern Ireland was in another hemisphere. I was making a move that would change my life entirely. Immense loneliness set-in but I had made up my mind — my life was with Julie. I would follow her to Mars if I needed to. It wasn't so much that I was in love — I had never met anyone like her and I wasn't going to let her go!

What had I learnt through this whole process of moving hemispheres? What was clearly evident was God's continual goodness to me, even at times when I did not deserve it. I am of the opinion that God is involved in the very fabric of our lives, shaping our life's pathway, bringing key individuals into our lives at certain times of our lives ... doing all this for our benefit and our good. You may disagree with me and that's entirely your right and I respect that, but could you honestly say that all I had just mentioned was purely coincidence?

So I arrived in Northern Ireland. Everything had gone smoothly at Heathrow. I had all the necessary immigration paperwork from Hamilton Road Presbyterian Church. I nearly missed the shuttle flight from London to Belfast but I was finally here — *Northern Ireland, my new home!*

Mum and dad on their wedding day

My playground (1972)

With cousins (1973)

With my cousin Hester (1975)

P7 Form Class — Norma Road Primary (1981)

Primary school rugby team

Sunday School Camp (1984)

Final school year (1986)

Andy & Vic – SU (1988)

Warren & I — Youth Week 1989

Andy – SU Camp 1989

My sister Glenda

Cape Evangelical Bible Institute — Last week of college

Cape Evangelical Bible Institute graduates (1990)

Donald's speech at my 21st (1990)

Gus & I in Cape Town with Namibia teens (1990)

Dad, mum, Sharon & Glenda (1991)

English High School — first coaching role (1991)

Ingo & I leading worship — St Timothy's Church of England (1992)

Doing mission in Rundu — in the Caprivi Strip, Namibia (1992)

Teaching at English High School (1992)

Men's Softball (1992)

Stomping maize — with the Umbukushu tribe (1992)

Ingo & I — fishing cabin (1994)

Julie & I out for a night (1997)

Graduation day — Queen's University (2003)

The family — Giant's Causeway, NI (2014)

Muizenberg, Cape Town (2016)

Friends for life; Bags, Jake, Ric and me (2019)

Loyalty! (2017)

Young men! Our boys (2019)

Chapter 10: The Land of the 'fast-talkers'

When immigrants live in your land with you,
you must not cheat them.
Any immigrant who lives with you must be treated
as if they were one of your citizens.
You must love them as yourself,
because you were immigrants in the land of Egypt;
I am the LORD your God!

(Leviticus 19 vv 33-34)

It was great seeing Julie and her parents again. We made the drive to Bangor and I walked into the little terraced house, rented to me by one of the members at the church. Everything had been pre-arranged. I had everything I needed. Julie and her parents had ensured that I had the necessary bits and pieces that come along with a house. They had bought groceries, toiletries and so on and helped me settle in. Then they left! I had promised mum that I would call to let her know that I had arrived safely. I then went for a little dander, familiarising myself with my new surroundings and found a telephone box. I called home and reassured mum that I was okay. Then it arrived ... loneliness! I was alone in a new country. I had no friends, no one I could pop into and just say 'hello'. Julie lived about twenty miles away and her parents about sixty. However, I knew that I would see her ever so often after school but I now had to pull myself together. I had made a choice to move countries — I just had to get on with it. *'Grow up Vic! This is your life!*

Congratulations! You have just been appointed as a Youth Pastor at a local church. Good news, yes, but the reality and responsibility of your new job soon kicks in when you have some time alone to yourself. You are concerned about what impression you will make — will the young people like you; will they get on with you; are they different to the teenagers back home; what if my relational model of ministry does not quite work here; what about building organisational structures; what if there are structures already in place which I disagree with; what if you don't get on with someone in the staff team; what if the parents of the teenagers you are working with simply think that you are just a big kid in an adult body — questions, questions and more questions! Sleep was hard to come by that night. Suddenly the words 'peaceful sleep' don't quite apply to you! I was afraid I would fail! However, I just needed a strategy — a way forward — a 'business plan'!

The first problem in 'Norn Iron' was that people generally spoke very fast and I struggled initially to understand them. However, having known Julie for five years, I was slightly used to it but some people spoke faster than others and that took some getting used to. People in Hamilton Road Presbyterian Church were very friendly and pretty soon I was starting to meet people and actually hang out. Steven and Gillian Gourley were so good to me in just allowing me to visit and drop in at any time and I honestly appreciated that. I'm sure there were times when they saw my car pull up and thought 'oh dear, not him again', but if they had, it was never ever communicated — not verbally or in their body language. I owe them for their hospitality but also for their goodness to me. I started playing football for '3rd Bangor Boys Brigade Old Boys' and that was good. It was another great way of making friends. I was settling in. It was all very new and very exciting.

The speedy talking was tough but soon I also faced a second issue — a political one! I was now suddenly labelled a 'Protestant'. There seemed to be this idea that because I worked within a Presbyterian Church I automatically fell into this category of the great divide in Northern Ireland. No one ever took the time to ask me what my opinions were on the topic, so I started to refer to myself as a 'Jesus-follower', rather than a Protestant. On government application forms I often ticked the 'Protestant' box and then wrote the phrase 'Jesus-follower' below it. I felt this immense pressure of being labelled — and I hated it! Of course I did not understand the intensity of the political conflict here but I did know a little about church history and theology. I was ignorant of the emotion in Northern Ireland which came along with 'the Troubles' — but so too were some people about the Reformation. So, my learning about the Troubles began — this being the historical political conflict which raged in Northern Ireland since the 1960s to the official end of the conflict at the signing of the Good Friday Agreement, although violence and turmoil still continued thereafter on a lesser scale. The Good Friday Agreement, also known as the Belfast Agreement … was a document signed on Good Friday in April 1998 between the British and Irish Governments — and all political players in between with regard to how Northern Ireland should be governed in the future.

Who was to now educate me about the political divide in this country? Who was to be my teacher? Each time I saw politicians on television, they were blaming the other side. No one party ever took responsibility for their side of the problems in Northern Ireland. I needed an impartial teacher but no one seemed to be! I therefore decided to learn from scholars on both sides of the divide, trying to keep balance in my thinking and thereby educating myself about the issues before making a personal judgement on political matters here.

Doing an A-level in Politics at Belfast Metropolitan College was an interesting experience. My lecturer was a Nationalist and very switched-on politically (a Nationalist being someone who seeks the unification of Northern Ireland with the Republic of Ireland, so as to no longer be under the rule of the British government and to ensure this form of independence through the process of the ballot box, as opposed to securing it through violence). We had very interesting conversations about his view of 'the north of Ireland' and I appreciated his honesty. I started reading about the conflict here — books written by historians on both sides of the divide. I also had the opportunity a few years later, to attend a conference where I found myself sitting across the table from an Irish Republican, that is individuals who sought to free themselves from British rule via the gun. This individual had made a decision to leave the gun behind and to now serve his community as a politician. I was one of a few youth leaders who had the opportunity to engage with him and have him field questions from us. Discovering that I was a non-white South African, he appealed to my sense of 'knowing what it felt like to be oppressed'. Later during lunch that gentleman sat on his own. It was obvious that no one wanted to speak to him. It was clear that everyone in the room knew that this gentleman had a tarnished reputation. What would Jesus do if He were in this room? Would Jesus ignore this man?

Maybe the organisers of the conference had planned to join him for lunch but hadn't done so as yet. It was evident that people returning from the lunch queue made their way past him and chose not to sit next to him. The hour I had spent alongside other youth colleagues chatting to this gentleman was an insightful experience — now he was sitting on his own. What would Jesus do here? What would Jesus expect me to do? Was I to be a Jesus-follower in name only? I took my lunch tray and walked over to the gentleman concerned and had my lunch with him. I would never be in his company again, but each time I saw him on television, I listened intently. It was clear that he and I would never agree about things politically but one day this gentleman too would have to stand before God and account for his life — as would I. On that day I would be as guilty as he. On that day there would be no category of sin, no distinction made between 'crime and white-collar crime', no distinction between the terms 'terrorist or freedom-fighter!' It would not matter whether he had a history of terrorism or whether I was responsible for burning a meat truck in my youth! My hands would be as guilty as his — for we both carry the scourge of sin! Before God, I would be as guilty as he and he, as me! We would both have to give account as to our response to the saving work of Jesus on the cross. Both that gentleman's destiny and mine would be determined by how we answer that question! Many years later after a gruelling illness, that gentleman passed from this life. His name was Martin McGuiness ... a former Republican activist who became Deputy First Minister of the Northern Ireland Assembly (the executive body which governs the people of Northern Ireland).

My learning continued! I started chatting to close friends — one of these conversations would happen a few years later at a caravan site in France, over a cold beer or two. I sat intently and listened to their individual experiences of life in

Northern Ireland. What a useful conversation that was. My learning continued! I ended up asking myself the same question over and over ... how would Jesus approach this were He in my shoes? One thing I knew was that He would not hate. Jesus would not keep driving a wedge between people. He would reconcile people! 'Love God and love your neighbour' — a constant reminder, like a piercing light in a dark tunnel. When looking at the Bible from cover to cover, it is evident that it deals with one key issue — reconciliation! The message of the Scriptures teaches the reconciliation of God with mankind and mankind with one another. The sacrifice of Jesus via crucifixion at the hand of the Roman authorities, therefore becomes in essence ... an act of reconciliation! This would therefore be my purpose. If I was to make Northern Ireland my home, my purpose would be to bring people together. That is what I would communicate and live out. This would be my life's goal!

Yet, how do I do that? I have no understanding of the hurt caused in Northern Ireland. What if I met people who lost loved ones at the hands of gunmen on both sides of the divide? Would I simply communicate words without understanding? Life's events have a way of becoming a teaching tool to all of us, if we simply take time to listen! I had only been in Northern Ireland a few months when an Irish Republican Army bullet pierced through the chest of a young British soldier, who fulfilled his duty at a check point. He was eighteen — a year younger than Calum is now! Something was not quite right here! We were away at a youth camp with young people from Hamilton Road Presbyterian in August one summer, when we received news that a car bomb detonated in Omagh — a local town in Northern Ireland, which resulted in the deaths of many innocent people and scores more injured! The news reported that those responsible were from the Provisional IRA, a new group who opposed the ceasefire implemented by the IRA at the installation of the Good Friday Agreement. More deaths, more innocent deaths —who cared if they were Protestant, Roman Catholic, Muslims, Bahai, etc. —these were people out shopping. They were innocent! Irrespective of their political views or their personal opinions about conflict in their country, no one had the right to snuff-out their existence! My learning continued! This cannot be right! Indiscriminately taking people's lives because of a 'cause' cannot be right; some took up arms to oppose Apartheid in South Africa too — it wasn't right there either! So Jesus, how do I actually 'Love my enemies' within this conflict? If I am to be a 'Jesus-follower' and communicate that to people I meet, how do I consciously love my enemy? How do I actually forgive those who are simply intent on destruction and death and who seem to get away with it? What would my response be if my wife or sons were to be innocent victims of a future Omagh bomb? How would I respond? I know for a fact that the condition of my own heart is the one thing that I am in control of. In 1985 during the 'troubles' in South Africa, my heart had nearly turned to stone and I could not allow myself to be in that position again! How do I become a peace-maker here in Northern Ireland? How can I help in reconciling and bringing people together? Historical wrongs had been done on both sides of this conflict — however, what about this current generation in which I now live? How do I communicate 'Loving your neighbour' to my generation?

I had a great boss in Reverend David Johnston, who always allowed his staff to get on with things. I had a strategy of what I wanted to achieve and Gary Millar was a tremendous help. He mentored me through my first year, giving advice — assisting me in re-thinking one or two things and outrightly disagreeing with me when he needed to. I was implementing a ministry model which was very much the ministry model at St James' Church years earlier. The bedrock of our youth ministry had been effective volunteers. This was now my starting point! I had a great team of leaders and we worked well together. The youth ministry at Hamilton Road was growing and things were going well. However, I hadn't moved to Northern Ireland just for a job — I moved here because of Julie. It was time to progress my relationship. I spoke to Julie's mum and dad in early January 1997 and asked for her hand in marriage. As conversations go I informed them that the summer was a good time to be married. Six months! Julie's mum felt that it was quite a short time to plan a wedding. She was right — but I wasn't waiting any longer!

Julie and I went to Belfast one Friday evening. As we shopped, I chatted to her about visiting a jeweller's while we were there. I told her that I was planning to marry her at some stage and that this was a good enough time as any to purchase an engagement ring. I wanted her to pick her own ring. She was going to wear the thing, not me and I wanted her to wear a ring she loved. So we shopped — not for clothes this time, but for an item she would wear for the remainder of her life! I only had a certain amount of cash and was happy for her to 'top-up' if she wanted anything more expensive. I am a realist and having seen how my parents struggled with paying back debt over many years, I was not going to borrow money in order to purchase an engagement ring either! I had seen people splash out thousands upon thousands of pounds on a wedding, only for the marriage to later dissolve! A ring was a symbol — nothing more! I wanted Julie to wear something she loved. We made a purchase and I took the ring home and stuck it in my draw. *Step 1 — done!*

Julie and I went out for a meal one evening. Those of you who know me well know the problems I have with my knees due to football. Now I had to get down on my right knee! In the middle of the restaurant she said 'yes'. I hadn't really con-templated the thought of her saying 'no'. What if she had? I would've looked a right idiot! Anyway, all went well. Julie was delighted. I was relieved. *Step 2 — done!*

Now came the next step — an emotional next step. When I was about seventeen I made a vow to myself that I would not get married until I owned a home. I spent fifteen years of my life living in a garage — my spouse and my kids would never be in that position! Purchasing a home was our next priority! We started looking! Nice house, nice house, very nice house — and so on and so on! We looked at a few within our price range. Then we found one we liked. We received the keys two months before we were married. Julie moved in while I was still in the terraced house in Bangor. Another opportunity to reflect on God's goodness — another opportunity to weep. My fiancé was in her home — not a garage! I wept before God and was thankful to Him for His goodness. Faithful to the end — God once again doing His thing!

"Yes, dear! I agree, dear! Go ahead, dear!" Julie was in her el-ement with all the wedding arrangements. Julie's mum and dad had been more than generous in their financial contri-bution to the wedding but Julie and I decided to keep our wedding small as such and put the majority of the money we had into the purchase of the house — which was more the priority than splashing out on a wedding celebration. I was so pleased that we were getting married here and not in Cape Town. My extended family is quite large and contem-plating who to invite and who not to, would have created a family war! Anyway, a few days after the engagement I spoke to Gary to see if the church could give me half my salary and bank the other half for me. I needed to get mum and dad here for the wedding. I had spoken to Boetimann, a close friend from Namibia who had emigrated to Holland with his girlfriend about being my best man. So that was sorted too. However, having mum and dad at the wedding was my number one priority.

The church handed me an envelope alongside my pay cheque — a cheque for three thousand pounds. It was their wedding gift to Julie and I. The cheque needed to be used for one thing only — flights, not just for mum and dad but for my sisters Sharon and Glenda as well. The tears thing again! That evening I rang home and spoke to mum and dad. My father was speechless when I told him about the cheque — and then it arrived, the realisation that dad ... for the very first time in his life would have the opportunity to board a plane and journey outside South Africa! It was an emotional phone call! How does God do that? Was this just a matter of people feeling sorry for me or was this truly a case where God moved people's hearts to give? Often there is a tremendous joy in giving and I'm sure those at Hamilton Road Presbyterian who were involved in making that decision, felt immense joy when my family eventually set foot in Northern Ireland.

The night before my wedding, we had a little family meal at the home of John and Pamela McDowell, who were good enough to allow my family to stay in their home while they were away on holiday. It was a nice meal ... mum and dad, sisters, my best man and his girlfriend. The problem was that I could not relax. I was starting to feel afraid — not so much about the wedding day but more about being a husband! I excused myself right after the meal, much to everyone's astonishment and made my way to our newly acquired home. I got home and went up to what would be our bedroom. I knelt down and intently started to speak to God. I had never been a husband before and the responsibility of it all started to overwhelm me. What if I was bad at being a husband? What if two, ten or twenty years down the line things didn't work out? How do I now make the transition from thinking about myself only — as I had done for years, to now thinking about someone else? I had got to know myself very well. I was innately selfish — those fellas standing behind pulpits would call that 'sin'! I wasn't like other guys who couldn't wait to married. On the contrary, I was afraid and I needed to talk to Jesus about all that! He knew me intently. He alone would understand what I was feeling. I had often heard or knew of circumstances where couples could not wait to be married and a few years later it all came to end. Was I to become a divorce statistic in the future too? I needed peace before the sun rose the next morning and I needed to talk to my Creator, for it was He alone who could give me peace about this thing called ... marriage!

Wedding day! Julie looked lovely. I'm not sure if she was nervous but she seemed to walk up the aisle quite speedily — completely out of step with her friend Yana's playing on the organ! Boetimann and I looked alright in our twenty-five pound suits which we hired at a shop in Bangor! I could not fathom having to spend hundreds of pounds on a suit which Boetimann and I would only wear for a few hours. People were gathered outside St Matthews church in Richhill. It was Julie's home church and I felt really honoured to be married in the church where she felt most loved. My sister Glenda sang as we signed the register — which kept the guests entertained. It was a special day too for our parents. Julie and I were the first ones in our individual families to be married, so it was a new experience for all concerned. The parents got on well. So did our siblings. Later on we had our reception at the Palace Stables in Armagh. At eight that evening, our wedding day was over and we made our way home to Bangor, to our new house, to our new life together.

Wedding over. Marriage begins!

Chapter 11: Namibia 1999

*God uses men (and women) who are weak
and feeble enough to lean on Him!*

(J Hudson Taylor: 1901)

Things were going well in my new job at the church. Our volunteers were exceptional and gave their best to our young people. With the assistance of a few of the elders responsible for the youth ministry within the church, we had successfully integrated all the various youth ministries under one umbrella and I was now content that we had cohesion within our work with young people. I also ensured that we had designated leaders and my role was now one of co-ordination and management. However, there was one thing I wanted to initiate — I wanted to give our young people exposure to life in Africa. I wanted them to experience life outside of their comfort zones and give them a brief snap shot of what the world was like for young people like themselves in my home continent. It was my ambition therefore to take our young people on a mission to Namibia!

It is fair to say that in my six years living in Namibia, I had fallen in love with the place. I wanted our young people therefore to not only be exposed to the beauty of Africa, but more importantly to have a taste of what mission in Africa is all about, be it in a short-term capacity. I shared the idea with Rev David Johnston, our minister and staff-team leader and he was in total agreement. The elders were very supportive of the idea too and our Youth Committee received the green light to make this happen. From the outset, I wanted to ensure that all young people had the opportunity to attend this trip — not just the ones whose parents could afford it. My own personal experience had taught me that money should never be an issue, for I had seen God make provision in my own life. The key therefore was to have an effective team — young people who would all make a contribution. The other important factor was finding the right co-leaders.

I played football with Jeff Bingham. Not only was he involved in our youth ministry but he was also a 'Boys Brigade man'. Having heard from Peter and Lisa Campbell that they were not able to co-lead the team with us as Julie and I had hoped, David suggested that Jeff and Karen would be the right couple to ask. Having spoken to them about this possibility, I was delighted when they agreed! We worked very well together with regard to the planning of this trip. We complimented one another. Julie and Karen concentrated on the finer details of the trip while Jeff and I looked at the 'broad strokes'. The church already pre-paid the hire of the vehicles as well as the accommodation, in order to make good use of the phenomenal exchange rate. Now all we needed was our team of young people. The teenagers went through an interview process. We couldn't take everyone. We wanted to ensure a total mix of teenagers. Some candidates nearly picked themselves — for they excelled in their interviews. Some we had to re-think but eventually we had our team ... we were going to Namibia in the summer of 1999. Julie and I had made the decision to start a family but that was now on hold until we returned from Namibia. The focus now was take these young people to Africa and more importantly, to return them back safely to their parents.

Our departure day arrived. Knowing my personal trait for being on time, Jeff and Karen rang to say that they had slept-in and would be late in collecting us for the airport. They knew that this would be the kind of thing that would annoy me but lo and behold, it was a total wind-up! They rang me while sitting in my drive way and we all had a good laugh! It was a good way of starting life together for the next three weeks. Jeff and Karen ... co-leaders; friends for life! We arrived at the airport and prayed with the parents and off we went. While sitting on the plane I was overcome with fear! I was now responsible for the safety and lives of these young people. They were going to Africa where 'health and safety' was a foreign concept. I was taking them to a country of snakes, big bugs, wild animals, etc. In my mind I quietly prayed: *Lord be with us every step of the way. Help me get these young people safely back to their parents, please!* Soon we were on our second flight from Heathrow. Next stop — Windhoek, Namibia!

The pre-paid arrangements had all taken care of itself. The mini-vans were ready and waiting and soon we made the journey from the airport to the capital city, Windhoek. It was Sunday morning and Windhoek was fairly quiet. As we were about to make the four-hour journey to Swakopmund, we gave the young people an opportunity to stop at a local shop in Windhoek. They could not believe their luck! They now began to realise how they benefitted from a strong currency. Twenty pence for a two litre coke — so they bought five ... and so on. They were in their element! Soon we were off to the coast — to the place Julie and I met and worked in years ago — to the place I loved, Swakopmund!

Johann Cilliers — my former mentor and Chair of the Trustees for the Youth for Christ office in the town, was an estate agent by profession. We had organised accommodation through him. It was so good to see him again. The house we stayed in was great — it met our needs! Once we settled in, we took the young people to the beach to relax — for the journey had been very long. I bumped into Ingo and Suann — colleagues and close friends who brought me to Swakopmund years earlier. They were in the town on holiday too. It was so good seeing them again.

We had arranged with the principal of Tamariskia Primary School—the school Julie worked in years earlier, to do a children's club as part of our two weeks there. Our young people had pre-prepared materials and booklets for a maximum of sixty children. In true African fashion, the principal of the school collapsed the timetable each morning, for he wanted his entire school involved in this club. Now how do you run a club with an entire school? Simple — you think on your feet and plan accordingly! As the first day was all about getting to know the children, we played activity games, which allowed us time later on to plan for the remainder of the week. It was crazy, but what an experience for our teenagers. They were thrown in at the deep end and they were swimming!

The team had the opportunity to work in the English High School, where I had previously taught and it was here where they engaged with young people their own age. It was great seeing them lead youth activities with their peers and I was slightly proud — not in a cynical way, but proud that they were coping at the task of being able to share Jesus with pupils their own age. That's hard to do ... and they were doing it! Our time in Swakopmund soon came to an end and we embarked on the journey north to work alongside a missionary couple there. It was here where our young people had access to the classroom in another school setting. The highlight of that week was the local lads playing football against our 'missionary team'. Peter McIvor was our star that day! 'Magoo' — his nickname, got the ball going into the opposition net on a few occasions and we won that day — but man were we wrecked! The heat, the dust, the tired bodies! Great fun!

The last part of the journey, was a few days spent in Etosha, Namibia's largest game park. Our young people had the opportunity to go on safari and see animals in the wild! It was so satisfying seeing them experience new things. Although westernised and some lacking for nothing back home — they were so vulnerable. The opportunity to be on this mission was a life-changing experience for them. They would never forget it as long as they lived. It was an experience I wish all our young people at Hamilton Road Presbyterian could have had! Eighteen months of planning had come to an end. It was time to head home — although Julie and I would not join the team on the return flight back to the UK, for we had other plans — a short two-hour flight to visit my family in Cape Town!

As with all things, one gets to a point of personal 'debrief'. What did we really achieve in those three weeks? We spent all that money on flights and so on — yes, our young people had a great time — yes, we implemented aspects of mission but did we truly do something beneficial for the Kingdom of God? I guess what I'm trying to say is who really benefits from short-term mission — the recipients or the missionaries? I guess the answer is both! Taking individuals out of their comfort zones and watching them deal with new experiences allows them to develop something within themselves — a spirituality and faith which is personalised! They begin to own their faith, each one using their own journey of faith as a tool of communication, as a means of telling young people about the impact Jesus has on their own life. I am of the opinion that young people must take opportunities like this to see what God can accomplish through them if they but simply trust Him and avail themselves to His work, to the building of His Kingdom throughout the world. The bi-product of the available life is the further building of one's faith, for once we realise our individual feebleness and frailty we cannot but trust in His strength and ability. When realising that mission is all about Christ's ability outplayed within our weakness, we become part of the crowd at the Mount of Olives, witnessing and listening to the words of the ascended Saviour saying, *"Go into the world and make disciples ... and yes, I am with you, until the end of this age!"* (Matthew 28)

However, what about the impact of short-term mission on the recipients? The danger of short-term mission is that the missionary can fool himself into thinking that he/she can change the context of the local people to whom they minister, seeking to bring about change to 'our kind of thinking and our way of life'. This arrogant mind-set once permeated throughout many churches who sent missionaries — alongside the military, to the 'dark corners of Africa' and we ended up calling this 'colonialism'. Our role as missionaries in my opinion is two-fold — to share the message of the life, work, death and resurrection of Jesus and to encourage people to spiritual transformation. Secondly, to assist others to live for Christ within their own individual cultural contexts. By doing this, we create impact, life-change and contextual transformation. You see, these go hand-in-hand. We cannot change people — that's what God does, but we must provide individuals the education and skills to apply their faith within their personal context. Is this not what the Apostle Paul did? Often we read within the Book of Acts as well as his Letters, how he shared the Good News and encouraged people to faith in Christ and then he stayed with them for a while, teaching them the truths of the Gospel so that they can possess the skills to stand firm. Once Paul accomplished this goal, he not only moved on but later wrote to them to ensure that they were implementing what he had taught them while he was with them. Isn't this short-term mission in a nutshell? Isn't this the impact we hope for every young person going on short-term mission? Alan Burricks — a graduate of CEBI and a fellow missionary in Namibia — who spent years working with the Umbukushu tribe, once informed me about the importance of earning the right to share the news about Jesus and one earns the right through becoming part of the community that one seeks to share the Gospel with. The Apostle Paul did precisely this!

The Parable of the Sower teaches us that our responsibility is to preach and God does the rest. Does this parable justify the 'going in and going out' approach that sometimes we apply to 'mission'? What did the young people in Namibia learn about our team during their time there? Did they view our young people as being lucky enough to be on a trip like that? Did they wish that they too had the opportunity and financial means to make such an international journey and did they remember the truths about Jesus which we shared during our time there? I guess God alone knows the impact that trip had on its recipients. He promises however, that He has the ability to water and bring to completion the preaching and sharing of His Word. Mission works, because mission in itself is all about partnership ... our ability to share the message of Jesus and God's ability to work within the life of the recipient. I am of the opinion therefore that if one of those children or young people in Namibia came to an understanding of who Jesus is and what He came to do for us at some stage in their lifetime, then 'Namibia 1999' was a phenomenal success. Therein lies the Sovereignty of God — we make our plans to 'do mission'; we wonder if it has been a success; we pray for those we leave behind when we return to our homes; we most likely will never encounter those individuals again. However, Mission ... be it short or long-term, allows God to do His thing in the world.

My 'world' starts with those close to me ...

Chapter 12: "Welcome to the world my son!"

No love is greater than that of a father for his son!

(Dan Brown)

There was a time when each of us looked through the eyes of a child, for that is who we once were. It was a time of education, learning from those we called parents — witnesses to their laughs, their joys, their indiscretions, their strengths and their weaknesses. As we observed their lives, we formulated opinions about who they were as people, how they adapted to times of difficulties and so on. We made decisions to aspire to be like them in some ways, never to be like them in others and then we judged ... pointed fingers when their mistakes were exposed to us and we vowed that we would do things differently when it was our turn to be parents ... and soon, we were!

Julie and I, having now returned from our trip to Namibia, had decided that the time was right for us to embark on the next stage of our lives ... pregnancy! The realities of life meant that we could possibly be one of those couples who sadly cannot conceive and therefore undergo the emotional trauma which comes along with that. One never really considers difficulties like that until one longs to have a child and then it suddenly dawns on you that you may not be in a position biologically, to have one. Many a couple have known the heartache which comes along with a scenario like this and soon we would find out if this too, was our fate. We discovered however, that we were expecting and the realisation of a baby was a moment of immense joy but also one of fear. We were now parents and the time would soon arrive where we had to care for and raise this child. I had gone from being single, to being married to being a parent ... all in a space of five years!

Calum was due the Christmas-New Year week and like many first-borns, he never played ball with the due date. Julie was eventually called in and we made our way to the hospital as a couple, soon to return with a bundle of joy. It was a long labour and Julie was exhausted. Calum was not for arriving! After many an hour, the foetal heart showed signs of distress and the surgeon spoke to both of us about the need for a caesarean section. We agreed and we made our way to theatre.

Now I have a very inquisitive mind; I always had. Having attired myself with the medical gown and paraphernalia, I held Julie's hand as she was wheeled into theatre. I then took up a position right next to the surgeon. I was going to be a witness to all the biological goings-on of this procedure. The surgeon encouraged me to move lower down the table toward Julie, for he feared that I would possibly faint at what I was about to experience. I informed him however, that I was 'good to go' as I watched him make an incision in my wife's body. Soon I saw this baby inside his mother and my heart leapt. Calum was removed from Julie's body — was cleaned, weighed and so on and brought to her arms. He was screaming! We started to talk to him and soon he stopped! He recognised the voices. All those months of talking to 'the bump' had paid off. He had been listening to our voices all this time and he now recognised them. Julie went from being utterly exhausted to being mum. This experience was a first and we now went from being a couple, to being a family! We had spent weeks considering names and we finalised on two, were it a boy. Julie's choice was 'Benjamin' and mine was 'Calum'... a Gaelic name meaning 'messenger of peace'. However, I wanted Julie to name him for I was happy either way. She named him 'Calum Benjamin Coert' and as she named him I prayed to my Father that this baby would one day share His peace with others!

I made my way to Julie's mum and dad, who were awaiting the news. They were delighted. I made a call to South Africa and congratulated my mum and dad on their new role as grandparents. Julie needed rest but that was the last thing on her mind. I was so proud of her. From the moment she knew she was pregnant, she cared for the well-being of our son. He was here and tiredness was not in her thinking. She held Calum as if she had been doing it all her life, but now she needed rest and the midwifery nurses were excellent in their care of her and our new son. I arrived home later and spent time on my knees thanking God for Calum's safe delivery and prayed for Julie. I walked in and out of what would now be Calum's room ... all ready and waiting for him. He would be home in a day or two and our lives would never quite be the same again. I was now a father and as I sank into bed that night I realised that I knew nothing about what it meant to be a father and it scared the life out of me! I needed to sleep as I needed to be up at four the next morning. I had an examination the next day and further study and preparation was still required. *Good night my son!*

Caleb and Joel soon arrived. Caleb's claim to fame was that when he was born, he spent a moment urinating over everyone, including his mother! God had been good to us. Our boys were all healthy at birth and we thanked God for that. Unbeknown to me, all three of our boys would later teach me about what being a father is all about and Calum in general, was a good teacher! While raising him in his early years I discovered that he only had one requirement of me, namely my time!

At age four, Calum was to teach me something I will never forget. I had arrived home late from school one Wednesday evening and consumed a plate of food before rushing out to the Bible Study. Calum stood at the top of the stair case and said 'Daddy, are you going out again?' It was a comment and a facial expression to match that cut through me. He was noticing something, I always seemed to be too busy to spend time with him! I caught Julie's eye and there was something quite uncomfortable about this moment. My son was feeling insecure! The person who was to provide him with that security, was a transient member in the home. Calum had possibly waited all day to see me and I was becoming a stranger to him because of my busy life and my obligations. Needless to say, I hardly thought of anything else at the Bible Study and it was then that I made a decision ... I would make time for our boys, even if it meant sacrificing certain things deemed important. A few years later Julie and I had a strong disagreement one evening which resulted in me getting into my car and going for a long drive, to kind of clear the mind as it were. I wasn't home by the time Joel's bedtime arrived. I discovered later that he cried himself to sleep because he feared that I was not returning. I made Joel a promise thereafter, that I would always come into his bedroom when arriving home late at night, even if he was asleep and I would whisper to him that 'daddy was home.' The boys taught me one valuable lesson in my early years of being a father ... kids need to feel that they are loved and they need to know that they are safe and secure. Being an absent father was not part of this parent-deal! Our sons taught me that!

It has been a pleasure and a humbling experience watching my boys grow up. Caravanning in France each summer, became the highlight of our year as a family. Life gets so busy during the academic year that sometime all we need is to take stock and recuperate as families. Going to France each year was our time of getting off the proverbial treadmill. It all started in June already — weekends of preparation, getting the caravan ready, doing the bits and pieces of preparation and the necessary DIY. Preparing to go to France was very therapeutic; not only did it bring to fruition the end of a very long academic year, but it also built expectation of a few weeks of rest, relaxation and some much needed sun! Time away with my wife and boys was priceless and I so looked forward to it. People have no idea how pressured an environment of education and teaching can be, particularly as a head teacher and the morning one leaves for holiday you literally feel the pressure slipping off your shoulders. I cannot accurately describe to you the immense feeling of leaving one's office at the end of a school year and the longing for a few weeks of relaxation with the people you care most about. Absolute bliss!

Over the years, the journey to the ferry commenced the holidays for us. I must say that the boys were always good travellers and they always seemed to get on really well on the journey in the car. Life is about new experiences and I simply loved watching the boys learn about French culture. The new experiences came in the forms of visits to medieval villages or theme parks or the many visits to different campsites and geographical areas over the years, including a day visit to the city of Monaco. However, I loved watching the boys interact with people whom they met at the campsites and the way they simply seem to pick-up the French language and engage with others they befriended. The joy of my life was watching them compete at sport at the campsites over many a year — from football to table-tennis to French bowls and so on and the many lessons they would learn from it, not just about communicating with others in a different language but also about how they portrayed themselves as people in victory or defeat! Life lessons! Time was also spent simply reading and relaxing, not to mention the fun times in the swimming pool and the many hours spent on the bicycles — including the many early morning cycles with Calum — he working on his fitness for football and me trying to keep up with him! Then there were the moments of simply watching my boys spend time with their mother — the relaxed moments when they simply threw their arms around her or times when they were deep in conversation on issues or simply lying on her lap in the sunshine while they were reading ... and the feeling of contentment which overwhelmed me. My family! My wife! My sons!

I must confess to you — I cannot live without our boys — they are my heart-beat! I am so proud of the individuals they have become ... each of them having faith in Jesus, watching them wrestle through, debate and chat through mysteries of the Bible at after-dinner devotions in the evening. Already, they are developing traits of being sound Jesus-followers and having mind-sets for grappling with matters of theology. I don't know what God has in store for their futures but Julie and I will continue to work hard at developing their unique characters.

Calum possesses tremendous leadership skills, character traits he seemed to have had from fairly early on in life! I remember him at about age six, holding a conversation about grand prix racing with a few men in church and not even being phased by the fact that he was in the company of adults. Then there were the many years of captaining his football team and the respect his peers and even referees had for him. During his years of playing table-tennis locally and in Dublin, Calum developed the discipline of concentration and taking ownership of self ... so different from the team-sport dynamic of football. Becoming Deputy Head-Boy at Clounagh Junior High School and Portadown College has allowed him to further hone his leadership skills and it is my hope that he uses these in whatever capacity, in the service of his Father in the years to come.

Caleb is, in many ways, like his dad — in physical stature and also in temperament. Caleb has been blessed with an intelligent mind, evident not only in his schooling but also in his ability and love for music. Ever since he was a toddler, he concerned himself more with Lego and books than footballs and other toys. However, I find myself most impressed at his passion for thinking through matters of theology and areas in the Scriptures he finds a struggle. There have been numerous evenings after family devotions at dinner time, where Caleb and I would find ourselves chatting through 'areas of difficulty' within the Scriptures — everything from the existence of angels to the reality of death. His inquisitive mind is evident in his ability to formulate and hold an argument on areas he is most passionate about and what really excites me about him, is his passion for following Jesus. Caleb has a good heart, evident in the many times he communicates his love to his parents and his brothers. Caleb regularly tells us that he loves us. It is simply just something he does and as his father, I could want for nothing more! Like his older brother, Caleb has tremendous leadership abilities which resulted in his appointment to the position of Head Boy at Clounagh Junior High School. Caleb amazes me with his music ability and the hours of dedication he gives to the piano, the guitar and even the drum kit. His outstanding feature is his caring nature and the way he works hard at keeping his social circle together.

My baby boy just loves life! Joel is the sparkle in our family! He just loves having a laugh and being with his older brothers. Joel's smile is infectious and his zest for fun is simply contagious. He will not go to bed until he has read his devotional booklet and prayed with his mum or I. His spiritual development is evident and though at times he lacks the patience and maturity to discuss in-depth spiritual matters at his age, his curiosity for spiritual matters is clearly evident. When playing football, he reminds me so much of myself. Joel would be in tears after losing a game — for his determination to win comes from within. I guess as the baby brother he is constantly fighting for recognition, whether it is beating his brothers on the Xbox or trying to dribble past Calum in a game of family football. Like his older brothers before him, Joel was recently selected as Head Boy of Clounagh Junior High too — three brothers achieving positions of deputy or head boy in the same junior high school. We look forward to witness the development of Joel's leadership and we pray for God's continual goodness towards him.

In my professional capacity, I constantly see the damage done by absent fathers — particularly at the teenage years. Sometimes I wonder if these dads have any idea at the damage caused in the lives of these young men and women, for young people need their parents! The sad reality is that this absence becomes a vicious circle at times, detrimental from generation to generation. Teenage boys in particular need their fathers — they need their fathers to engage within their lives — they need their dads to be role-models they can look up to. I would be the first to admit that fatherhood is not easy. At most times it requires sacrifice! Once you become a dad you lose the right to want your own time. Show me a son or daughter who is balanced in their thinking, respectful in attitude, studious in learning, friendly in manner, passionate in things that are of interest ... and I will show you a father and mother behind the scenes who are investing in their child!

I thank God daily for our boys. I would let you into a secret ... I don't think I could endure life without them. You speak to my wife and she will tell you that. I love my boys with every fibre of my being and I thank God for each of them. Nick Lachey is right when he says ...

> *'To me, having kids is the ultimate job in life.*
> *I want to be most successful at being a good father'*

To this end I commit myself!

Chapter 13: 'Catching up'!

Vitally important for a young man or woman is first,
to realize the value of education and then to cultivate
earnestly, aggressively, ceaselessly ... the habit of self-education!

(B C Forbes)

Like many Coloured or black pupils thirty-five years ago, I was expected to finish school, find a job and contribute financially to the family home. University study was beyond our reach financially speaking, therefore the expectation was to go to tech — learn a trade and step immediately into the realm of employment. What was I going to do with my life? Well, that question ultimately led me to the doors of the Cape Evangelical Bible Institute, which allowed me to study Theology. I was now employed as a Youth Pastor, but could I really do this for the rest of my life? I was married, had a house and was about to start a family.

God has a way of looking after us! The Apostle Paul would call it God "working for our good" (Romans 8). It seems that God has this ability to set plans in motion, which allow strategic individuals to cross our life's path which results in positive outcomes for us. It was clear that as much as I loved being

Youth Pastor of a very special church, I could not see my-self doing youth ministry indefinitely. I now found myself in a catch twenty-two situation; in order to progress myself financially I needed to study and in order to study I needed additional finance. There was simply no way that I could pursue further study on my current salary other than taking a student loan which I would have to repay. In the midst of all this uncertainty and angst, God however was doing His thing! I got an invitation to coffee!

My contract at Hamilton Road Presbyterian was due for re-newal. I could either remain as Youth Pastor for another few years or grab an opportunity which I was about to be offered. Unbeknown to me, conversations about my future were be-ing had behind the scenes and during coffee with an elder — who was also a businessman, I was afforded an opportunity to attend Queen's University Belfast to read Theology. This opportunity would include the financial cover of my tuition while embarking on an undergraduate degree, all expenses covered with regard to books and a monthly stipend as well — my current salary for three years. God had done this sort of thing before in my life — but at that very moment I was silent! My reply to the gentleman who made the offer was 'I would have to speak to Julie about this'! I was gob-smacked! I didn't quite know what to say. I was given an opportunity to do a degree and it would cost me nothing!

A few years earlier, I had visited Queen's University and had a conversation with the Theology faculty to see what accreditation I would receive for having completed a diplo-ma in South Africa. The simple answer was — none! I was informed that irrespective of my qualifications in South Africa, I would need to do a GCSE in English, Mathematics and an additional GCSE subject of my choice. (GCSEs or General Certificate of Secondary Education are the baseline examinations at the completion of compulsory second-ary education within the United Kingdom, done at age six-teen.) I was also informed that I would require an A-Level in a subject of my choice before being considered for entrance as a mature student into the university. (Advanced Levels are subject-based qualifications completed by pupils at post sixteen years who seek in-depth knowledge of three or four subjects only, which will lead both to university placement and a future profession in those particular subject areas). Having had that conversation, I went down to Belfast Tech (now Belfast Metropolitan College) and registered to sit my GCSEs, about three weeks before the GCSE examinations started. I made my way to a local bookshop and purchased a few self-help books to assist me in preparing for these GCSEs. I received international accreditation for English and therefore did not have to sit this exam as such. However, I had to do the Religious Studies examination and enrolled in a night class to do Mathematics the following year. These exams came and went and the grades I received meant that I could now pursue an A-level in a subject of my choice, name-ly Religious Studies — a two-year course completed in one. I spent two hours each Monday evening travelling to and fro Belfast Bible College in my pursuit of this A-level and at the end of sitting the exam, my result was good. I now had what I needed to get into university as a mature student.

Julie got home from school that day and I informed her about my appointment over coffee. We agreed that it was a great opportunity for us and we accepted the offer. Things progressed very well in my job as Youth Pastor and the Youth Committee were in agreement that the prudent thing to now do was to employ my successor and allow a time of overlap for a period of six months, in order to give the new Youth Pastor an opportunity to learn the ropes and settle in under my tutelage. I wanted to ensure continuity, so that the structures we had worked so hard to put in place over four years, would not now fall apart. The elders were in agreement and Peter Douglas was appointed as my successor.

I was now a first year mature student at university, sitting alongside eighteen and nineteen year olds. I was the older statesman as such. I loved Union Theological College. I could not believe that I was so blessed to have the opportunity to study at a prestigious university like Queen's and a Theological school like Union College. I wanted to do well academically as a means of demonstrating my gratitude to those who had invested in me! They afforded me an opportunity and I was not going to waste it! The first two years flew by and very soon I was about to start my final year! I was intent on becoming a minister and therefore had an interview to become a candidate for the ministry.

The interview went well. However, with the set questions all but over, a comment was made I was not expecting! Maybe the panel wanted to be straight with me! Maybe they wanted me to be under no allusions or maybe they were looking out for my best interest. To this very day I'm not sure what their motive was but I was informed that the likelihood of me being called to a church in Northern Ireland was very small — due to the colour of my skin! Did I pick that up correctly? Did I just hear what I thought I heard? We were in the new millennium and this was not South Africa right ... and the colour of my skin was still an issue — is that what I just heard? I walked out of the interview and joined Julie in the car. Maybe it was the look on my face or maybe it literally was the colour draining from my complexion. I felt like I had just been hit with a baseball bat! I told Julie what happened at the end of the interview — and we looked at each other trying to make sense of it all! Maybe the panel were correct.

Maybe I would have struggled to receive a call from a local church ... but wasn't that God's call to make?

'Well, if that's the case then why do you not consider teaching?' Julie asked. Yes, Religious Studies is a curriculum subject in the UK. In South Africa and in many parts of Africa, Religious Education is a one period a week add-on to the timetable. Here it was a subject, all the way to A-level. It was February and if I had any notion of pursuing a teaching certificate I had to enrol very quickly. We stopped at the post-graduate school and grabbed an application to do a Post Graduate Certificate in Education (PGCE). Having returned to my church in Bangor I relayed to my minister what was conveyed to me about an hour and a half earlier. He was quite annoyed and wanted to make a call just to get some clarification. I told David that it was not necessary for I loved the idea of teaching. I made application to do a PGCE and got an interview. I was made aware that numbers to this post-grad were limited! Having interviewed, I received a letter to inform me that I had been successful. I got in! Now I had to concentrate on my third year finals!

During my three years of study, Calum arrived and it so happened that he was born the night before I had a mid-term exam! God has a sense of humour! There was now additional pressure to have some extra money. Julie was off on maternity leave and we required added funds! I took a small amount of my student loan to ease the financial pressure in the home, knowing that I would have to eventually pay it back. However, I needed a part-time job that would fit around university and family life. So I job-hunted! I got a job at NEXT — the clothing chain. This job however was not on the shop floor as such, but on the delivery shift — four till eight thirty each morning. I took the job! Alongside the A-level in Religious Studies which I completed a few years earlier, I also now embarked upon an A-Level in History and a year later, one in Politics. I had to catch up! If I was going to enter this very competitive profession of education, I needed to make myself as marketable as I could, for if I had ambitions of entering this profession, I would have to sit an interview alongside many other candidates and I needed to do all I could to be the candidate any school would want to employ. I needed additional subjects as part of my CV and doing additional A-levels at the same time as my degree, would eventually stand me in good stead. During the summer, I enrolled in a Summer School Sports clinic at Queen's University — doing a Level One Coaching course in Rugby, Football and Hockey! I needed to do everything I could to get myself in front of an interview panel.

My time at NEXT was a fantastic experience. It was great working alongside people — who in many ways had no affiliation to church at all. I left home at about three thirty in the morning and took a walk to work — starting at four. Finishing at eight thirty, I made my way down to the train station and commuted to the university; sat in lectures all day; worked in the library until five, walked down to Belfast tech for six in the evening; did my A-levels until nine-thirty at night; jumped on a bus and got home at ten thirty; chatted to Julie for an hour or so; completed some homework and then slept for three or so hours. I completed the same routine again the next day and the next! Soon I was given an opportunity to work on the shop floor on Saturdays which was great and the added income would be most welcome. I was then also asked to work on Sunday. Now, I am not a Sabbatarian as such. However, starting at midday meant that I would miss church and I was not happy with that. I had got on quite well with the manageress and had an honest conversation with her about my faith and the importance of me attending church. I inquired as to the possibility of starting at one and suggested that I would work the additional hour on Saturday in order to make-up the required hours. It was either that or I would terminate my contract. Church fellowship was important to me. It was her call. Michaela was happy with that arrangement which therefore resulted in some additional income! No use worrying about the opinion of fellow Christians about me working each Sunday. They were not in my position! I had a responsibility to my family. If they objected to the fact that I was working on Sunday — well that was just too bad!

I was catching up academically. No need feeling sorry for myself. I had to get on with it. My family were counting on me! I was doing this to give my family a future. This too shall pass! Calum had arrived and he was going to have a better life than I did. He was not going to struggle! He was not going to wear clothes from a factory shop. Julie and Calum became my motivation. I loved him more than anything in the world. I was going to give him a life I never had! This was me ... doing this now in order to provide him with opportunities never availed to me. Each time I got tired or had to study for exams, I thought about my wife and my son. The studies and the hours had to be done — short-term pain for long-term gain.

Suck it up Vic. Work hard. This too shall pass — but for now, this is your life!

Chapter 14: God ... always working for my good!

Commit your work to the Lord,
and your plans will be established!

(Proverbs 16 vs 3)

I enjoyed my Post Grad year, learning about education and writing schemes of work in preparation for teaching my subject area. Soon it was March and my classmates and I were frantically making application for jobs. University was fun, but now we had to get into the real world — we had to find employment. I had set out to achieve a two-one-degree classification, thereby providing myself a good opportunity to get an interview! I had completed a Bachelor of Theology degree, was about to complete a Post Graduate Certificate in Education, attained three A-Levels and Level One coaching courses in three sport codes ... all in a time-frame of four years. I now lived in a country with just over one and a half million people — jobs are tight to come by and I had to put myself in a good position to get a teaching post! I could not have done this without the financial support which was afforded to me and my gratitude to those individuals will be life-long!

Grab the newspapers. Check the websites. Job-hunting! I eventually found two available teaching posts which raised my interest — one a Teacher of Religious Education and the other a Head of Department of Religious Studies. The latter was a long shot, as one normally needed a few years of teaching under one's belt before a promotion to management of any department. I was desperate for employment and so I applied to the second post as well — not really expecting a reply. However, I got one. I was called for interview to Antrim Grammar School. Although I was delighted, I started to wonder why I had? How come a grammar school decided to interview a candidate with no experience of teaching in Northern Ireland, for a Head of Department post? Could it be that my management experience gained over years in Youth for Christ and Hamilton Road Presbyterian Church, plus a good degree, those A-levels and those coaching courses ... got me to this door? The Governors of that school gave me an opportunity to be part of their staff team — now I had to formally prove that I was good enough to join them. I needed to get ready for an interview! How do I do that? Last time I interviewed for formal employment was years earlier at Hamilton Road Presbyterian but this interview was going to be very different. I needed to prepare — and prepare well!

I had a few weeks left doing my post-grad at university and while making my way to the Students' Union for coffee one day, I saw a poster which caught my attention. The university had arranged an 'interview skills' event and it was open to anyone, at a price of course. I paid some money for that event and booked in. It was money extremely well spent. I learnt so much practically about doing an interview — how to sit; what to do with your hands; portraying confidence; etc. I also engaged the help of a friend at a school in Bangor who provided me with incite as to the roles and responsibilities of a Head of Department. Lots of reading and preparation about education in Northern Ireland; lots of early morning studying, lots of ringing of the bedside alarm clock at four in the morning ... and so on. I simply had to prepare well! The time arrived — interview day!

I sat in the car park of the school, awaiting my time slot! I had prepared as best I could. Now I had to deliver. For any of you who have sat an interview you know how nerve-wrecking an experience it can be. I was nervous, which meant that I would talk fast! I needed to settle! I needed to implement all I learnt at the interview skills event ... but I needed to settle myself. There was only one Person who had the ability to do that, so I started speaking to God. I asked God to give me clarity of thought and to remove the sense of nervousness from me. You see, there was a lot hanging on this interview ... Julie and Calum! I started doing the one thing that would settle me. I stopped thinking about myself and started worshipping God for His goodness in shaping the pathway of my life to that very moment. I sang — my eyes closed and fixed on the Sovereignty of God. He made this interview possible and worshipping Him for His goodness to me, changed my focus! My time-slot arrived. I was ready. I was now in a place of humility. I did not deserve this interview but my Father in heaven was in the business of blessing His children. As I walked to the front door I remembered the words one of my Bible College lecturers prayed over me when I left Cape Town for Namibia. It came flooding back into my memory — "I know the plans I have for you (says God); plans to prosper you — plans to give you hope — plans to give you a future." (Jeremiah 29vs11) I was ready! Julie and Calum ... here we go!

It was over. The nerves had gone. I spoke clearly. I was relaxed. I sat the way I was taught at that skills event. Job done! I was not in control of the outcome! The Governors were! Now I had to play the waiting game. I drove back home and collected my son from my in-laws. We stopped in the village for some milk and my phone rang. "Congratulations Mr Coert ..." I listened intently to the Chair of Governors who informed me that I had been recommended to the local Education Board for the post of Head of Department for Religious Studies at Antrim Grammar School. It was simply a recommendation at this stage and would be finalised after a police and medical check. He went on to inform me that the Principal would be in touch and so on. After pleasantries on the phone I said my goodbyes. I removed Calum from his car seat and held him tight as the tears rolled from my eyes. We did it! We got a job! God, yet again did His thing. A Head of Department without having previously taught in Northern Ireland! I couldn't believe it. I kissed my son. The God of grace blessing us when we least deserve it! How does He do that? Julie was speechless! I called my financial supporters in Bangor, shared the news with them and thanked them for all they had done for me. I had a few weeks left to complete my PGCE and it was good to know that I could now finish and walk straight into a job. In a few months I had to lead a department and there it was ... the fear suddenly set in! Could I really do this? All those things I said in the interview, could I now actually implement that? I decided to do what I always do when I'm under pressure — commit the issue to God and deal with it!

I started planning and preparing. The principal — Janet Williamson ... an impressive school leader to say the least, kindly allowed me to purchase whatever I required within the department. I got my classroom all ready. I cleared out and binned loads of material no longer relevant to the current curriculum and purchased what I needed. The Governors and principal had put their faith in me. Now I had to come through! God had done His thing by getting me this job, now I had to do mine!

I had a good first year. As any Head of Department would tell you, you are only as good as the examination results gained in August. Results were positive. My department was now growing. More and more pupils wanted to do my subject at senior level. I needed added resources and additional personnel within my department. The principal informed staff that some additional funds had been made available for departmental usage. The difficulty was that Heads of Department had to formally bid for this money before the Board of Governors. I prepared well. My punch line was clear — I have more pupils doing my subject. My results were very good! I was doing what was expected of me, now please "show me da money!" I was successful with the bid and was pleased with the cash injection into my department. Now to persuade the principal and Governors that I needed another theology specialist within the department! Sharon was appointed. We could now share the responsibility of planning schemes of work, etc. Sharon was responsible for all things in junior school and she was a tremendous asset in co-teaching external exam classes. A few years later, after things were progressing within my department, I started to get bored and needed something more to get my teeth into. In reality, I could teach the course with my eyes closed! I applied to join the examination team at CCEA — the body responsible for external examinations in Northern Ireland. I became an external marker for A-level Religious Studies. I was also working in the boarding school at the Royal School of Armagh as a counsellor twice a week and was involved in bits and pieces in my local church. I enjoyed good working relationships with staff and pupils and the pupils were excelling academically, but I needed more. An opportunity arrived for senior management. I applied and got an interview!

I was unsuccessful. The leadership of the school had changed and I was aware that the new Principal was now forming a new team leadership team who could work closely along-side him. I understood that. The successful candidate was well-deserving of the post. A year later I had another go at a Senior Management position. I didn't get that either. Seeds of doubt started dripping into my brain. Maybe I wasn't as good a teacher as I thought I was. Maybe teaching within the classroom is what I excelled at and though I thought I was management material, maybe I wasn't after all. Then I started doing a bad thing — I started to get bitter! I started finger-pointing and started finding reasons why I should have been appointed over and above my colleagues. That's not me! What was happening to me? My life was slowly heading out of balance! There was once a time when I believed that God had organised this job for me. A few years ago I was humbled and blessed at the opportunity to teach. Now I thought I was deserving of it all! I had lost my focus! My spiritual life was taking a hit. My life was out of balance and it was about to get a whole lot worse!

There are things in this world beyond our control ...

Chapter 15: The realities of life!

The greatest certainty in life is death.
The greatest uncertainty is the time!

(Carl Sandurg)

Manchester United had won that afternoon and therefore it was a very satisfying "Match of the Day" on the television — a very popular Saturday night viewing of the Premier League football matches that day. It was a pleasure to now sit up late and catch the highlights of the matches. Having just switched off the television after midnight, the phone rang. The phone hardly ever rang this time of night and it was obvious that someone either ran out of fuel and needed my help this time of night or something was wrong in Cape Town. To my horror, I heard my mum's voice on the line ... "Victor, your daddy has had a huge heart attack."

I had heard those words many times before. Having been a smoker all his life, dad had his first heart attack at age thirty-nine and there were a few since then. Dad had survived many a medical scare which included surgery for stomach ulcers and cancerous tumours which resulted in half his stomach being removed. This obviously resulted in major loss of appetite and with smoking continuing later on, a noticeable loss of weight. Between continuous heart attacks, there was the replacement of his trachea, worn away by the effects of tobacco poisoning. He now had a plastic trachea which allowed him to breath a lot better and though quitting cigarettes for a little while, he succumbed yet again to the addiction of tobacco.

Mum however was more concerned about this heart attack than the previous ones. She informed me that the paramedics had arrived and were now working on dad. I was glad to hear that my sister and brother-in-law were with her and that they were getting ready to take dad to the hospital. Mum also informed me that the paramedics seemed quite concerned at dad's condition. A neighbour, who was a nursing sister by profession, worked with the paramedics to try to get dad conscious before embarking on the journey to hospital. The plan was to get dad there as quickly as they could. Mum told me that she would ring me from hospital in an hour or so in order to provide me with an update on dad's condition. What mum failed to tell me was that dad's heart had stopped on two occasions while the paramedics were there.

The phone rang just before two in the morning. My sister Sharon was in tears and informed me that my aunt and younger sister Glenda had arrived at the hospital too. Sharon was not quite sure how dad was, for although he was stable the medical staff were awaiting news from the cardiac surgeon. I planned therefore to call back in about two hours. After the initial phone call I informed Julie, who then went back to sleep — as we had been down this road a few times before. At four that morning the phone rang yet again. Dad's condition had deteriorated. I therefore asked mum if I could speak to the cardiac surgeon. The gentleman informed me as to how dad was doing. The news was not great. I eventually asked him "Doctor, should I be on a plane home?" "As quickly as you can", came the reply. This was serious. Dad had had a few heart attacks since I moved to Northern Ireland and not once did it ever get to a point such as this. I needed to get home. I got to my knees and for the first time in a very long time I made a personal request to God. I asked God to hold dad until I got home. I simply wanted to see my father before the inevitable was to happen, for I knew now that dad was dying.

It had been many a year since I last prayed that fervently. The last time was the night before I was married. Back then I feared the whole journey of marriage. Now I spoke to God again with that same trepidation. This time it was not the fear of failing as a husband, but the fear of not seeing my father before he passed. I reminded God that night of how, since the age of six, I availed myself to His service, how being the only Christian initially in my home I had remained faithful to Him; how as a teenager I made social decisions based solely on His will for my life; how I decided to pursue life as a missionary, and so on. On the basis of these things, I begged my heavenly Father to hold my earthly father until I got back to Cape Town. Bottom line ...I bargained with God!

It was now about eight or so in the morning. Julie got some clothes ready for me while I spent time booking a flight online. Then, the phone rang. It was my sister Sharon who informed me that dad had died. Instantly, something in my heart grew cold, so much so that I never even shed a tear at the news. God couldn't keep his side of the bargain! I suddenly turned into business mode. I called my school principal — Stephen Black and made arrangements to take time off. Mr Black was very good to me with regard to time in Cape Town and told me to contact him again if I needed to stay a while longer. My mum in law arrived from across the way

and helped Julie get some things together for me. My mum
in law called me into the kitchen and handed me a cheque to
cover the flights and she wanted no talk of me refusing this
money. I guess it was her way of helping. My parents in law
had always been good to me and yet again they gave of themselves to help me. Alastair, my minister, arrived and prayed
with us as a family and soon I was off to Cape Town.

Sitting in London awaiting the flight to Cape Town I sent
some texts to friends and colleagues, informing them that I
would not be in school and arranged some work for my classes. While on the flight, I started making a list of things to do
when arriving in Cape Town and the various bits and pieces
of funeral preparation. Needless to say I couldn't sleep, but
kept thinking about dad. Memories now came flooding back
and many of those memories made me smile. However, not
once did I shed a tear.

Arriving in Cape Town I was met by my mum, sisters and
brother-in-law. Our first destination was the mortuary at
the hospital, which looked like something out of the third
world. The barbed wire and security doors were signs that
the hospital was right across a gang-infested part of Cape
Town. The fresh blood lying outside the front door was evidence too that lovely corridors with matching curtains was
not a characteristic of this place. Apparently the paramedics had to get dad to the closest hospital they could and believe me, this hospital looked like it belonged in a war zone.
However, I was grateful to the surgeons and nursing staff
who I then had the opportunity to meet, for it was they who
had worked so tirelessly in trying to save my father's life.

We were escorted to the back of the hospital and pretty soon
we arrived at the mortuary. The gentlemen who led us slid
out a slab which contained the body of my father. This was a
first for me. I had never experienced this before. My father

whom I loved very much was still and cold. Two bits of paper were taped to his body which contained his name, date of birth and time of death. I felt mum's touch on my shoulder and heard my sisters crying behind me. I never shed a tear. I held mum and told her that it would be okay but now for the first time I tangibly felt anger toward God. Dad's body was moved to the funeral parlour later that day. We organised a meeting with the management to discuss the necessary details. Arrangements were made and a coffin chosen. A cost was settled on and we moved on to our next meeting, dad's employer. Again paperwork was looked at and condolences received. Our visit there was very awkward, for the company was having a Christmas party for their staff. However, they were very good to us. Explanations were made regarding finances entitled to mum. The company had made a decision that due to dad's exemplary service over many years, mum would remain on their medical records indefinitely and that they would pay for any medical expenditure mum would incur in the future. I was extremely grateful to the management for their kindness. It was evident, that although retiring on health grounds years earlier, dad had been a valued employee.

I found it very difficult to fall asleep that night but eventually got there. The next morning, I made my way to mum's bedroom, slid in beside her and started to cry. I missed my father. I was now angry with myself that I was not home sooner to be with him. Truth be told, I started to feel guilty ... guilty for moving to Northern Ireland and not making more time to see him during my time there. I suddenly realised that I will never again have the opportunity to speak to my father. I recalled the conversation dad and I had one morning via telephone when he told me that he had been in my home church at St James in Kenilworth with his sister and that he had given his life to the Lordship of Jesus. I recalled the promises of salvation in the Scriptures, reminding myself that God had promised eternity in His kingdom to those who sought the salvation that He alone offered. I took great comfort in that and got up and made some coffee. Soon we were giving away dad's clothes to a few of his friends. Unpacking his cupboard was difficult but ever so often I found little notes dad had written. Mum then asked me to consider preaching at dad's funeral. I agreed, as it was something she wanted. However, this request meant that I had only two days to prepare. Although it was an honour to preach at my father's funeral, how was I going to do so and keep my emotions in tact at the same time?

The day of the funeral was difficult. I was surprised at how full the church was. My aunt (dad's sister) was slightly late but I informed the minister that we could not start without her. Soon she arrived and the service commenced. My sisters paid tribute to dad by playing a slide show to some music, which brought many smiles. Soon it was time for me to preach. In preparing, I tried keeping in mind the many people who would be there. I endeavoured to maintain a balance between biblical truths and speaking into the grief experienced by so many of the family who I knew would attend. In striving to this goal I started to speak:

"Dad loved watching movies ... and I guess he passed on that love to his three children. Many a movie became famous for its classic one-liners .... Humphrey Bogard's "Here's looking at u kid" in Casablanca or Marlon Brando's "I'll make him an offer he cannot refuse" from the Godfather. My personal favourite one-liner is from the movie Gladiator and it is this ... "what we do in this life, will be echoed in eternity". The reason I love that statement is because the statement itself is all about legacy. Every single man and woman at some stage in their lifetime, questions as to whether or not they have achieved something great with their life. Key questions begin

to occupy one's mind ... "have I made a difference; have I achieved anything of value; are other people better people because of me" ... and so on!

When we are faced with questions like these, we soon come to realize that money, possessions and status mean absolutely nothing. We come to realize that the truly valuable things in life are those things which money cannot buy ... honour, respect, work-ethic, family ... and in many ways Victor Abraham Coert exemplified these valuable qualities in the way he lived. He may not have achieved the mountain top of financial success, or brought into submission his own struggles and personal demons, he may not have achieved his dream of going to Poland to see Auschwitz ... but you and I are here today because dad left us an amazing legacy. Dad was successful in the one thing that Jesus Himself was successful at ... and it is this ... daddy loved people!

In John chapters 12-17, Jesus' love for people is clearly recorded by John, His closest friend. John informs us that Jesus finds Himself in the garden of Gethsemene ... and though crucifixion and death awaited Him in the hours to come ... we are informed that He was not concerned about himself, not concerned with His own destiny ... for His thoughts were always about his disciples, His friends!

As we reflect briefly upon dad's favourite Bible passage, there are two key things I'd like to share which I do hope will bring us peace and hope in our time of sorrow.

Firstly ... that Death is but a door to the Presence of God.

I teach Philosophy — as part of Religious Studies to 17 and 18 year olds back home in Northern Ireland ... and the issue of death is the one topic which creates tremendous discussion among students each year. In all our technological advancements as mankind, death however remains the great unknown. While informing His disciples about His approaching arrest and death, Jesus sees the fear in their eyes ... He recognizes that they are troubled with all this talk about betrayal, denial, death ... and so Jesus, in chapter 14, now seeks to put their mind at rest.

In Philosophy we talk about a Parallel Universe... the idea that there are two roads to this life ... running side by side, parallel to one another. There is the physical dimension to this life, which is seen by the eye ... and as we sit here, we are very much part of this physical universe. However, running next to the physical dimension is the spiritual one ... which is unseen, but which is very much real. Death therefore is simply the doorway which allows us to move from this physical universe into the spiritual one. Death simply becomes an entranceway to the very presence of God.

Tell me friends ... what can be more joyful than being in the presence of the Father. The Apostle Paul later reminds us in 1Cor 15 that death no longer has a surprise for us, that it no longer comes to bite us in the backside, that it no longer has a sting. Paul reminds us that no longer do we have to approach death with fear and anxiety ... and though we are mournful in losing dad ... we are not sorrowful in thinking that this is the end ... for behind that door for dad, for you and me ... lies eternity ... behind that door awaits the joy of meeting God ... face to face.

Though we await our turn to place our hand on that door-handle of eternity ... daddy has already entered in. Already he has had his turn in meeting his Maker face to face. Already Victor Abraham Coert has given an account to God the Father ... of what he has done in this life ... and already daddy has experienced what awaits us all ... the judgement, the grace, the mercy, the forgiveness and the blessing of God. Let us therefore rejoice in our sorrow, for dad now finds himself in the presence of the Almighty God.

Secondly ... for those of us who mourn, let us remember that ...

In death, we receive Comfort

Jesus knew that His disciples would be fearful when He left. He knew that after His death, they would be extremely sorrowful, fearful and in emotional turmoil. Jesus therefore promised them that He would send them the Comforter, the One who will provide them with strength to endure the days ahead, the promised Holy Spirit.

But, how does the Holy Spirit practically comfort us? Well firstly, He reminds us of what we have just spoken about ... that for those who have died and have acknowledged God in their lifetime ... for them awaits eternity in the presence of God. But secondly, the Holy Spirit comforts us through the memories we have of those who are departed.

Dad left us with amazing memories. My father taught me to swim on one of our memorable day trips to Simonstown ... the Coerts, the Cupidos, the Osbornes and of course Aunty Janie. Who can forget the way dad simply had to cover himself in an entire jar of Vaseline before sun-tanning. Who can forget that somehow, every domino game with the Coerts, the Osbornes and George Thompson always seemed to end in a singing festival ... dad knowing all the words of course. Once I got my driver's licence and took dad for early morning Sunday drives, we never ever headed for the lovely sights of Cape Town ... it was always, "take me to Sonny, take me to Francis, take me to Bux, take me to Myrtle and Abe" ... and when returning from aunty Myrtle … we always had to make another stop ... "take me to Johnny." My father loved his brothers and sisters and uncle Johnny and aunty Elaine … and though uncle Sonny was the one to whom he looked up to, dad had no favourites. He loved his brothers and sisters and he missed uncle Charlie very much.

To aunty Francis, aunty Myrtle, uncle Bux, Uncle Abe, uncle Johnny and aunty Elaine ... you are the ones who knew dad much longer than the rest of us. Besides mum, you are the ones that dad loved most. In your sorrow, let the Holy Spirit comfort you in the memories you have about dad.

To mum, the one who knew dad best ... you alone knew the good and bad to daddy. You have remained at his side in the good times and the bad times. Mummy, as we honour daddy today, we honour you.

In your time of loneliness may the Holy Spirit be close to you and strengthen you as you now prepare for a life without dad.

To Sharon, Glenda, Cecelia, Donovan and Cameron ... as you miss dad, remember the values he taught us, the virtues dad installed in us. Our responsibility now is to honour him in the way we live. Let us now teach our own children the values daddy taught us ... and let us share the memories we have of him with our children too. May God's Spirit be with you as you mourn.

To dad's nephews and nieces ... from Randall downwards ... and for those of you who have married into this great family ... thank you very much for the incredible love you had for my father. Thank you that you made his life richer by always making time for your uncle. In your sorrow, may God's Holy Spirit now strengthen you in the days ahead.

And finally ... to those of you who were dad's friends ... those of you who knew dad from his very young days in District Six and remained his friends to this very day ... many of you who worked alongside dad and knew him in a professional capacity ... those of you who sat on the stoep (the porch) chatting with dad and to those of you who were his neighbours in Bannockburn Crescent ... thank you all for the way you grew to love my father over the years and in your sorrow, may the Holy Spirit comfort you with fond memories.

I have no doubt, that the love daddy had for his family and friends ... now echoes in the corridors of eternity. Dad was right ... in his Father's house are many mansions ... so through our sorrow, let us be joyful ... through our despair may we experience hope and as we think about the life that dad lived ... let us all take comfort from the words spoken by our Saviour himself:

> *'I am the resurrection and the life. He who believes in Me will live, even though he dies.' Let's Pray.*

I made it through the sermon. Needless to say I was emotionally spent! This thing of 'keeping it together' for mum's sake was turning out to be a lot more difficult than I had expected. At the conclusion of the service, my brain seemed to engage itself to the reality which was ... the loss of my father. I was never going to see him or speak to him ever again. My heart was ripped in two. When the time came for the coffin to leave the church, I hugged my uncle Johnny and informed him that this was possibly the hardest thing I had ever experienced. As a family, we then privately made our way to the crematorium and said our last goodbyes. I was the last one to see my father. I stayed with the coffin until I was told 'no further' — and that was it! Returning home, we found many of the extended family and friends staying for some tea and sandwiches. I was emotionally drained and slipped away to mum and dad's bedroom and cried myself to sleep.

The days which followed were difficult, as my time in Cape Town was drawing to a close very quickly. The thought of leaving mum was tough, although I had no option but to make my way home to Northern Ireland. The inevitable chapter in one's life had now come and gone ... the experience of losing a father. Earlier that week, while packing up dad's clothing and so on, I found this little diary in his draw. I purposely decided not to read it until I was back on the flight home. When having the chance later that week to do so, I turned over the cover and started to read:

I was born in a small village called Elim, approximately 200 kilometres from Cape Town on the 30th December 1942. The second world war was three years old and already the tide was turning against Nazi Germany and the Japanese Empire. My parents, Abraham and Petronella, moved back to Cape Town a day or two after my birth. We lived in the heart of Cape Town in Mechau Street, near what is today called 'The Waterfront'.

I grew up with four brothers and two sisters. Their names, from eldest to youngest namely ... Theodore (Sonny), Francis, William (Bux),

Myrtle, Charles, me and Abraham. I grew up as a happy child with loving parents, especially my father with whom I had a unique father-son relationship. I really loved him.

When I was about six years old, our family moved house to a flat called 'Canterbury' in Constitution Street, in what was regarded as a crime area called 'District Six'. We moved into flat number seventy-two which had a back-view of Table Mountain. It was beautiful. I was happy to live there. I was enrolled at a new school called Moravian Zinzendorf. I loved my new school. I also loved my teachers, especially Mrs Abrahams. I started coming first in class and rapidly passed from standard to standard, much to the delight of my father. Soon it was time for high school and I enrolled at Roggebaai High School which entailed travelling by bus.

Being seventeen I was now close to becoming a man and my hormones were working overtime. She was sitting two desks behind me and I could feel her eyes on my back and when I looked round she would give me a seductive smile. Was I imagining it? She was very pretty and a Muslim. Her name was Amina and we started having our breaks sitting together. One Friday I suggested walking her home. We arrived at her house in 'Bo-Kaap'. She asked me to come in and meet her mother and we then started to date. Soon it was time to write our Senior Certificate Exams and we were all excited about passing. I had my biggest disappointment of my scholastic career, for I failed my standard 10 exams. How was I going to tell my father — he would be very disappointed. That night I summed up the courage and told my father about my failure. As expected, he was disappointed but understanding.

It was now time to get a job and get on with my life. I was increasingly getting interested in politics. The white ruling party called the Nationalists Party, was becoming a real pain in the butt with the laws they were making. Their laws made your decisions for you — laws that told you where to live, what books to read, what movies to see, who you could marry, what job to do and everything else. These laws were draconian and it was strangling us. Although the older people had this overwhelming respect for white people, including my father ... it caused a lot of arguments between us. The Whites came first, Coloureds second and Blacks third. The Blacks had to carry a document called a 'pass'. If they were found in a White area after dark, they were liable to be arrested. I really grew to hate the National Party.

Sport started to play a big role in my life. I loved rugby and played wing for a team called Wanderers R.F.C. I swam for the Erica's Swimming Club and ran for Silverleaf Athletics Club. I received a diploma and a small trophy for coming first in the mile. There was no school Matric system yet. That came later. I was now working in a printing factory. My mother had a firm policy with regard to earnings — never open your pay packet! So everything went to her, including my overtime pay. But I didn't mind and throughout my life at home she received my salary ... sealed. I received seven shillings and sixpence pocket money. It wasn't much but I didn't mind as I knew my mother had a lot of debts. Besides, it was enough to take a girl to a bioscope (cinema) and for buying her a chocolate. The movies began to be an integral part of my life. It was an escape from everything and I took a real interest in movie making. My obsession with the Holocaust was beginning to be obsessive. I bought every book I could afford relating to that topic and at times my thoughts about it became so real that I seriously considered becoming a Jew in the faith, so that I could suffer their pain. My favourite movies were musicals made by MGM and Vincente Minnelli was my favourite director. My all-time favourites were Seven Brides for Seven Brothers. They were really great movies.

I had quite a few friends by now, especially one called Tommy, who had the most beautiful sister called Joan and by now I was madly in love with her, or so I thought. A few years later Tommy died and I was very sad. My twenty first birthday wasn't far off and I was looking forward to that. I would be twenty-one and it afforded me *new heights in which to dream from. I also met a new friend called Ronnie Theys. We found we had a lot in common — dreams about the future, singing, music and sport. We also both had a desire to get out of the area, live in a house with a garden, speak English more often, start a singing group and sing on stage. Ronnie's dream materialised — mine did not. He joined the Eon Group — which was a cultural society to promote talent among us Coloureds. He sang very well, but I still had my dreams and this burning desire to visit Auschwitz Concentration Camp in Poland. I wasn't going to give up that — but a dream it remained.*

By now we considered ourselves to be in a sense, a sort of a gang. We congregated in the entrance to the stairs every night and we sang songs. We prided ourselves in the way we sang. No one was allowed to sing false. We sang harmoniously and that became our trade mark. Our so-called leader was Hector and he had a forceful way about him. I felt myself following him. He was fairly intelligent and therefore could hold a nice conversation which suited me very well. We developed a new thrill — jumping on and off moving buses. It was exciting but also very dangerous. In the end it was very satisfying to our small egos ...

And that was it! Nothing but empty pages followed. I felt like I had been robbed of a chance to get to know more about my father in his early years. For some reason he never got an opportunity to further pen his past. I closed the diary and allowed my thoughts of my dad to cloud my thinking. Many a happy thought followed and I now wished that dad had an opportunity to write more. There was so much about his youth I was still ignorant about and I must admit that I now felt slightly cheated. *Perspective Vic — you were blessed enough to have some of dad's early life! Perspective mate!*

I wasn't there that morning, when my father passed away
I didn't get to tell him, all the things I had to say
I think I caught his spirit later that same year
I'm sure I heard his echo in my baby's new born tears
I just wish I could have told him, in the Living years!

(The Living Years: Mike and the Mechanics)

The flight back to the UK was one of tears, reflection, memories, sadness and pain ... and the pain was about to create turmoil!

Chapter 16: Dealing with GRIEF!

The irony of grief is that the person that you need to talk to about how you feel, is the person who is no longer there!

(Unknown)

Returning home to Northern Ireland, I started a very slow journey of self-destruction! I had met her once before — this lady called grief! It was many years prior. Having had Calum, Julie and I lost our second baby a few days before her birthday, fairly early on in the pregnancy. I guess Julie felt that entire experience a lot more than I had and I guess that's very natural. However, I never really grieved this loss at the time. I had to be strong for my wife and in many ways, was very 'matter-of-fact' about the whole thing. I had been a bystander to the effects of miscarriage before, watching a couple in church undergoing this experience. I bore witness to the pain in the life of others but now it was experiential and very real. I worked hard at supporting Julie through this trauma — doing what I could in the home to help ease her grief. However, three months later the pain was tangible!

Looking out across the countryside while cleaning the kitchen one evening, I suddenly started to cry! It was evident that

I could not stop, for now I found myself clearly weeping. My heart was experiencing something it had not known before — the loss of a child ... and it hurt! People who are supportive of the 'pro-choice' camp within the Abortion debate, would tell you that the foetus is not a real human being as yet and so on. Well, I disagree ... for the reality of the pain experienced is testimony to the fact that there is an innate bond between the parent(s) and the living foetus, whatever the stage of gestation. This pain was real and the grief unbearable. I never felt an emptiness like it. I'm fairly hard-wired when it comes to my emotions but that evening in the kitchen I experienced pain like never before. We had lost a baby ... but God in His greatness blessed us a year later with Caleb.

Dad's death, I was now to discover, was pain on a completely new level. Memories and thoughts about dad continued to flood my mind those few weeks after returning from Cape Town. Christmas came and went and three weeks later I turned forty. I had asked Julie not to arrange a party for my fortieth birthday as I was not in the frame of mind to enjoy the company of others. However, she did. Maybe she thought it would be a good idea to celebrate this milestone but also that having friends around would help emotionally. I spent my fortieth birthday with my friend Jake — playing golf, apparently organised by Julie to get me out of the house for the day while she made arrangements for the party to come. It was good to see everyone that evening, including Jake — who never mentioned a word about this while playing golf.

Though I enjoyed having everyone around that evening, I really wanted to be alone! Personally I was so mad with Julie. She had no idea what I was experiencing and having asked her not to arrange a party, she had gone ahead and organised one. That evening I was asked to say a word or two. I had to stop myself from being cynical. For those of you reading this and were there that night, you may remember how awkward my little 'speech' was — not quite the Vic who generally is polished when communicating publicly! I wanted the night to end. The guests were my friends — good people I knew and respected — but I was not in a frame of mind to relate to them. Anyway, it was so good of them to attend. When it was all over I sat down and watched television — working my way through a bottle of red wine I received as a gift that evening. I was encountering a double-barrelled phenomenon at the same time — grief, having lost my father and guilt, as I now blamed myself for not making more time to see him in South Africa. Maybe I should have visited dad and mum a lot more; maybe I should have made the effort to be more involved in their lives than I was; maybe I was so caught-up with life in Northern Ireland that I inadvertently neglected my parents! I very slowly started to be consumed by this tsunami of thoughts which seemed to attack me from all sides. Was this now my first experience of clinical depression? My one saving grace was that dad got to see all three his grandsons six months earlier, as Joel had been the new addition to our family. The thought of dad having met Joel alongside Caleb and Calum softened the pain ever so slightly! Had that not been the case it may have mentally tipped me over the edge!

I'm generally level-headed and would consider myself to be fairly intelligent but something was happening to me over which I had no control. The guilt of losing dad was now slowly affecting my behaviour. I was getting annoyed and angry at Julie and the boys for the slightest thing — issues which previously would never have bothered me now seemed to get under my skin. I started to become very critical about people and sceptical about their motives ... and I was about to do something I will regret for the remainder of my life.

That summer we returned from a holiday in France. It was a difficult holiday for me personally but now I was back home and could get my head focused on school again ... for work was the only positive thing in my life at that stage. I unhooked the caravan at home and headed to the shop to get some fresh milk and bread. While there I bumped into three people who verbalised their anger at decisions made in our local church. Something had obviously transpired while I was in France over the Summer. Rather than point them to the minister which I should have done, I involved myself in an issue that I had no right to. I became a listening ear to the discontent, which pampered my arrogance and air of self-importance. The issue later spiralled out of control and became a mess of my own making.

Challenging and disagreeing with anyone publicly is never a good idea but doing so within a church context is even worse. It was the first Sunday of the new year and Alastair was talking about loving one another. I was of the opinion that our church at that time wasn't quite doing that. I could no longer take what I viewed as hypocrisy. I got up and challenged the minister, my friend ... about what he was saying. The fall-out of my actions had long-term consequences. I contemplated the thought that I would most likely be asked to leave the congregation. If I survived that, the possibility of church discipline for an extensive period was high. Church protocol most likely determined that the minister needed to report this incident to his superiors, which possibly meant being kicked out of the denomination. I also contemplated the possibility that I would not have the opportunity to preach in that church ever again. I now also considered a scenario where my family would be in this congregation without me, a congregation I had personally invested a lot of time in. The problem was that I simply did not care! I had no idea what was happening to me. I was in a place where I no longer cared about anything.

The minister was my friend! I let him down badly ... I get that now, but I was oblivious to the relational damage I caused at the time! I got home to a very angry and tearful wife. Julie's reaction didn't really bother me! I couldn't care what the elders of the church thought either. As far as I was concerned, I owed one person an apology and that was the minister who put so much of his faith in me in the years prior. However, I was not even at a place mentally at the time to go and see him and make my apologies. Inevitably, the phone started to ring ... members of the congregation, friends, some of the elders and so on. Around the Sunday dinner tables that day I guess I was the topic of discussion. Rumour had it that I had planned to challenge the minister publicly all along. Nothing could be further from the truth. The gossip came hard and fast and sadly one cannot control hear-say. The problem was that I was about to lose one of the most valued and constant foundations in my life, namely my church family ... and I couldn't care less!

There was now no longer any need to attend church! The one thing I never contemplated ever doing in my life — seeing no need for corporate worship and koinonia (fellowship), I was now happy to do. I stopped going! I was awaiting news from the elders about kicking me out, which never materialised. I therefore decided that unless they kicked me out I would remain but not attend. So I stayed but I felt no obligation to attend! So Sunday mornings ended up being 'staying at home and watch sermons on YouTube' mornings. It was just over one year since losing dad. I couldn't care what people were saying. Apart from being at school, I spent much of my time alone and it was in moments like these when I started to encounter my demons! It's not nice meeting the dark-side of yourself; it's not easy coming face to face with the depravity of your own heart, your motivation for doing things, the wickedness within your thoughts and so on. One's personal demons often manifest themselves in your behaviour and before you know it, you are out of control!

Another Sunday morning of avoiding church — another argument with Julie! I had a headache and popped yet another preventative Nurofen, the only thing that worked for the migraines I regularly seemed to get. Having spent another night without sleeping, it must have been about four in the morning when I started having a conversation with my deceased father. I spoke to dad in the kitchen as if he was in the room with me. Later that morning Julie thought it best to take the boys over to her mum's. My mother-in-law arrived. It was possible that having been a nurse all her professional life, she noticed that my pupils were dilated. She noticed me grabbing another Nurofen and enquired of me as to how many I had taken. I had no idea! I had lost count! She encouraged me to go with her to Accident and Emergency, just to make sure I was okay. I agreed! I love my mother in law and though I ended up being nasty to her and my father in law, she loved me enough to make sure that I was physically okay. Having met with and spoken to the doctor after treatment, I was issued with an appointment with the clinical psychologist for the next morning — standard procedure I guess for the predicament I was in.

I arrived and was taken into a room with the psychologist and her assistant. Then the questions started! I got to about the third question when I informed the doctor that I had an issue that she could not help me with. I informed her that she was not going to put me off school — for it was the one normality in my life at that stage. I also told her that she was not going to medicate me either! I told her that unless she was God Himself, me being in her office was wasting both our time, for my issue was with God — who was not able to keep dad alive until I got to Cape Town. With that statement made, I got up and left!

Summer holidays were fast approaching and we were making plans for yet another summer in France, except that this holiday was either going to save or break our marriage. It was a beautiful morning on the French coast and like every morning in my life I was up at five. I got up and went for a run. Getting to the beach dawn was breaking and I sat down on the sand looking at the ocean, wondering why I felt so alone! I started to cry as I thought about dad. Since his death, my life had spun out of control! I never got to say goodbye to him, never got to apologise for the things I needed to, never got to say those things a son and father should share before death and I never got to hold his hand. I never got to tell him how much I loved him and I never got the opportunity to tell him that I forgave him for so many things mum never knew about, but which I carried in my heart since childhood. I wept as I thought about the night he died — was he thinking about me, was he wondering if I was making my way home to be with him, was he asking where I was in his mind, although he couldn't verbally utter the words, or was he wondering if I had abandoned him? Maybe there were things he needed to say to me, things he needed me to know, thoughts he needed to share, reserved only between father and son. Would it have been enough for him to simply have held my hand? I would never know! I felt as if life had cheated me out of the one thing that truly mattered in my life ... being able to tell my dad that I loved him before he passed.

The guilt overwhelmed me! Irrespective of how much I loved my father, the bottom line was that I was not there to say goodbye! I wept! I would never have the opportunity to say another word to him. I was inconsolable. How was I ever going to move on from here? In a three-year period, I had wrecked every friendship and relationship I had, which included in-laws, my wife, Jeff and Karen, Alastair and one or two in the church family. How was I going to get out of this hole of grief and depression? I looked up at the horizon as the early rays of dawn licked across the ocean and that's when I heard it ... deep in my psyche as if it was audible to me. In the depths of my being I heard God say to me ... *It's okay Vic, I'm here!* I cannot possibly or adequately explain to you God's presence at that time but I heard God speak to me as if He was literally sitting in the sand right next to me. God understood, for He too lost someone for a period of time — His own Son. He knew my pain and He told me that it was 'okay'. In a matter of minutes while sitting in the sand, I moved from a position of despair to hope. I got up and jogged back to the caravan, with renewed hope in my heart. I woke Julie and said to her ... "I'm going to be okay" and that was that!

From that day to this I am rebuilding my life and the relationships I destroyed in those three years. I never expected that guilt would destroy me, but it very nearly did. God intervened into my life yet again at the most appropriate of times and he continues to be a Father to me. I am at peace, but ever so often I long for my dad. There are things a son cannot say to his spouse or anyone else. There are times that a son needs to take his father for breakfast and share things about life. There are moments when a son needs to see pride in his father's eyes and no words need to be said. These are the times that I miss! Do I still feel guilty that I failed to be with dad at his death? Yes, I do ... but more at a cognitive level these days, not an emotional one as such. I treat it more as a matter of fact, but it remains an emotional scar ... ever present, but kept in check. I have made peace with the fact that God knows best. He alone knows why I never got to see my father. Maybe all I had been through for those three years was something I needed to go through. Maybe one day I may have the opportunity to sit next to a friend who may encounter the very same scenario and I could both empathise and assist him in his own grief. If I believe that God loves me, then I must hold to the fact that He loves me even at my worst. One day in eternity I will know the reason why God chose for me not to be at my father's bedside when he died. Until then, I will live by faith, trusting in the fact that my heavenly Father knows best! Those three years was the worst I had encountered in my fifty years on this planet. Grief had done its job — it nearly ruined me ... but God intervened at the most appropriate of times, as He always seemed to do!

So what did I learn about myself in all of this? My personal demons had now culminated in the breakdown of relationships many years in the making! These now needed repair and I had to embark upon a process of restoration and reconciliation. The church should have disciplined me and they had more than sufficient grounds to do so. My marriage now needed work and so too relationships with close friends. Lessons learnt. Grief dealt with. Live and learn. Now time to move forward, time for humility and apologies, time for coffee shops and chats, time to acknowledge failure, time to revel in the strength and love of my Father in heaven. Time for taking stock, but most importantly — time for healing! *Come now Vic ... time to move on!*

What would have happened to me were it not for God's intervention on that beach that morning? Would our marriage have survived? Would the trauma of dad's loss still be eating away at me? Would I still be so self-absorbed with my own pain? Having undergone that entire experience of grief and its negative effect upon my life, I ask myself but one question ...where would I be had God not intervened? Where would

I be had God decided to withhold His grace from me? The good news is that He did not. In the mess of my grief, He applied His grace at a time when I needed it most.

> *God of grace I turn my face, to you I cannot hide*
> *My nakedness, my shame, my guilt, are all before Your eyes.*
> *Strivings and all anguish, grief, in rags lie at my feet*
> *And only grace provides the way, for me to stand complete*
>
> *And Your grace clothes me in righteousness*
> *And Your mercy covers me in love*
> *Your life adorns and beautifies*
> *I stand complete in You!*
>
> *(Chris Bowater)*

Thank you for looking after me, Father!

Chapter 17: "Mr Coert, you may have a brain tumour!"

*... we rejoice in our sufferings, knowing that suffering
produces endurance and endurance produces character,
and character hope ...*

(Romans 5 vv 3-4)

It was Christmas-New Year week and I was invited to play golf alongside a few friends from church. There was a little snow on the ground and the air was chilly, damp and cold. I struggled through yet another round but enjoyed playing golf as always. About a day or so later I got a cold, from which I couldn't quite recover. It lingered — finding its way eventually into my chest. Now we all have colds from time to time so I wasn't fussed at all but things were about to take a turn for the worst. The cold lingered and my chest felt tight, with the odd pain now and again! I had mentioned to Julie that this stabbing pain in my chest seemed to intensify ever so often but I had put it down to muscular pain from swimming — or so I thought! While driving home from school one afternoon, this pain hit me like a bolt out of hell! Thankfully my journey home each day took me close to Craigavon hospital and that afternoon I drove myself straight to it!

I'm from bad stock — heart attacks run in my family! While driving I was convinced that this was my first heart attack. Like my dad before me, it was now my turn! Heart issues had taken my father's life — well to be more accurate, years of smoking did. I had been so careful over the years — I never smoked ... other than my three-week addiction alongside Gary as a six- year old, never took salt in my food, swam regularly as a means of keeping the weight off — now that days of football and rugby were well behind me and so on! The pain just wouldn't go away — in fact, it was getting worse! I was now slumped over the steering wheel while driving, anticipating another stab of pain as it arrived every few seconds. I made my way to the hospital and parked my car, walked into the emergency room and made my way to the information desk. Informing the duty nurse about my pain and probably observing the sweat on my face, I was rushed into a room. Pretty soon nurses arrived with a crash trolley. Wires and sensors were connected to my chest as the medical team talked about heart rate, etc. As they asked the necessary questions, I had informed them about my family medical history. It seemed that I had an irregular heart beat and my blood pressure was high, but I wasn't having a heart attack. They also could not account for the stabbing pain in my chest but having been held for a few hours for observation, I was sent home to rest for a few days and given medication to help the flu-like symptoms. I was informed that the medication would improve my conditions in a few days — but the improvement never came!

It was nearly March now and I was off school for about six weeks. I had lost weight and just looked withdrawn. I had been in and out of hospital and had numerous scans. I eventually got a note from my doctor stating that there is a possibility that I may have a tumour in my lungs. I was called in for an appointment. It was explained to me that medical dye would be injected into my blood stream just prior to the scan and if I had a tumour, the dye would highlight it. I was also told that I would most likely end up with a splitting headache. So an hour or so later after the scan, I awaited the doctor to tell me what the scan revealed and yes, I had a splitting headache. The doctor arrived and informed me that all was clear. Joy and relief flooded through me! I was determined therefore that I would go back to school and carry on with my life. I lasted one full day in school and was back in bed!

Now let me explain something. I'm not one of these people who take sick days! I watched my father go to work every day — six days out of seven. Staying at home because you are not feeling well is alien to us as a family. However, I was now at home for two months and I was not getting any better. My next appointment was to be a brain scan. Doctors were convinced that three months of medication and tests had led to nothing. They were clueless. The only other explanation left was that I had a brain tumour. I was called in for an appointment — one of those 'camera up your nose into your brain' appointments. The surgical team explained to me what the procedure would entail. This was it — my fourth scan! If there was bad news, well then so be it. At least I'll know.

My buddy Johnny Nesbitt drove me to the hospital and prayed with me before I got out of his car. While in my room and having been prepped for surgery, I sank to my knees and prayed earnestly. I thanked God for my many years of good health. I acknowledged that if it was bad news — if I had a tumour, there was nothing I could really do about it. I asked God to give me the strength — if this was the case, to share that news with my wife and boys. It was then that the fear came — my wife and sons! How I loved them. Would I now have to consider not seeing my boys grow up? Is it inevitable that Julie would have to raise them on her own? What if my time on earth had come to an end, would I expect her to remain on her own? Would she possibly meet someone else later on? Would my boys have a new father? Would they be okay with that? The thoughts kept coming like a whirlpool. The door opened. It was time to head to surgery!

A short time later I was sipping tea and having some toast in the recovery room. The surgeon arrived with three young trainee doctors. I braced myself! Last time I felt that immense amount of fear was many years ago — when Mr Cloete, my primary school principal, opened up his cupboard and instructed me to choose one of his five canes, one which was to connect with my buttocks a minute or so later. The surgeon chatted away and suddenly uttered the words I had hoped he would say "Mr Coert, we could not find any tumour ..." The relief! As the doctor explained things, I don't think I heard much else. I'm sure as surgeons this sort of thing is quite routine but it was a few seconds of relief before I was back up to speed with the conversation. The team was now in discussion as to why the pain in my chest would not stop. One of the young doctors then asked me if I had ever broken a rib? I replied and stated that I had broken a rib playing rugby in my early teens. The doctors then discussed the possibility that as the rib broke, it may have scraped and scarred the lung. I was sent for another x-ray immediately. It was confirmed. One part of my lung wall had a weakness. That area was where the infection occurred. I was suffering from pleurisy! The area was treated with very strong medication and soon I was on the road to recovery!

Broke a rib playing rugby? Now how do I put this in a way that does not cause offence to those in my extended family? How could I tell the consultant that my rib was not broken playing rugby, but broken with a cricket bat at age thirteen — swung at me by my own father in another rage of anger?

Growing up, I was used to getting beatings and so was everyone else back in the day. This idea of not smacking your kids due to the fact that it was 'unlawful' was very much a foreign concept in the seventies and early eighties in South Africa. Smacks and beatings were a regular occurrence and some were worse than others! The broken rib was not the worst though! Dad once lifted a piece of hose pipe and used it across my back and legs one Saturday morning while mum was at work because I refused to go and queue at the bookies and place a bet on a horse on his behalf — as I had to do most Saturday mornings before heading to football. My first appearance at the bookies was about age eight and by age fourteen, I knew quite a bit about race horses, placing bets and the likelihood of a horse winning by what I saw on the television screens. The hose pipe stung and it left thick swollen lines across my back and legs, my bottom and the top of my thighs. The broken rib however, was a result of getting home late one evening after playing cricket at the Howard's place. I made the silly mistake of leaving the cricket bat accessible. I hadn't got my sisters bathed and had not cooked any rice for our meal, as I would have done each evening from age six. I paid for that indiscretion! Mum applied some ointment to my ribs and tightly wrapped a towel around it. I looked like the 'Michelin man' going to school the next morning. I would never forget the pain. Nearly thirty years later that broken rib would come to haunt me again in the shape of pleurisy. However, I'd rather deal with pleurisy than with a brain tumour!

The good thing is, that I have long ago forgiven my father for the many beatings, which my sisters often bore witness to and could testify to. I often intervened also when they were the target of dad's anger and many a time I would lock them in the bathroom while dad 'expressed' his anger on me. It was only while working with young people in Namibia, when

I realised that even though dad had moments of rage, my sisters and I were lucky in comparison to some of the young people I was encountering. Some were experiencing the trauma of neglect, absent fathers, being disowned by family, etc. It took a phone call one Monday morning to dad from Namibia, to tell him that I loved him and that I forgave him for the many wrongs experienced. If truth be told, dad and I developed a good relationship only after I had left home and even though the time we had would be short, and even though I would move hemispheres, my father and I became friends ... the way it should be between father and son!

A time will come however, when I will receive bad news with regard to my health, for we are all mortal! Our time as individuals on this planet will cease and the frailty of our bodies means that we will succumb to cancers, serious illnesses, heart attacks, etc., as things in our physical bodies start to go wrong. My time will come, no doubt! There will be a time when I will be happy to trade a broken rib for cancer or some other serious illness. When that time of illness comes, how will I approach it — knowing that my time on this planet is short and time-bound? Will my faith in my Creator be evident for the world to see? Will I approach illness with dignity — resting in the fact that I have been so blessed to see fifty plus years, while many have not? Will I glory in the fact that illness, which most likely will lead to death is simply part and parcel of what it means to be human? Will I fear death? Do I have to be apprehensive about it? Does the great unknown bring a sense of trepidation with it?

The Apostle Paul reminds us in 1 Corinthians 15, that for people of faith who believe that Jesus conquered death ... the great unknown holds no fear. Paul gets to a point where he seems to mock death and taunts it with regard to its hold of power over humanity. The Apostle asks ... "Death, where is your victory? Where is your sting?" The Apostle goes on to explain that death is a consequence of our sin and if Jesus freed us from our state of sinfulness, then He has freed us from death too. Paul reminds the recipients of his letter, that the breaking of the Law requires payment, namely our death and that we are powerless to free ourselves from this fate. Therefore, he introduces Jesus as the Saviour of humanity, who literally pays the punishment on our behalf. Paul therefore argues that due to the redemptive death of Jesus, death no longer has power for those of us who entrust Jesus with our lives, for we have received grace through the Cross which brings us freedom from sin and its consequences. Jesus literally, swops His life for ours. He fulfils the requirements of the Law on our behalf! No wonder the Apostle is confident that we no longer need to fear death, for our future as God's children is life after death, paid for and secured by the blood of His own Son. Death now is simply the door to eternal life!

What will it look like — this thing called 'death'? If I adhere to the fact that my body is but simply a biological machine and when it gets to a point of being damaged beyond repair, we deduce that it will shut down for good. Agreed? However, at what stage do I cognitively know that I'm dying? Will I be blessed enough in my process of death, to actually know that I am dying? What if I encounter death very tragically in the form of a car accident and there are but mere seconds between the point of impact and the moment of death — will I still cognitively be aware of my pending demise? No wonder death is the one thing we fear most.

I was in my late teens when I came to the realisation that my time on this planet is limited. We are all going to die, but it's the 'how' that scares us, isn't it? I often think about the possibility of Jesus' involvement at the point of my death. If I were to be a road accident statistic and undergo the process of death behind a steering wheel — alone and most likely afraid, would I hear His voice saying *'Vic, it's okay'*? Personally I cannot believe that Jesus would be so callous as to leave us to our own demise with regard to the one thing we fear most — the moment of our death. When some people on a hospital bed pass this life with a smile on their face, are they doing so because they now see what those standing around the bed cannot — the meeting of the physical and spiritual world? Is it at that point when my belief and faith in Jesus now become spiritual and physical at the very same time? Will I therefore physically see the face of my Saviour at the process of my death? Do I therefore need to be afraid?

I cannot definitively tell you that this is what it will be like at the moment of death, for I am yet to embark on that journey, as will you! I know that I will take comfort in the fact that Jesus will journey with me. If I do not have that assurance of Him assisting me through that encounter, then death will be the scariest road I am yet to travel. *"I will be with you always"* Jesus says, "even to the end of this age!" (Matthew 28 vs 20) Would it be more comforting to you and I if Jesus stated *'I will be with you always, even to the end of YOUR age'*? Whatever death looks like, I do not welcome it but it will knock on my life's door pretty soon. What I do know is that I will hold my Saviour's hand very tightly when my time comes and it is my hope, that at the point of my death ... the words of the Apostle Paul will echo in my mind: 'Oh death, where is your sting?'

As I have trusted You in life Lord, I will do so too in the process of my death!

Chapter 18: Where it all began!

We travel not to escape life, but for life not to escape us!

(Unknown)

At the heart of every teacher lies the need to make your subject area relevant to the lives of the young people you teach. I loved teaching Religious Studies and my thirst to teach was coupled with my thirst for learning. Teaching New Testament and Church History, I longed for the opportunity to one day visit the place of Christianity's fiercest opposition at that time ... Rome! Having looked at a brochure and having sought permission from my principal to take my students, I was off to Rome on a school trip!

Here I was, a boy from the back streets of Cape Town living his dream! Most of my fellow countrymen back home would never have the opportunity to fly abroad, let alone walk the streets of this great city. I felt privileged, yet humbled — humbled at the fact that I was afforded an opportunity not many in my community would ever have. I was hungry for knowledge, taking in everything the various tour guides informed us about. I was like a thirsty antelope in the Namibian desert, drinking from a water hole on a dusty and sandy plain. Although professionally I was the teacher in the group, I was simply like every one of my pupils — a learner.

The Colosseum blew my mind — the size of it all, the large chunks of cut stone, one placed on top of the other. I could not wait to see the arena and soon there it was in front of me! I wondered what it must have been like all those years ago — the place filled with crowds, watching people battle for their very lives — gladiators wooing the crowds and the Christians awaiting death — opening the door from death to glory! The single wooden cross in the Colosseum said it all — commemorating the saints who had gone before. Men, women and children ... killed for sport for the simple reason of bearing the name of Christ! I was lost in my own thoughts amidst the clicking of cameras as pupils took photographs. As a Jesus follower, this was not just a tourist attraction to be visited, for the Colosseum was more than that. It was a reminder of the cruelty of man and the cost of discipleship. Two thousand years later and things haven't changed much!

The visit to the Roman Forum was exquisite — although now, just piles of stone everywhere. One could imagine the busyness in this part of Rome all those years ago. My mind was intrigued and sadly for most of the pupils, having to imagine what Rome was like back then, was a little too much and for some boredom set in. However, we were soon to visit the one site every visitor to Rome must encounter ... the Vatican!

The Papal Basilica of St Peter's was phenomenal. Designed by Renaissance gurus like Bramante, Michelangelo and so on ... this building, completed in 1626 replaced the old St Peter's basilica. I was taken by the architecture and the various sculptures within the building. No expense was spared here! My thoughts then centred upon the many who made pilgrimages here and the thousands upon thousands who like me, were simply tourists. I saw people kneeling in prayer at the many side altars and others awaiting their turn at the confession booths. Ever-so-often, the teacher in me came to the fore, as the pupils raised a variety of questions — but like them too, I had questions of my own! Soon we made our way out of the cathedral and joined the queue to see the Sistine Chapel.

Once the official chapel of the Papacy, the Sistine Chapel took my breath away. Having turned right to the door through which I entered, there it was before me ... Michelangelo's work of the Last Judgement. Depicting Christ's second coming and man's eternal destiny, Michelangelo conveyed through his art, the journey of the soul of man. This was his personal interpretation of Dante's Divine Comedy — an Italian poem about a vision of the afterlife. I stood and watched in amazement, trying to imagine in my own mind what Michelangelo was trying to convey through the muscular and naked images within this fresco. Was he in some shape or form making a statement? His very rebellious relationship toward the papacy was very well known at the time and was this his way of getting back at the church leadership?

Having stood intensely looking at the Last Judgement, a nun approached me. She was an American, and addressed me in Italian, until she realised I spoke English. She asked if I was 'of the faith' and politely I replied that I was not. 'You are a Protestant then' she inquired — and I told her I was not! With a perplexed look on her face I informed her that I would personally consider myself to be a Jesus-follower. We discussed my self-designation and how the word 'Protestant' was often used today by people who had no faith in Jesus and used simply as a means of disassociating themselves from Catholicism. We agreed that in the same vain, people often refer to themselves as Christian, to disassociate themselves from Islam. Although I would be considered a 'Protestant' in the broad sense of the word and align myself to the views of those who reformed Christianity, my sole aim is to live my life for Jesus — not the church as such! She got that!

I was impressed with this nun, for it seems that she had left a seminary in the USA to further her theological studies at the Vatican. As we traded pleasantries it was clear that she was obviously very switched-on intellectually. Having got the 'why are you not a Roman Catholic' thing out of the way, we started to chat about the fresco. It was obvious that we were both widely read in matters of theology and we had a great time debating matters of faith as seen within this fresco. She then walked around the Sistine Chapel with me as we debated Michelangelo's work on the far wall. We also debated the use of colour in the frescos all around the Chapel, the considerable amount of royal blue used by the artist. It was great to debate matters of theology depicted through art and the mutual respect we had for each other's personal belief simply added to the intensity of the discussion. I was blessed that day to meet someone so intelligent and so engaged in her faith, but I was also concerned. It was evident that we both loved Jesus and our individual devotion to Him was obvious. However, we disagreed on one key fact — her devotion to the Scriptures was viewed through the prism of the Church, and mine to the Scriptures itself! The great thing was, we never judged one another when debating this very issue.

A trip to the Catacombs in Rome was something to behold. As the burial place for many a Christian in ancient Rome, one could not escape the feeling that as you walked around those narrow underground corridors, you were in fact beholding something awe-inspiring — history and faith before your very eyes. Christians lived in these catacombs, hiding from the authorities as their faith in the 'Risen One' grew, as they shared what they had with one another, doing as Jesus

taught them to do, which simply was to *'Love your neighbour!'*
What amazed me was the many vents they had, allowing oxygen to freely flow into the corridors far below the surface.
Here they lived, among the many who were also buried here
... literally living amongst the dead. For these people, faith in
Jesus meant death! It was part and parcel of following Him
and yet they were prepared to face this ordeal. They often
chose death rather than denying the name of Jesus. Their
deaths inspired others and due to these people who chose
death rather than life, Christianity developed to what it is
today. Martyrs, saints, regular people ... call them what you
like. They were normal people, some who encountered Jesus
personally and others whose lives were changed by the things
they heard about Him. Some key individuals were later can-
onised by the Roman Catholic Church, while the names of
the many will never be known. They had one thing in common with Jesus-followers today ... they loved Him and could
not contemplate life without Him, even if it meant death!
What a challenge to you and I! The great thing about having
a personal faith, is that I too am I pilgrim! What started out
as an academic trip to Rome, ended up as a pilgrimage of
faith and it simply wet my appetite for the ultimate pilgrimage — a visit to Israel!

Having taken pupils to Rome for a few years now, I spoke
to my principal about taking pupils to Israel. He agreed but
due to the issues of security, we thought it prudent for me
to do a 'recce' and scout-out whether a pupil trip would be
feasible and safe. Arriving in Tel-Aviv at two in the morning,
I made my way alongside many others, to passport control.
The passport control officer, dressed in military uniform
questioned as to why I was travelling on my own. She asked
to confirm that I resided in Northern Ireland and I did so.
She lifted her telephone and pretty soon I was escorted by six
military personnel to a side office. For the next three hours I

was questioned over and over as to my visit to Israel. Having to unpack my bags, I was asked to undress down to my underwear. I informed the officer that all they needed to do was access my school website and look at the staff list, where my name and subject area would appear. He was not interested.

At about five that morning, there was a personnel change — as the night-shift staff were now getting ready to leave. The new officer in charge was female and we went through the same issue again. This time she did as I asked and uploaded my school website. Five minutes later I was given permission to leave! Due to my interrogation, I had missed the bus I booked, which would take me to Jerusalem. I had no choice but to hire a taxi. Due to my three-hour ordeal, I fell asleep as soon as the taxi left the airport and awoke as the taxi stopped, right outside the old city of Jerusalem. Wow, the walled city — the old city within the modern city! I was here, the city in which Jesus would spend the last days of his life. Once again I became a pilgrim!

I got out of the taxi and collected my suitcase in the boot of the car. As I paid the taxi driver at the airport before the journey, there was now no need to access my wallet again and I waved him goodbye. As I watched him drive away I suddenly wondered where my ruck-sack was and then it hit me ... it was at my feet inside the taxi and I had forgotten to lift it! My ruck-sack contained my passport, my wallet and my phone! I had just spent the night being politely interrogated as to the reasons for my visit — and now a few hours later I was black man from Northern Ireland in one of the most dangerous cities in the world — without a passport! As it was early morning, there was no one in sight. *Stay calm Vic — don't panic! God, I need Your help here!* As I looked about, I saw a police officer speaking to some soldiers. I walked over and told him about my predicament and requested him to take me to the

British Embassy. As we chatted in the car, he pointed at a taxi rank who shuffled people between Tel-Aviv airport and Jerusalem. He told me that the owner spoke English and that we should stop there for a chat. Low and behold, the owner of the taxi rank studied at Edinburgh University! He had a chat with the policeman and informed me that he would look after me and that I had nothing to worry about. He would find my ruck-sack. He called his drivers together and asked me to describe the taxi driver to him. An hour later my ruck-sack was in my hand. During that hour of waiting, the owner had organised me some breakfast and showed me tremendous hospitality. *God, You are amazing! When I needed You to intervene, You did just that and You even organised to feed me as well!*

I entered the walled city through the Damascus Gate and turned left. I was so impressed at the narrow cobble-stone walkways. It was so busy with early morning traders — Muslims, Jews and others selling their goods in the morning trade. I turned left toward St Stephen's gate and made my way to the convent I was staying in — accommodation for students and scholars. I had booked the cheapest room and made my way toward the church — having been invited by one of the sisters. As a non-Roman Catholic, I was so thankful at being asked to attend morning worship and I grabbed the opportunity with both hands. Here I was, a pupil once again — observing worship, looking at their architecture, relating knowledge I taught as a professional to the very building I was in. I was an invited guest and I was so thankful for the opportunity.

At nine in the morning, the heat was unbearable to say the least. I stopped at a local small holding and ordered two litres of water and some round baked bread. I made my way up the Via Dolorosa, where two thousand years ago Jesus walked with a beam across His shoulders as He made his way to

Golgotha. My mind was envisioning Scripture and history, trying to imagine how on earth Jesus made his way through such narrow but crowded streets. I stood at the corner and had a moment. Yet again I became a pilgrim! I made my way to the Church of the Holy Sepulchre — the site which is believed to be the place of crucifixion. I walked inside and due to the fact that it was just after nine, I was one of but a few inside. I made my way around the various key areas inside the church which included the Altar of Anointing, the Altar of the Crucifixion, etc. Suddenly a bus load of South American tourists arrived. I stood to the side as many surrounded the altar of Anointing. Soon, photographs of loved ones etc., were placed around the altar as these pilgrims started to pray. I was astounded at this devotion and watched as many a tear flowed down the faces before me.

About an hour later I made my way to the Jewish quarter in the old city. Having spent ten minutes undergoing security checks, I made my way through a tunnel-of-sorts and upon exiting it, there before me was the Western Wall of the ancient Jewish Temple — built by King Solomon, destroyed by the Babylonians and re-built and further completed by King Herod — only to be destroyed again, this time by the Romans during the siege of Jerusalem in AD70. The Western Wall is what remains of the Jewish part of the Temple — as opposed to the other part of the ancient Temple which is adorned by the Dome of the Rock ... the shrine of Islam. I stood for a while and observed the Jewish men worshipping and praying, their bodies rocking back and forth in rhythmic formation. Here too I witnessed it — utter devotion and faith — both at work! Men of all ages, devoted to God and bringing their various needs to Him. It was time for me to head back to the convent. Rest was required. A big day of travel lay ahead of me the next day! I was looking forward to seeing that which I read about as a young boy in our primary school library many years ago ... Masada!

That evening I sat on top of the convent roof enjoying the cool air. Now some of you may wonder why I was sitting on a roof — well simply because houses were built with flat roofs back then. This was where everyone sat and chatted at sunset. I started speaking with a gentleman and his wife who had just arrived that evening. They were from Canada. He had just retired from many years as an international banker. As a couple, they had spent many a holiday in Israel, availing themselves to excavation teams all around Jerusalem. We started talking about Jesus and he shared with me his story of faith. What a story! Here was a man who lacked for nothing materially but the emptiness in his life started a search which led him to faith in Christ. His search for meaning in life had now led him to a practical search for artefacts, which would continue to ground his faith in history. I was impressed by this couple! Both of these people were intellectuals and far more intelligent than I would ever be and yet they gave of their personal holiday time to excavate, as a means of literally cementing their faith in history!

It was a long journey to Masada through the Judean desert and the heat was incredible. On arrival, I made the decision to use the cable car up to the fortress, which would allow for an easier walk down. This mountain fortress was impressive and I now imagined what it must have been like for the many Jews led by Eleazar, who made their last stand against the Romans ... after the fall of Jerusalem in AD70. The history of what happened here came flooding back. I made my way to the western part of the fortress and saw what is left of the ramp the Romans constructed in order to make their assault on the Jews. As I walked around I couldn't but help to think how cheated the Romans must have felt, spending months building this ramp and looking forward to the attack and the victory to follow ... discovering on their arrival however, that every Jew lay silent and dead. Rather than give the Romans the glory of conquest, Eleazar and his generals decided that they alone were the makers of their own destiny, opting for suicide rather than defeat in battle. As I made my way down Masada, I was deep in thought as to what happened here!

It was Palm Sunday and so much was planned in the old city that day. I had heard that there was to be a procession from the Church of Bethphage on the Mount of Olives that afternoon — the historical village where the disciples found the donkey upon which Jesus sat. The procession was starting at two thirty that afternoon. I made my way through St Stephen's Gate early that morning, crossed the main street running around the Old City and walked into the Garden of Gethsemane. I entered into the Church of All Nations or the Basilica of the Agony as it's also called, which houses the said rock upon which Jesus prayed. I spent upon an hour there ... thinking! Obviously sceptical thoughts ran through my mind — thoughts like "surely this couldn't be the real rock, could it?" The church itself was dimly lit, so as to set the mood of silence and contemplation. The rock itself was surrounded already by a few early morning worshippers, rosary beads in hand and fervent prayers being offered. Then the spiritual side of me reminded my brain that whether it was or wasn't this particular rock, surely it would not matter, for here was a reminder once again of the agony which Jesus underwent. I had a long conversation with one of the monks as to how this rock had been identified and preserved over the years. As I enquired as to the initial Crusader church which was the first to house this rock, he realised my interest in things theological and availed himself to give me a private tour of the Garden of Gethsemane. After spending about ten minutes with me, the monk returned to the basilica. I then had a quiet walk in the garden on my own, contemplating the best way up or around the Mount of Olives to my destination of the Church of Bethphage. I couldn't stop what then happened — tears slowly rolled down my cheeks at the acknowledgement that the Saviour I pledge my personal allegiance to, once possibly walked the very soil upon which I was now standing. The connection between faith and history combined yet again to allow me to ponder the realities of my own soul.

I made my way up the Mount of Olives. As the procession would later make its way down the side road around the Mount, I decided to climb it. Nearly getting to the top, I sat down and had breakfast and there it was ... the Old City before me in its splendour, with the Dome of the Rock sticking out over the walls. Here they were — Judaism and Islam side by side, a reminder of the Crusades, the quest for occupation of the Holy City. It would be a quest which was all in vain, for Jesus was seeking to conquer our hearts, not these city walls before me. I thought about how many a life had been lost during the Crusades, both Christian and Muslim — soldiers fighting not just for ancient walls but also for dominance and recognition. The 'Holy City' — torn apart by so many years of war. The Babylonian conquest, then the Roman siege, the Crusades and the continuation of modern warfare between Jews and Palestinians. Did Jesus see this with His mind's eye when He arrived into Jerusalem on the weekend of his death? When Luke reminds us that Jesus wept over the city on His approach, did He cry because of the unbelief of its citizens at the time or did He also see the future, where men would put one another to the sword in order to have dominion over these walls? Did He weep because men and women like us, would forget that the Kingdom He came to establish is not one made of stone and mortar, but one of faith?

Arriving at the Church of Bethphage, there was already so much busyness. The little village was packed with tourists, all getting ready to join the procession. I started a conversation with one of the security gentlemen and requested permission to take some photographs. I joined the procession. It was one of the most unforgettable experiences of my life — a walk from the top of the Mount of Olives to the Old City with people waving palm branches and singing as they walked. It was an experience, an opportunity to connect history with faith. Once again the teacher became the pilgrim — the tourist became literally … a disciple. What joy people in that procession displayed. Immediately my mind raced through the accounts of this event by the Gospel writers who wrote about Jesus descending into the Old City from this hilltop village. I wondered what Jesus was thinking at the time when He saw the crowds smile and celebrate, waving their palm branches cut from many a tree in that area. If they only knew what He knew. If they only knew what awaited Him in that city. The hero-status He was experiencing at that point in time would end up hours later in death! Had I been in the crowd all those years ago, would I too be experiencing joy and celebration or would my mouth quietly verbalise my thoughts and say … *"Behold, our God!"*

My time in Jerusalem became more than a destination for a school trip. As it turned out, I never got to spend time there with my pupils due to the fact that I ended-up moving schools, but the visit was a spiritual re-awakening, a literal reminder that Christianity is not just steeped in history, but has its roots in a Man who was just like us, an individual who lived in time, had parents and siblings, lived within a community, had friends, laughed, used the loo, got tired, got hungry, smelled of sweat, pulled wood splinters from his hands, went to social events, etc. — a man who was so like us, but also so unlike us … a Man who was God!

As I was encountering the streets of where He too once walked ... was He possibly walking with me?

Chapter 19: So, you're a school Principal?

Great leaders don't set out to be a leader;
they set out to make a difference!

(Lisa Haisha)

We all aspire to leadership, don't we! Irrespective as to what it is we do, a promotion is a sign that others have seen qualities within us necessary to move forward an organisation, a team, a department, etc. The qualities of leadership displayed by an individual, results in others entrusting the individual with the future of an organisation or institution. Leadership is often described as a lonely business, requiring objective decision-making which may at times be unpopular to the masses. I had been a teacher for nine years and spent two as Vice Principal, but the ultimate challenge was still to come — leadership in the form of a Head Teacher.

My predecessor often joked about me sitting in his chair when the time arrived for his retirement. Often it was pretty awkward because I never quite saw myself as being a school principal just yet, for I was relatively new in education. However, the thought had slowly but surely begun to appeal to me. The difficulty was having to undergo two interviews and gain the necessary knowledge required for these and convince governors that I had the necessary skills and qualities to make it as a school leader. The added complication was that if I was successful, I would become Northern Ireland's first non-white school principal. If I pursued this role of school leader I would have to give it my best, for surely the doubters with racist intent would be the first to point the finger at my inadequacies! *Do you want to pursue school leadership Vic? Yes!*

My predecessor took it upon himself to prepare me for the opportunity of headship by inviting me to various meetings. My training began — learning as much as I could about the finer details of school finance and so on ... all theory at this stage. Soon the time came for the Board of Governors to set the criteria for advertising the post. In order to apply, I needed to meet the criteria! I did! I could now apply, alongside others. I spent time putting my application form together, ensuring that I answered the questions correctly and sufficiently, demonstrating knowledge with regards to key areas raised within the form. I met the application deadline and awaited the short-listing to see if the Governors were happy to call me for interview. It became apparent however, that no one else applied! I'm sure this caused a problem for the Education Authority (one of the governing bodies which implements education objectives set by the Department of Education in Northern Ireland), in that they possibly required more candidates to make the interview process robust! Normally in a case like this, the job would be re-advertised. Most likely, the Governors of my school thought that I deserved the right to interview, seeing that I had taken time to apply. It is quite possible that the Authority met the Governors half way, for I was therefore given the opportunity to interview before the school Governors. However, I needed to do well enough in the initial interview to merit the Authority calling together the Teaching Appointments Committee, for the second.

The interview before my Governors went smoothly. No hiccups! I prepared well and delivered! Now for the second interview! I knew that this interview would be much more demanding and most likely I would be clueless as to the make-up of this panel as well. While preparing, the doubts arose! Could I really do this job if I got through the interview? One early Sunday morning, the week of the interview before the Teaching Appointments Committee ... I contemplated the person of Nehemiah in the Old Testament and how he availed himself to journey back to Jerusalem after the Babylonian conquest with the sole purpose of rebuilding the city walls. Once given permission by Artaxerxes, the king of Persia ... Nehemiah took along with him a small cohort to embark upon a considerably difficult task. That Sunday morning, I wondered what went through his mind, knowing that the city most likely would now be occupied by bandits. How would he protect his men and embark upon a building project at the same time? It was clear however, that Nehemiah trusted God with this project and in the same way, I now needed to do the same.

The day of the TAC interview arrived. If I were to be successful here, I would have to produce within the twenty-five minutes or so allocated to me. I had prepared well but like all interviews the planets have to align as such! Sometimes it all goes pear-shaped, irrespective of how well you prepare. You get off to a poor start and you simply do not recover. Sometimes you blow the presentation at the very start and the questions which follow are simply a blur. Sometimes you speak too fast and you lose your train of thought and so on. Those of you who have sat interviews know exactly what I'm talking about! Everything has to come together in those

few minutes to put yourself into the window of possible appointment. If not, you walk out of that room and intellectually move on. Sometimes you wonder if the panel who just
interviewed you, considers you an idiot but you just have to
put it behind you. It's happened to me before and I'm sure
to you too. Sometimes you simply require the experience of
sitting an interview at the next level — more as a learning experience, knowing that success most likely is a long shot. The
bottom line is that if you aspire to leadership, interviews are
one of those hurdles you must jump through. No one likes
them; it is simply just part and parcel of professional life.

The problem with interviews, particularly within the profession of education in Northern Ireland, is that those twenty-
five or so minutes do not tell the full story of the candidate.
There are some very capable people who cannot sit through
an interview due to nervousness and so on. However, given
the chance, they would most likely excel at the role for which
they are applying. Many a school, seeking to appoint a subject teacher have now introduced teaching a lesson as part of
the interview process, in order to ascertain a candidate's performance and ability to relate to young people within a class
setting, prior to the formal interview. Thinking back to assessment day of the Professional Qualification for Headship
(PQH), which was without a doubt the toughest assessment
I have done ... I am of the opinion that a multi-faceted assessment like that would give a decision-making panel seeking to appoint a Principal, an opportunity to assess multi-
ple disciplines and not just the candidate's ability to answer
set questions. I am aware that the Education Authority has
put measures in place to do just that, with regard to new appointments at school leadership level.

I sat in the car just before my interview and spoke to God. I
needed only one thing ... clarity of thought! I thanked God for

bringing me to this point in my life and asked that I would be content if the decision went against me. I got out of the car and made my way to the EA building in Armagh. It was then that I saw him in my mind's eye ... my father! How proud he would have been. I swallowed hard and really could not allow myself to have these emotional thoughts just yet. Then the pressure came — I would be carrying the hopes of all non-white educators who aspired to school leadership in Northern Ireland. I would become the bench-mark! I needed the education fraternity in Northern Ireland to know that any non-white teacher, foreign national or ethnic minority had the potential to be a school leader, if they had the necessary qualities to do so. This was not about race but all about leadership. However, if I was successful I would raise hope within the minds of all non-white educators, that anything is possible given the opportunity. As I walked into the room and introductions were made, I realised that this panel included current and former principals, ministers, the chair and vice-chair of my Governors as well as individuals from the Education Authority and possibly one or so from the legal profession. I recognised three people on the panel — two members of my governors and Graham Montgomery, former principal of Cookstown High School and currently a close friend and Principal of the Royal School Armagh. The time had arrived — I was in the lion's den. Let the games begin! I was ready! *Now Vic — you have one stab at this. Don't screw it up!*

As I was the only candidate, these people had all gathered to give me an opportunity. Normally, they would assemble for a full day and interview a few. They were all here for me! However, most likely other schools were interviewing for Headship posts too but in the case of my school, I was the only one. Breathe! Smile! Take one question at a time! First question is vitally important. Settle yourself. Speak slowly!

Take your time! Due to the fact that I had to do a presentation in the first interview, one was not required for this one. The panel was introduced. I remember the training session on interviews I attended years' prior at Queen's University — find the friendliest face on the panel and look at that person while you speak. Friendliest face found — now relax! There were six questions I had to answer. The first went well but the second and third questions were tricky. I could feel the panic rising inside me. Prior to the fourth question being asked, I said to myself … *"Pull this together Vic — you must succeed with the next three. Wake up!"* The questions which followed went better. I felt a little more relaxed as two of the last three contained my strengths — issues relating to Pastoral Care. The final question was on finance and I had done my homework in that area. However, did I do enough in the interview to merit a positive scorecard from each of the panel members? Well, that was beyond my control. I thanked the panel and left. It was over!

As I had the morning to myself after the interview, I popped into Joel's sports day to relax and unwind. While there, my phone rang — I got the job! The preparation had paid off. I was now a school principal — in name only of course! I still had to do the job but I was delighted. I called Julie and some other key people and felt a tremendous sense of achievement. I was now a Head Teacher of a high school, eleven years after entering the profession! All I wanted to do was call my dad and tell him. How proud he would have been. I now needed time to get ready and become acquainted with the finer details and the ins and outs of the school, which prior to my success at interview, I was not privy to. The paperwork which I now needed to see, lay inside the filing cabinets within the current principal's office! I needed time to digest all this information and I had the perfect opportunity to do so, five weeks of summer holiday in France.

Being involved in education these past eighteen years has been an interesting experience, particularly in the financial climate in which education finds itself. It has also had many rewards — young people achieving academically, tremendous parental support and so on ... but ever so often there's a day that makes one question whether or not school leadership is for you. This day could be classed as being my most humiliating experience in my role as principal.

I had been sworn at once or twice before by a pupil in the past, but on this particular day I had to stand and listen to a pupil call me everything under the sun — while other pupils had no choice but to stand by and watch. While driving home that evening, I started to get really angry — not at the pupil as such, for the system in some shape or form had failed him. My anger was toward the education system itself, for placing school leaders and teachers into situations like these — where pupils can say what they like to staff and after a period of suspension, they return to school as if nothing ever happened. I started to think about how the system by its very nature was stacked against the very teachers the system is supposed to protect. I started to wonder while driving, if this sort of behaviour would be accepted in any other professional sector? Educational bodies — whether locally or internationally ... are often more concerned as to whether or not the member of staff has followed procedure while disciplining a pupil — rather than addressing the core issue, namely the behaviour of the pupil itself. Ever so often I'm outraged at the fact that I am working in an environment where procedures and processes are often vastly more important than whether a situation is in fact morally right or wrong. Of course procedures are vital, but even after obvious and clear-cut issues of poor and detrimental pupil behaviour, pupils walk free of a situation due to one aspect of the procedure which had not been followed. Sometimes school procedures are dealt with as if it were a court of law. They are not! Schools are relational institutions of learning, where the behaviour of one impacts upon others and unlike a court of law where the perpetrator is removed from those he/she had offended ... within schools however, other pupils and staff are expected to yet again relate to that pupil and treat that pupil with dignity and respect, with no guarantee that the respect will be reciprocated.

Our schools are victims of a societal problem! I do not have to tell you as to the shift we have seen in societal behaviour among teenagers these past two decades or so. The use of foul language, the lack of respect for those in authority, the way children communicate to their parents, the use of the phrase 'oh my God', explicit use of sexual language in 'normal' conversation and sexual images on Snapchat and so on ... are now the norm in our teenage world. This type of teenage culture makes its way into schools every single morning and as teachers, we are not only confronted by it, but also have to deal with it on a daily basis. In no other profession would this type of behaviour be allowed, but for some unknown reason there is an expectation that teachers should accept it as 'their lot'! Thankfully the vast majority of pupils behave in a manner conducive to education and it is my hope that positive behaviour throughout our schools, not only overshadow the negative but also become the norm!

In a world of increasing concern for pupils' mental health — and rightly so, concern must also be expressed for the mental health of school staff. How much disrespect, verbal abuse and excessive workload do teachers have to take before getting to a point of saying 'no more'? Surely encountering rudeness and disrespect on a daily basis from a tiny minority affects the mental health of teachers as well? There are times where I wish parents had a glimpse into their child's behaviour in school. Sometimes I wish parents could see what their child becomes when they walk into school. For ninety-five percent of parents, I can guarantee you that your child would make you proud — for the majority of pupils in schools are dedicated to their learning and committed to respecting both their peers and teaching staff. However, there would be other parents who will be ashamed and embarrassed at the behaviour of their children if they had but a glimpse into their child's day at school. You see, teachers availed themselves to this profession because they care about children and young people, because many of them view teaching as a vocation, a spiritual calling, an innate emotion to give for the benefit of others, to educate and provide guidance to young people in a structured setting. We teach because we care! We teach because we love! How often has a teacher encountered negative behaviour and looked behind that behaviour and realised the hurt and pain that pupil is undergoing ... due to something outside of school directly affecting that pupil? How often has a teacher gone out of their way to say a kind word or demonstrated a supportive gesture minutes after being disrespected by that very same pupil? That's what we do! As teachers we give emotionally every single day! As educators, we find ourselves in the position of being teachers, social workers, counsellors, surrogate parents, mums, dads, philosophers, encouragers, etc. Our job is not just teaching and marking, it's also about caring, giving, supporting, assisting, listening, empathising, crying alongside and so on and ever-so often that amount of giving has an impact on our mental health too! We live in a culture which seems to operate an 'open season' policy when it comes to telling teachers what they should be doing! It is my hope that the state would one day awaken to the fact that they need to value teachers, not because of who they are within the professional standing as such, but for what they do ... both educationally and relationally!

I have another frustration; each time the Government needs to tackle a societal issue — whether its matters of sexuality, issues of ethics or areas relating to crime, the cry is the same ... "our schools should be looking at curriculum change to address these issues!" Not again! How much do they think we can cope with? Budget restraints in education mean that schools are cutting down on teaching staff while pupil numbers are increasing. Areas of responsibility therefore increase while your compliment of staff are less, which results in added work-load for all concerned, which further results in longer working hours at home in preparation for the next day! The problem with teaching is that it is a sixteen to eighteen hour a day profession! You see, we don't switch off the computer at five and arrive back at nine the next morning to switch it back on and resume the project worked on. No, teaching is relentless! Once you have spent your day in school, teachers rush home to collect kids, make tea and so on like everyone else! Once kids are in bed, the marking commences and after that, the preparation for the next day! Our professional day is not quite over as yet! We slip into bed and then it starts, the worry and the 'what more can I do' conversations we have with ourselves! "What more can I do with Johnny, or Mary, or Steve, or Margaret, or Kelly, etc.? What more can I do within the classroom to engage Susie in my subject?" Then there are moments of despair and self-doubt — "am I failing Mary, Johnny etc. They just don't get it! Is it my teaching?" Then too the tears — "how much more rudeness can I take from that pupil? Do the pupil's parents really know what an impact his/her disrespect and rudeness is having on me? Am I just supposed to stand there and accept being disrespected constantly?" These are the thoughts teachers have which parents rarely see or understand! Then as the teacher drifts off to sleep, there remains the worry about a meeting with a parent tomorrow — the parent who is renowned for defending their child to the hilt, irrespective of the situation — everyone else's fault but my child's. Then there's my favourite, "my child behaves that way because your staff are not engaging him in the classroom!" *Oh really?*

Then there are the moments of magic in teaching, the days which make you smile as an educator, the moments when parents ring you out of the blue and thank you for the great job you are doing as a teacher, or the moments when after a school trip the pupil you would least expect, drops a 'thank you' card on your desk, or the parent who sends the staff scones each year, even though her child has left your school years ago ... not to mention the encouraging comments and smiles from pupils, or the engaging conversations with senior pupils about life! What about the pupils who impress you with their resilience — the ones who may be in the average band, but who consistently improve and achieve beyond their potential. What about the moments of singing and prayer time alongside pupils in Scripture Union or playing football with the senior pupils and the mutual laughter and banter when one pupil slips the football through the teacher's legs? What about the pupil who on results day is full of smiles and makes his way to his teacher and says "I could not have done it without you, Sir!" What about the parent who weeps in your office and explains to you that her partner has left the family home and that his leaving may most likely affect her child's academic performance, but tells you that school is the one place that her child feels most secure? What about the moments when a colleague arrives in your office, sheds tears of frustration but then picks herself up and returns to her class ready to face another challenge of poorly-behaved pupils and the immense pride a principal has at the resilience shown by that colleague? What about the magical moments when your personal assistant arrives with a cup of tea and a bun, as its already well after five and you are still engrossed in planning a budget for a Governor's meeting? What about those moments when a pupil simply says "Thank you, Miss" for something insignificant and finally, what about the moment when a parent conveys to you that, according to their child ... you are the best teacher he or she has had in their entire school life? Moments of magic!

Next time you are tempted to make a cheeky comment about teachers having six weeks off during their summer, think again! Ask yourself the question: would you trade places with them for a week? Would you be happy to place yourself in a position where you are both educator and vulnerable to the negative behaviour of someone else, on a daily basis? Could you cope as an adult, when a fourteen-year old decides to verbally abuse you in front of thirty other watching pairs of eyes who are now interested to see what your reaction is going to be? Could you operate on sixteen to eighteen hour days and understand the immense amount of accountability you have in your job, knowing that you are accountable not just to your line-manager, but to the Principal, the Governing body of your school, the Education Authority, the Department of Education, the Government and the parents of those children you are educating? Could you deal with that amount of accountability? Welcome to our world!

You see, as educators, we are not just principals or teachers ... we are in fact much more than that! I will let you into a secret; we have a superpower! Our power is that we TRANSFORM THE LIVES OF CHILDREN AND YOUNG PEOPLE! You see, sometimes as parents we are so intent at pointing fingers at the teachers of our kids, that we forget to take a step back and contemplate the thought that our kid could actually be at fault. Teachers need parental support, not parental condemnation; teachers require parents to discipline at home so that the following of rules and guidelines are part of the child's psyche before they even get to school. The responsibility for raising our children are ours as parents and we should never abdicate that responsibility to teachers!

One of my frustrations as a Principal in Northern Ireland is that many of our pupils do not realise what a fine education system they have here. They don't seem to realise that there are pupils across the world who would give their left arm to be in a school like the ones we have here in Northern Ireland. Our pupils take so many things for granted, with the result that they do not appreciate what they have within their local school. I have seen pupils vandalise school property because they have no concept that things cost money. I have seen others drop litter, stating that it's the caretaker's duty to clean the school, not theirs! The good news is that the vast majority of pupils in Northern Ireland appreciate what they have and it is the minority who, at times, bring shame to their school and their parents because of their behaviour. Head Teachers across the world will tell you that five percent of disruptive pupils take ninety-five percent of teacher's time within the classroom. The problem is that unlike the ninety-five percent of pupils who value their education, this minority are disengaged from education because of situations often outside of school. How do we educate pupils like this? How do we make parents of these pupils understand that we need their support? How do we make pupils like this understand that their negative behaviour is harming not just their own future prospects, but also the future prospects of their peers within the classroom?

Leading schools through the COVID crisis has been an interesting experience for all Head Teachers. Leadership is tough at best of times when things are running as normal, but throw COVID, lockdown and predicted grades into the mix ... leadership rises to a completely different level. Communication is key during any crisis and keeping parents informed has been my number one priority. Part of our role as Head Teachers is to correctly interpret the guidance issued by the Public Health Agency and the Department of Education, contextualise it to our individual settings and thereafter communicate that guidance to our wider school family. The sad reality is that a minority of parents do not seem to realise that Head Teachers do not write the guidance, for we simply implement the guidance issued by those in authority over us. A minority of parents, who hold differing views to the guidance issued, seem to take it upon themselves to argue with local schools about the validity of the science, wearing of personal protection equipment and so on. Why? Sometimes I wonder if certain parents don't realise that our role as school leaders is to protect everyone within our building, as well as the family members and grand-parents our pupils go home to. I cannot tell you the amount of hours my vice-principals and I have spent talking to parents who have differing views to that of the government and the PHA. Why fight with us over PPE implementation in school? Would these parents not make better use of their time calling the PHA and speaking to them directly about these issues and explain to the PHA why they as parents have a difficulty with the science and difficulty with their kids wearing PPE? Why fight with us?

I have also been astounded by a tiny minority of pupils who simply refuse to wear PPE within school and who constantly have to be reminded to do so, claiming that the "guidance is not mandatory". Sometimes I'm aghast at the parent's inability to convince the pupil otherwise, for it seems that in these small cases the pupil seems to have the authority in the home and not the parent. On the other hand, it has been a tremendous blessing to see the very large majority of pupils simply doing what they have been asked to do and getting on with it. It has been a blessing to have so many parents support Head Teachers in the decisions which have had to be made within this crisis. As school leaders, this support has been invaluable. Who knows what lies in store for us as schools in the very near future? Whatever may come, our role as Head Teachers will be no different than what we are currently doing, for our role is to lead, to bring calm in a deadly situation like COVID and to educate our pupils even within a crisis. It is what we have been called to do.

Many a morning when arriving to school, pupils pass my car and may wonder why I'm still sitting in my car. Sometimes I'm in the middle of listening to a song and it would be a shame to let good music go unfinished! Other times I'm simply sitting quietly in contemplation. Reason being ... I'm speaking to my Father and asking him for strength to deal with whatever the day may bring, whether that is a meeting with a parent which has the potential to go sour, or being straight with a member of staff about an issue that occurred the previous day. Whatever a school day brings, Head Teachers and Senior Management Teams across the country require one thing — wisdom! Make a right decision and things go well; make one wrong decision and you find yourself accountable to parents, tribunals and possibly courts of law. That's the nature of leadership and that's why I will encourage you to pray for your school principals and teachers, whoever they may be. We require wisdom daily and therefore we need you to pray that God provides us with the insight we require! Leadership — there's nothing quite like being a Head Teacher!

We are in this profession because we love; we hurt when we see pupils make choices detrimental to their futures; we feel pride at those who excel ... we are teachers!

Chapter 20: 'Black in a White World'

It's no disgrace to be black, but it's very inconvenient!

(James Weldon Johnson)

Arriving in Northern Ireland in September of 1996, it was evident that I was one of but a few black faces in the country. It was therefore not surprising that no matter where Julie and I went, people would be looking and have the odd stare at the two of us holding hands! A few years later while in a food stall one day, it was clear yet again that we being looked at by our fellow shoppers, but this time it had nothing to do with me being black but simply because our three-year-old Calum decided to pull groceries off the shelves as he walked behind us — while we were oblivious to it. What poor parents we were right? Thanks boy! Anyway, sometimes I wondered what negative comments about Julie milled over in people's minds as they most likely contemplated her being with 'him'! There were times when you could read people's thoughts, for their expression on their faces clearly betrayed them. Anyway I was no longer in Southern Africa. I was now in Northern Ireland — a first world country where the colour of my skin was no longer an issue — or so I thought!

I had the privilege a few years earlier of visiting Julie's parents and making my acquaintance with Northern Ireland. Julie and I made our way up to the north coast for a bit of sightseeing. We popped into a coffee shop where I was introduced to what has now become a personal weakness — banoffee! A few tables away sat a mother and her very young daughter. Having a good look at me, the child said to her mum, loud enough for the world to hear: "Mummy, there's a black man!" Her mum obviously then tried to remedy the situation but Julie and I had a bit of a giggle. The message received from that situation, as innocent as it was — was simply this ... black people were very rare in Northern Ireland! However, I was soon to discover that many a situation to follow would not be as innocent as that.

While working in Hamilton Road Presbyterian Church, I enjoyed going to the swimming pool during my lunch hour. Having just finished my swim, a group of boys from a local school passed me while in the changing rooms. Pretty soon the monkey calls started and many a giggle was had at my expense. I had to remind myself that these boys were ignorant and in a group and most likely would never contemplate behaving that way were they to be alone as individuals. However, walking back to the church office I reminded myself that situations like these were possibly going to happen again and that I needed to prepare myself for further comments in the future. As much as I did not want it to happen, it was inevitable. However, I had to rise above it — I had no other choice! I could not allow myself to be reminded of days gone by in South Africa. I was now in the UK, Northern Ireland, Ulster, the north of Ireland — call it what you want ... I reminded myself about all the good people here who had welcomed me with open arms into their beautiful country. I had to look beyond this incident, annoying as it was — for all over the world there were ignorant young men and women who still had a lot of learning ahead of them.

It was a funny thing which seemed to become a habit — I found myself greeting every black face I saw in the street. It's uncanny, but it became a thing to do! I guess it was just a reaction to being in the minority. One day while in Cork and walking with Jake — a friend and colleague, a black fella walked past us with a 'ghetto blaster' (a large tape deck or CD player) on his shoulders. The two of us immediately greeted each other and Jake and I had a good laugh as to how he felt left out in that situation, as he was not 'a brother'. It was a funny moment, but it seemed that prior to the year two thousand, people of colour were very rare on this island — be that north or south!

I had been informed that my appointment as Vice Principal became a talking point to a few in the community of Kilkeel, the summer before I took-up post. The point of discussion to a minority, was not that I was qualified to do the job, but that I was black — though I suspect the majority could not have cared in the slightest. I was the first non-white Vice Principal to be appointed to a school in Northern Ireland and no matter which school I was to be appointed to, it was going to be an agenda item for discussion around some family's dinner table! Anyway, I spent my life being resilient and fighting racism and this was now just simply another challenge in the story of my life! Before I even started my first day in my new school, I knew it was going to require every ounce of strength of character. It was clear — I was different! I was black in a white community; I was a city kid in a rural town; I was an outsider and, a 'blow-in' and often people fear or despise what they don't know. *Strength required Lord Jesus!* However, I had nothing to worry about, for the community accepted me with open arms, although I clearly wasn't everyone's cup of tea!

On the second day of the first term, I had two visitors in my office on separate occasions — one a member of staff and the other a senior pupil who started his last year at school. The member of staff came to see me in order to pray for me as I started my new post. It was a kind gesture and one which I appreciated. About an hour later, the pupil arrived. He sat down and started to speak. He informed me — just so that I was aware, that he did not consider me to be his Vice Principal as such and just to let me know that he and his family were not in support of my appointment. There it was — as stark as that! According to that young man who continued to air his opinion about my appointment, I was not welcome in the community! I thanked him for his time and off he walked. On results day a year later, that young man walked back into my office and with tears in his eyes and apologised for the conversation he had with me a year before. I shook his hand as tears trickled down both our cheeks. It was evident that we had both been on a journey that year and we both were now better individuals for it.

It was not too long into my new post when a racist comment from a parent would come my way. I was in discussion with a parent on the telephone regarding a disciplinary matter which involved his son. He was not happy and I was not going to bend the rules over something that was pretty clear in our school policy. Then it arrived — "but you're just a monkey aren't you" As he was now in free-flow, other comments included "if I was on the governors you would never have gotten that post!" I reminded the gentleman that I was well within my rights to pursue his comments through the courts. He tried to retract the comment and muttered some sort of apology. Having completed the phone call I made my way to my principal and told him about the call, for I'm sure he knew the parent. I needed to verbalise my anger and my principal was gracious enough to allow me to vent in his office. It was clear in my mind — there was more to come! I told myself that I was not in control of what came out of people's mouths but that I was in control of my response. I decided that if I was good at my job, it would earn the respect of the community. This therefore became my motivation! A comment from one parent only — reading between the lines would mean however, that I was accepted by the majority of the school community!

One thing that raised its head from time and time in Northern Ireland, was the scourge of sectarianism! Individuals across the country have worked consistently over the years to help change perception about 'the other side'. The Shared Education initiative was introduced into education in Northern Ireland — an initiative which allowed pupils from a Catholic and Protestant school to collaborate with regard to the curriculum, allowing pupils from each school to access subjects in the other school and therefore spend an academic year or two sitting within a classroom at the other school. This project was already operational in my school prior to my appointment as Vice Principal and it was good to see that respect for one another was already embedded. How could I further contribute to change in my school? How could the Shared Education initiative within the classroom have a wider impact upon community? What could I do as an individual to help build further relations between the two schools and in turn, enhance relations between pupils and communities from both schools? The opportunity was afforded to me through the medium of sport.

Rugby was once quite popular within my school but had now died a death. In trying to resurrect it, I had interest from a few boys in school, but not enough to start a team. I had a chat with the principal at the Catholic grammar school with whom we worked quite closely, to see if any of his non-playing GAA boys would be keen to play rugby (the Gaelic Athletic Association is an organisation which promotes Gaelic games such as Hurling, Gaelic Football, etc. and promoted in all Catholic schools across the island). There were a few boys at St Louis Grammar who showed interest and having chatted to them about the possibility of coming over to Kilkeel High School for a bit of training, it seemed we had sufficient boys to start a team. Our very first practice was an interesting one; the boys were courteous enough to one another but when time was afforded for rest, they seemed to only chat with boys from their own school. It was clear we needed to deal with the elephant in the room — this unease with 'the other side!'

We needed to talk about being from opposite sides of the community, from two different schools and what it now meant to be a team! My life's journey had allowed me to experience situations of segregation and reconciliation before but as I walked to the centre of the pitch on the drizzly, cold, late afternoon, I whispered "Jesus, I need Your help here!" I knew that this could all fall apart. I needed wisdom! I started to speak to the boys. We were a diverse mix in that circle — boys and Vice Principal — all from different backgrounds and experiences, all of whom I'm sure were impacted by 'The Troubles' in some shape or form. We needed to talk about being people, about rugby, about being a team. We also needed to make a decision — either we would forever be shackled by the past or respect the past enough to move forward together! These young men would be the future — future leaders within their respective communities, leaders in the town of Kilkeel, leaders within Northern Ireland. What if this little experience of playing rugby together would aid them in their development as people? What if this opportunity of playing rugby would be the initial step of character-building which would affect their lives forever in a positive way? However, there was also a flip side to that coin — what if they had family members killed in the Troubles? What if their dislike or hatred for each other was justified? What if their wider family backgrounds included affiliation to para-military groups? What was I about to uncover here? Agreed — this was a risky conversation to be had, but one which needed to happen! If Jesus took risks in order to reconcile people with God and one another, here was an opportunity which required just that! *Faith Vic! Choose your words carefully. Eye contact! Create change! Be Jesus to these young men!*

The boys agreed that we would be a team — and they were true to their word. Our very first game was against my old school at Antrim Grammar. I was thankful to Jake and to the principal for allowing us to come and play. We were hammered, but we scored one try. Progress! Teamwork, effort, resilience, communication ... things that we all need if we are to make any country better — all which was evident that day on that pitch. I was so proud of the St Louis Grammar School boys in the change room. Handing them the old Kilkeel High School rugby top, they never hesitated to put it on! There was the odd banter about the top, but smiles all round! They were a credit to their school, their families and their community. Captain and Vice-Captain were chosen by myself — everything based on merit, not background. The captain of our team was a St Louis pupil, the vice-captain from Kilkeel High — everything based on merit! Our team name was 'Kilkeel' — not Kilkeel High or Kilkeel High and St Louis, but just Kilkeel. The reason behind this was that the boys were not just representing their schools, but more importantly ... their community. I wish you could have witnessed the hugs when they scored a try. The score board was irrelevant but the joy of achievement was evident! We were well beaten, but we got to the try line — as a team! At the end of the game they proudly shook the hands of the opponents. I was proud — not so much as a coach, but more so as a human being!

The journey to and from the match was great — lots of banter, lots of laughs and chat. Then came the return leg a few weeks later — Antrim Grammar at Kilkeel. Now the boys had a few weeks to work hard on the training ground. They now had their own pupils and parents watching on the side-line, including staff from both schools. It was a few weeks after the first game — we had improved as a team, the game was a lot tighter, a lot more physical and we competed! We got beaten again, but we were close to winning. What an improvement this team had made during a few weeks. They had now earned the respect of their opponents. Boys from two teams, but three schools — playing a game they loved. Progress! If we were going to move toward reconciliation in our country, here was but a very tiny example of what relationships in our country could be like. At the end of that first year, we bought a trophy for 'Player of the Year'. It went to a pupil from St Louis Grammar School. Everything on merit — the way it should be!

However, something else was happening to these young men — something within their thinking and something within their hearts. Unbeknown to me, they were hanging out on social media and soon they came up with an idea of a new playing top. We had been playing in our old school rugby jersey and the boys felt that they needed a new top which reflected the badges of both schools. I was amazed at how far they had come as people — as individuals. This sport had now been an avenue to a process of change of which I was witnessing first-hand! I made an agreement with the boys that if they took time to design this, I would find funding to make this happen! Soon we had a new rugby top — a white playing top with the individual school colours on each sleeve. The boys decided that each school badge should sit on the opposite side of the other school's colours — to show the unity of the two schools. It was tight-fitting top, conducive to playing modern rugby and well designed. However, this top would cause offence to some in the community ... be it four years later!

As rugby developed, soon there was interest from girls to play as well. Still playing in our new kit, our girls competed in a tournament a few years later. It took one individual in the community to raise a question as to why the colours of the other school were present on the rugby top of our school. Sadly, the objection was not made to me in my office but on social media. Before we knew it, the entire community was now in discussion over a top created four years ago and which the teams had been playing in for years! It was national news in the Belfast Telegraph! I received phone calls that week about our rugby top from people I hadn't even met, which included a parent at St Louis Grammar School, people in rugby, colleagues in education and local and national press from both sides of the community. My comment to the newspapers was simple — "no comment". Thankfully, the majority of my school community were in support of the shared rugby top and in support of this joint initiative. Something was happening in my school community — there seemed to a sense of moving forward by the majority, as the minority who opposed the top now found themselves silenced by the rest!

Pupils from St Louis Grammar school were now very much at home in our school building — and vice versa. There now seemed to be a general acceptance of one another! About five years ago, a parent who was in a mixed marriage (Catholic and Protestant as opposed to a South African understanding of black and white) called me about enrolling her child in our school. She informed me that they lived within a Catholic community but had heard about how things were progressing in our school and she stated that she wanted to give her child an opportunity to broaden his thinking and to select a school where his worldview can be nurtured and challenged. She wanted him to be in a school where he would learn about life and how to get along with others. She loved the fact that we were involved in Shared Education and asked me as to how she could enrol her son in such a forward-thinking school. I was delighted to hear that our school community was now one where people from all backgrounds felt that this was the school for their children. It is evident that our schools and our communities are fast becoming more and more cosmopolitan. Our responsibility as educators is not just to provide our pupils with academic knowledge but also to develop their character and their thinking. It is the aim of any educator to produce the 'soft skills' within their pupils and challenge their thinking, in order to create within our pupils a mind-set of balance ... as they seek to become contributors to their wider world. As educators from both sides of the communities, we are to role model this ourselves!

Why therefore did I have to justify myself to others with regard to a rugby jersey? Why did an act of bringing young people together, become such an issue? Whether it is 'apartness' in South Africa or within Northern Ireland, it is slowly becoming evident that young people are stepping out of themselves and taking risks, pursuing friendships across the sectarian and colour divides and seeking reconciliation a lot quicker than people of my generation. Across the world it is young people who are transforming communities by reaching out and coming together. However, there are times when divisive attitudes held by adults are transferred to their children and sadly in some cases, this cycle still continues!

It's hard enough having to deal with racism personally, but when it's directed at your children, it becomes a different matter! Calum had the honour of captaining an exceptional team of players while playing for Portadown Football Club. He had earned the respect of many coaches, referees and people in football for his ability as a footballer but also as a leader. However, whenever they played one particular team, Calum constantly received racist abuse from one player and the father of that player who watched from the side-line. On a particular Saturday morning, the two teams competed again. Unfortunately, I had missed most of that game as I spent time watching Caleb play that morning. The two of us later rushed over to see if we could catch the final few minutes of Calum's match. Calum came off the pitch and the usual smile of victory was lacking. He got his bag and wanted to leave — immediately. It was unlike him, for those of you who know Calum, know how social he is. He loves being around people and enjoys a good chat, but all he wanted to do that morning was to leave as quick as possible.

I enquired of him if he received comments again. He had! Knowing the father and son concerned, I walked over to the opposition side of the pitch and requested of the father to leave my son alone. It had been a while since I was sworn at so profusely in such a short space of time! Unbeknown to me, Calum's coaches had heard the abuse during the match too and had followed me over. They too had now had enough of the abuse Calum was receiving. When playing other teams, he never experienced racism at all — banter yes, but not the comments he was constantly the recipient of when facing this team. I spoke to Calum's coaches in the car park and we were all in agreement that something had to be done! When we got home, Julie and I chatted to Calum. We discussed the possibility of either dealing with this or letting it lie, but the latter would most likely lead to more comments in the future. We were in agreement, these racists comments needed dealt with! The problem was ... how?

We decided that Calum should write a letter to the Irish Football Association (IFA), the governing body of football in Northern Ireland. He needed to explain to them the impact these comments were having on him. I too wrote three letters — one to the club concerned, one to the BBC in Belfast and one to the IFA. When writing to each organisation individually, I included a copy of Calum's letter and copy of the other two letters to each of the recipients. I had given the other club twenty-one working days to deal with the player and parent, else the letter to the media (which the football club concerned now had a copy of) would be initiated. The club and the IFA acted swiftly. The player and parent were sacked from the club and Calum and I received an invitation to meet with the newly appointed Northern Ireland manager Michael O' Neill and his academy director Jim Magilton. We spoke intensely about truly implementing the 'Kick it Out' campaign, UEFA's initiative to kick discrimination and racism out of football. It was a very positive meeting and these gentlemen could not have been kinder to Calum. This was a fight worth having and Calum never faced this type of abuse again.

It has been my privilege lately to contribute toward raising awareness of racism within educational settings here in Northern Ireland. I have been working alongside the Social Sciences department at Queen's University in Belfast, together with other ethnic minority professionals ... to educate students as to the challenges faced by black and ethnic minorities moving into the country. It has been a blessing telling my story and engaging students within their understanding of contemporary issues surrounding the black debate, recently high-lighted by the 'Black Lives Matter' initiative. I must admit that sometimes I feel quite out of my depth, due to the fact that I'm sharing a virtual platform with some really bright, intelligent and extremely articulate black contemporaries across the is-land - both north and south. I feel quite honoured to simply be part of the debate! Nevertheless, I thank God for the privilege of being asked by the university, to engage in the eradication of racism in a very small way here in Northern Ireland.

I have discovered to my detriment however, that the school system ... which is supposed to protect all teachers and espe-cially those of ethnic minority from racism in Northern Ireland ... clearly had no effective procedural mechanism to do so. I discovered that the odds were so stacked against teachers in general, that the organisation who employed us, had no formal procedures to protect staff like myself, from racist abuse. Had my colleagues or I been the ones making racist or sectarian comments to a parent or pupil, our employer would have sus-pended us immediately pending investigation and most likely would have required our resignation soon thereafter. It has been my experience therefore, that although my employer was in agreement that what happened to me was wrong — they were powerless nonetheless to procedurally protect me ... al-though the pastoral support I received from my employer was excellent and very much appreciated at the time. How do I live with this? What about other teachers of ethnic minority across Northern Ireland? Who protects them? Who speaks for them?

It was evident in my case, that legislative change was required in order to further protect all school staff ... and especially those of ethnic minority ... from procedural consequences, which have often been detrimental to both the individual member of staff and the wider school. Plans have therefore been put in place to remedy this and to update current legislation. My employer has therefore asked of me to assist the wider educational organisation, in developing systemic, legislative and procedural change ... so as to ensure protection for all schools and staff in these matters. That's immense! It provides me not just with a sense of hope, but a real sense of duty. If we can improve the system, the mechanics and legislation to support schools and protect staff against all kinds of abuse, then surely that's a good thing. Having met with key individuals in the Education Authority, draft proposals have been written so as to ensure that the system is a lot more robust. The key now is to further define these drafts, have them written into legislation, have them ratified by government ... to the point of implementation across all schools in Northern Ireland. I am so thankful to my employer for providing me the opportunity to be involved in this change, which will result in the further protection of all teaching staff, regardless of their nationality. I am also thankful to the CEO of the Education Authority in Northern Ireland for making available key members of her staff, to drive forward the change required in legislation. I am indebted however, to my Union representative who spent hours upon hours - working behind the scenes in supporting me to find a positive outcome ... in what was a difficult time.

It has been an interesting experience being black! In my lifetime I have been sworn at, disrespected, struck a few times by a policeman's whip, shot in the thigh with a rubber bullet, verbally abused, marginalised, discriminated against etc., ... simply because of the colour of my skin. If truth be told there were times that I truly despised being black and the implications and consequences that often came along with that, which include receiving an invitation to come and speak at a youth event or preach at a church ... and because you have a Dutch last name, they assume you are white and its only when you arrive that you see the disappointment in their eyes. However, because you have a task to fulfil, you pick yourself up and do what it is that you have been asked to do, irrespective of the emotion you are experiencing inside. Then there were the moments within my youth when I slept over at a white friend's house and woke up to the sound of raised voices, as his parents interrogated him as to why he brought me home. From the day I was born, I have had to fight for recognition, for the right to be treated as a human being. However, as painful as this journey of prejudice has been, I have come to realise that God has been gracious to me in this regard. It is He alone who has allowed me to undergo these experiences, learn from it and be a better human being because of it.

Every individual who enters my office at school, will see a framed photograph (copy of course) of Martin Luther King speaking in Washington DC in 1963. It was within this speech where he conveyed to his listeners, the hope of every black individual who has encountered discrimination and racism, and who has been scarred by its outworking at some stage. He stated: *"I have a dream that my children will one day live in a nation where they will not be judged by the colour of their skin, but by the content of their character."* I share this hope, not for myself but for my three sons. It is my hope that others are drawn to them because of their depth and strength of character and their love for Jesus, irrespective of the fact that their father is black and irrespective of the fact that they are mixed-race. A day will come when racism will no longer be, when we will no longer talk about black or white, when prejudice and discrimination will be a thing of the past, when terminologies like these will eventually be confined to the history for humankind. It may not be today, but it will come!

Lord Jesus ... let it please be so within my earthly lifetime!

Chapter 21: And then there were none ...

*"I've learnt that regardless of your relationship with your parents,
you'll miss them when they're gone from your life"*

(Maya Angelou)

It was a good Christmas and a few days of rest and relaxation from what was another busy term in school. A couple of days over the Christmas break is a welcomed time for teachers, for it allows both the opportunity to recuperate from a busy first term and to slowly prepare for the one ahead, which often includes mock examinations, reports, modular examinations, and so on. However, while many a teacher grabbed the opportunity to sleep as late as possible that week, unbeknown to the wider world something awoke within the Republic of China that particular week too, which was slowly causing a storm. They called her 'Corona' ... and unlike other viruses within our modern world, she was already causing a storm! What I did not know at the time was that the corona virus would forever be linked with my family for the remainder of my lifetime. It was February 2020 and the virus was sweeping across the European continent. Unbeknown to them initially, aircrafts most likely became her mode of transportation as thousands upon thousands of travellers became infected and carriers of COVID-19 at the very same time. By the time governments awoke to the need for shutting borders and grounding aircrafts, people were starting to die from this virus, not in their hundreds but in their thousands. Flights were grounded and travel restricted, as countries went into lockdown and waited to ride-out this pandemic!

"Hi brother. I don't want you to worry but mum is due for an operation!" I listened intently as Sharon began to explain to me that mum had a pain which needed checked. She had also been experiencing it seems, a speedy loss in weight and Sharon thought it prudent to have this checked. There was a possibility of a tumour in the abdomen, for it was this area where the pain was at its worst. I was just about to enjoy February half-term but now had to contemplate mum undergoing major surgery. Mum was in high spirits, for hopefully post-op she would find relief from this incredible pain. I awaited Sharon's post-op phone call which confirmed the presence of a large tumour and its surgical removal. Additional and surrounding tissue were removed for biopsy and mum was now to make her way back to Sharon's house to recuperate.

However, back in Northern Ireland, there was talk of closure of schools by the Education Minister due to the virus. With all the speculation surrounding schools, my role was now to keep my staff focused on teaching, make educational contingencies and upskill my staff for the inevitability of online teaching, all this while thinking and worrying about mum. A decision was reached with regard to the closure of schools across the United Kingdom due to the impact of COVID-19 and on the 20th March 2020, school literally stopped! However, due to the suddenness of the closure and the possibility of the arrival of children of key workers, I planned to be in school the following week. Little did I know that it would be a defining week within the relationship between my mother and I.

Mum was in good spirits, sore from the operation but glad to be over the worst. She was scheduled to receive the results of the biopsy first thing that morning and commence with the much needed chemotherapy later that day. However, I received a call from Sharon that Tuesday morning — the biopsy revealed that there was now no need for chemotherapy, for the cancer was at such an advanced stage that chemotherapy would be a waste of time. It was then that Sharon informed me that mum had lymphoma.

'Lymphoma' — what is it and what does it do to the human body? That Tuesday night, there was no thought of sleep. Once my family went to bed, I got my laptop and slowly started to research what lymphoma actually was and its impact on the human body. Educating oneself on that of which one is ignorant, is always a good thing but the information which presented itself on screen left me with a shiver. Phrases like 'impact on the immune system' and 'cancer in the lymph nodes' virtually smacked across my face as I slowly came to terms with this type of cancer. My fingers googled as quickly as I could … 'recovery from lymphoma' … but the more I read the more I understood that there was to be only one inevitable outcome here, which was that mum was not going to recover from this. The more I researched and read, the clearer it became … mum was dying.

It was but only a few days earlier when mum had spent a Sunday at my aunt's for lunch and although she was weak post the initial operation, I was pleased that she at least felt fit enough to be out and enjoy seeing family. Needless to say I video-called my aunt's that afternoon and had a good chat with mum, which included a bit of banter about her 'social-ising' so soon after her operation. In my mind, I considered the possibility that mum would most likely have a couple of months but already in the space of a few days, mum was get-ting weaker. Sharon had been brilliant keeping Glenda and I informed about mum's recovery but I knew it wasn't easy for her. With Glenda residing in Johannesburg, Sharon was mum's sole carer. As plans were put in place to provide mum some full-time care, I decided to inquire of mum's consult-ant what the prognosis was and what sort of time frame we were talking about here. It seemed crazy that mum could go from walking to being bed-ridden within a space of three days. Due to doctor-patient confidentiality and all that, my email to the consultant had to include personal details about myself which the consultant could verify with my sister prior to mum's medical information being released to me. The in-formation received was telling! It was now two in the morn-ing and I started talking to God. I had learnt many years ago, when dad was dying, that God is not to be negotiated with. Yes, I believe in heavenly intervention in praying for healing and so on but I also know that we have a designated time to be on this planet and considering the extent of the cancer, death was inevitable. Very soon the tears rolled — not be-cause of the state of mum's body as such but more due to the recalling of memories in years gone by.

Ever so often I smiled through the tears as I recalled fun mo-ments and so on. Yet again, the smiles were replaced by guilt as I recalled many an issue in my mind, which included an apology I owed mum, now long overdue. Then I started to weep from the depths of my soul — I was losing my mother! Mum would never see my sons be married, or experience the joy of being a great granny. She would never know how grateful I was to her for raising us the way she did. She had her faults, but so did I. She could be as frustrating as anything, but then so am I. If truth be told, I'm like her in so many ways. I chatted to God and thanked Him for the many years He gave mum. I prayed too that God would intervene in the unbearable pain mum was currently undergoing. In a short while I was fairly at peace about mum's impending death, whenever that would be — in a few months, maybe a couple of weeks but never ever realising that it would be a matter of days!

I made a decision that I needed to be strong for my sisters. In a period of days, it was evident that mum was now getting weaker and her strength was failing. I decided that in our communication with one another over WhatsApp, I would be as upbeat as I could possibly be with her. As governments were starting to lockdown and ground flights, I wondered how soon it would be before South Africa went into lockdown. The answer came as a bit of a shock ... two days! Due to the grounding of flights, Glenda was stuck in Johannesburg that week and could not travel. Sharon had mum with her in Cape Town and in two days the UK too would go into lockdown. Airlines were still flying to Cape Town from the UK, but quarantine would be implemented in South Africa the morning of my possible arrival. If I could get a flight to Cape Town, I would have to undergo quarantine for two weeks and would not be allowed to see mum. Also I had no guarantee when I would be allowed to return to the UK. I had a family and a school for which I was responsible and I needed wisdom as to what I would do. It was now about four in the morning and I sat with a sheet of paper noting the pros and cons of travelling to Cape Town. I made a list for my Vice Principals of what needed to be done if I were to be on a plane in the next two days. I made a decision to call the Chair of my Governors and the CEO of the Education Authority in Northern Ireland to request permission to take time off and head to Cape Town. I now had a decision to make ... do I travel and spend two weeks in quarantine before seeing mum or do I stay home and video-call and not see her personally?

I set out a plan of action and chatted to God. If these options were to be pursued, I would accept the fact that I should remain in Northern Ireland and not travel. If they opened, I would see that as a sign that God was preparing the way for me. I got onto Facebook and made a public announcement about the possibility of travelling. I received a few messages from friends in Cape Town encouraging me not to travel. The concern was not so much about arriving but about the quarantine and about the possibility that I probably would not return to the UK for another three or so months. One friend whose wife is a medical practitioner implored me not to travel, for they could foresee COVID 'having its way' in South Africa. I spent many a minute calling the South African embassy — both in London and Dublin. As I am a UK passport holder and had foregone my South African citizenship years ago, I needed to re-apply for a South African passport. Due to lockdown in the UK now, there was no one at the office in London. However, the operator manning the phones at the South African embassy in Dublin was very helpful. The bottom line was ... there was no way I was going to get documentation in twenty-four hours. A friend of mine in London was enquiring if his company jet was flying to Cape Town in the next few days. I heard back from him in an hour after speaking to him ... all company flights were grounded too. One by one the doors closed. One by one the options on my notepad were being scored off. There was no way I was getting to South Africa. *Corona virus ... I am starting to hate you!* My sisters were not expecting me to make it to South Africa either. In fact, due to the quarantine, they encouraged me to stay home. Having all these doors closed to me, it was evident that remaining in Northern Ireland was the prudent thing to do. I wasn't there for dad's death and it seemed that I would not be there for mum's either. It was now another tough pill to swallow!

My sisters and I were video-calling daily and I had various opportunities to talk to mum. By Sunday morning that week it was clear that mum had a few hours left. Sunday night the doctor arrived with Sharon and stayed with her. Monday morning came and the appendages of mum's body started to lose body heat. At about twelve that afternoon, I had the opportunity to video-call mum … about ten minutes before she passed. Now what do I say? It was clear that although her body was failing pretty quickly, she still had the physical capability to hear. Glenda had just called a few minutes before and said her goodbyes and now it was my turn. In the next minute or two I was about to speak to my mother for the very last time. What do I say? If these were the last words she would hear from me as her son, what would it be? Would I be strong for her? Would I shed tears and be emotional? If I were to be emotional, would that upset her? I made the video-call. Sharon held the phone to mum's ear. Mum was now physically a shadow of her former self. I decided to be as upbeat as I could possibly be under the circumstances. I started to speak. I heard Sharon's voice and that of the doctor in the background — mum's eyes were starting to flicker when she heard my voice. She started to grunt as she sought to reply. It was her son on the phone — she knew that and she could hear every word I said. I loved my mother from the very minute I was able to comprehend who she was as her son, to this very minute. Fifty-two years of memory was now compressed into three minutes. I started to speak. I told mum that I loved her and thanked her for raising us the way she did. I told her that we would not forget the values she sought to instil within us. I told her that her time had now come and that she could pass in peace, knowing that she would be with Father in His presence. I did not want to cry as

I did not want to upset her any more. I said my goodbyes and terminated the call after speaking to Sharon. Ten minutes later, my mum passed away. In true Victor fashion, I never shed a tear, but it would come in stages later on. However, I was content. I got to say goodbye to my mum — be it on a mobile phone. I never had that opportunity with my dad, but I did with my mum. God is good!

How does one make a mental switch about losing someone you love, especially your mum? One minute you have her and the next she is removed from your life ... permanently. No more phone calls, good laughs, serious discussions or even disagreements at times. No more verbalising 'I love you, mum' or birthday and Mother's Day cards specifically chosen to suit her personality or humour. No more thoughts about visits and taking her for coffee or lunch or picking her brain while you are in need of some serious advice. No more reminiscing about days gone by or laughter when you talk about dad whom both of you lost years before. How does one make that switch, that your mother now simply is ... a memory?

I am sure that the grieving process should go some way in assisting with the mental shift, but the pain of loss never quite goes away. I find myself thinking about my mum quite often and I am glad that the memories are good ones. God has allocated each of us a designated time on this planet. With life comes frailty of body in later years and the inevitability of death. This fact of 'the circle of life' by no means diminishes the loss we feel when loved ones depart. However, the hope that Jesus' followers have is that we will see our loved ones again and it is this hope that takes away the sting of loss and the hope of eternal reunion!

Loss ... even Jesus Himself experienced how much it hurts!

Chapter 22: 'So Black Lives Matter ...'

*"So Jesus was white huh? Innocent man, beaten, whipped
and hung ... that don't sound like a black man to you?"*

(@#AmBlack)

The death of George Floyd at the hands of a local policeman
in a specific street, in a specific city, in a specific country ...
has to date had a major impact upon our modern world, not
quite seen before. If truth be told, this kind of incident —
death by law enforcement, has historically repeated itself
over generations. Though the vast majority of police officers across the globe ensure that they comply to grounds of
acceptability when fulfilling their duties, there are incidents
where enforcement of law has led to the abuse of power, resulting in the death of the individual being arrested. Let me
affirm of course, that no individual joins the police in order
to hurt the general public. Individuals who join the police
often do so for a variety of positive reasons, which include
being a servant to the local community.

The question always is whether or not local councils or governments, view the death of the apprehended as unaccep-
table or simply as an unfortunate 'casualty.' Of course every

police force has its accountability structures and in an incident like that of George Floyd and others, positions such as the role of the Ombudsman often kick into place. Public frustration arises when officers, found guilty after due process ... simply receive official warnings or face short-term suspension after admission of manslaughter etc. The outcry however, comes when very few officers actually find themselves incarcerated. This frustration often leads to the obvious question as to whether or not local councils and judges are soft in cases of police brutality. The further concern is that where this sort of thing happens frequently, the general public begins to wonder whether or not local councils or national governments are sympathetic to 'mistakes' made by officers. The general public therefore can be forgiven into thinking that leaders within local police enforcement, allow for this 'sort of thing'. The outcry comes when 'this sort of thing' happens far too frequently!

The death of George Floyd resulted in an outburst of violence on the streets of America. Many across the world watched their television screens in horror, wondering where all this would lead to. Inevitably, every viewer not just became a witness to the violence but also began to formulate individual opinions on whether or not such violence was justified. I had seen it all before ... race violence! I had witnessed it! I was involved in it! What I saw on my television screen is what I personally experienced in 1985 ... an emotion of rage! As I saw young black and white teens, young men and women destroy cars, shops, etc. within their own communities, I could not agree with the violence but I clearly understood it. When one has seen 'this sort of thing' within the history of one's country and when it continues to this very day after years of campaigning for this to stop through movements like Civil Rights and so on ... rage is inevitable. As adults, we have the fortitude and wisdom to understand that violence never accomplishes anything, but try telling that to a sixteen or eighteen-year old who is formulating opinions about life, his community, his government, his country! As adults, it is easy for us to sip coffee and have astute conversations about government policy about 'this sort of thing' and rationalise as to why young people are engaging in violence, but often we forget the reactive nature of youth!

What became evident day after day and within city after city across America, was that criminals infiltrated the ranks of genuine protesters after the death of George Floyd. Soon genuine protesters removed themselves from the violence and adopted a 'modus operandi' which then took off around the world, namely non-violent protests! Every major city across the world was now engaged within protesting — not just what happened to Mr Floyd, but protesting against racism and calling for its eradication across the world, all under the auspices of a movement which seems to arise ever so often like a phoenix after injustice against blacks ... a movement called 'Black Lives Matter.' We cannot refer to BLM as an organisation as such, for in essence it is simply an international voice calling black people to action and to respond to government-sanctioned violence against black people. It also seeks to bring an end to injustice against oppressed black communities across the world and it envisions a world free of anti-blackness. It is a voice that now calls black people and all others who seek justice 'to arms', a voice getting louder and louder crying out ... "enough!"

BLM protest marches were now becoming a phenomenon across the globe post the death of Mr Floyd and I knew that it would only be a matter of time before it reached Northern Ireland. Inevitably a BLM protest was organised in Belfast city centre and I debated as to whether or not I should attend. As we were in the middle of COVID-19, having been instructed by local government not to be in crowds and to ensure that we stay home where possible, I had to make a decision as to whether or not I would break these instructions and journey to Belfast in order to make a personal protest to that which has affected me since birth. As racism is quite an emotive experience for me, deciding as to whether or not I should attend this event was not an easy decision to make. However, I had to weigh up the pros and cons, for COVID-19 was the overriding issue here. I decided therefore not to attend! We were in the middle of a health crisis and I could not justify voicing my opinion against racism within a health crisis like this. If I were to attend, would I possibly put my family at risk by mixing with people who may or may not carry the virus? Would I possibly be breaking the law? I had to do the right thing for me and not attending the protest was the right thing ... for me! However, what astounded me post this event, was that the Police Service of Northern Ireland decided to formally charge those who attended this BLM protest. Of all the countries in the world which had a protest march, Northern Ireland was the only state which sought to formally charge people for attending a public gathering during this health crisis. The justification was that the protesters were in breach of COVID-19 regulations with regard to social distancing and so on. Well, so too the many young people who gathered on a beach in Crawfordsburn, — a coastal town in Northern Ireland where teenagers demonstrated very little regard for social distancing guidelines. Were these young people formally charged too? No! What about the many who paid their respects at a funeral in West Belfast? At a time where lockdown guidelines included limited attendance at funerals, hundreds of people — including the Deputy First Minister of Northern Ireland, as well as other politicians ... completely ignored their own guidelines and attended nonetheless. Should all these people not have been charged either? How come BLM protesters are the only ones facing a legal sanction? Are the Northern Ireland Executive and the Police Service of Northern Ireland therefore, in these specific examples adding to the type of government-sanctioned injustice which BLM is seeking to address? If not, should these charges against the BLM protesters in Belfast not be revoked?

In the streets of England, a minority of BLM protests turned violent and in Bristol, the statue of Edward Colston — a merchant who financially thrived through slavery, was pulled down. Soon there were global calls for statues of people who were connected to slavery and injustice — to be removed. Local museums and councils were now coming face to face with having to make decisions about statues of those affiliated to historical racism, as the BLM movement pursued governments to deal with racism once and for all. As noble and right as this is, where do we draw the line on statues which cause offence? Which statues do we remove and which do we maintain? Inevitably, the majority of statues around the world — other than those paying tribute to soldiers who died in wars, are offensive to someone, correct? Surely when walking past a statue of Queen Victoria, one would be reminded of the days of British colonialism. Would this statue therefore not cause offence to anyone whose country was colonialized by the British? What about the Voortrekker monument in South Africa — does this reminder of Afrikaner dominance over blacks in South Africa not bring offense to modern-day black South Africans? What about the indigenous people of Canada — are they not offended by the likeness of Sir John McDonald on the walls of the city hall in the city of Victoria — an individual who was known for the genocide of the indigenous people of Canada? What about murals and street art glorifying terrorists or freedom fighters ... surely they too cause offence to some? What about places like Auschwitz — should we get rid of that too so that we do not cause offence to the modern-day German who may view this place as a scourge on his national identity? If we want to be an inclusive global community the way we should be, then all statues should be reconsidered and not just the ones pertaining to slavery, correct? Are we therefore currently in a position globally, where we are re-writing history? If we are, then where do we draw the line on statues and buildings of injustice? I am in agreement with the BLM movement with regard to re-considering statues pertaining to historical slavery and if this is the road they want to pursue, well then don't just stop there — deal with other statues too which have caused offence globally! In so doing we will implement and give to all people across the world that which was denied to us as black people over the generations … true global equality!

Marc Quinn, a sculptor … replaced the statue of Edward Colston in Bristol with a sculpture of Jen Reid, one of the BLM protestors. Soon this new statue was removed too. Surely there were protocols which needed to be followed in order for this new statue to be erected? Surely the council in Bristol should have been notified or a formal request made to have this statue erected? No protocols were followed. No applications made. No wonder Jen Reid's statue was removed by the authorities. Are we therefore at a stage where rules and guidelines now no longer apply in order to achieve the objectives of BLM as it seeks to eradicate racism? Does the end now justify the means?

Scholars, leaders, Hollywood stars, sports people, etc., have all contributed to the Black Lives Matter debate. Morgan Freedom, the renowned actor, emphasised that racism would continue if we keep talking about 'black and white'. He encouraged us to stop this talk of black and white and to simply talk about 'people', as opposed to 'black and white people.' Sports bodies too are implementing BLM 'protocol' by allowing players to express their convictions by the bending of the knee at the start of matches. This public display of support for the BLM movement obviously has its roots in the 1968 Olympic Games, when two black American athletes — Tommie Smith and John Carlos raised their black-gloved fist during their medal ceremony in support of black people in 1960s America. These gentlemen later acknowledged that they did so in support of human rights and not solely in support of black people as such. However, our current bending of the knee and raising of the fist in support of injustice against black people, are clearly modelled on this event. It took a tremendous amount of courage by both these men to do what they did at such a global event and yet they did as their convictions dictated. My problem with this current public display of bending of the knee is that it seems to be a trend and those not bending, seems to be looked down against. Recently, San Francisco Giants pitcher Sam Coonrod did not kneel in support of BLM, because his conviction dictated otherwise. While everyone else in his team knelt in respect of BLM, Coonrod decided not to. The sad thing is that Coonrod had to later explain himself to the American people. Why did he need to do so? This is my problem with this public display of support — if individuals do not bend the knee, they are viewed and looked upon with suspicion! Coonrod later went on to explain that as a Christian, he could bow the knee to no one else but God Himself. Coonrod stated that he meant no ill by standing but my point is simply this, why on earth did he have to explain himself? Are we moving toward a position of intolerance to those who don't bend the knee?

We had an interesting non-verbal dispute raised within Formula One recently which has simply added to the 'black debate.' The drivers agreed that they would wear 'End

Racism' t-shirts as a means of support to black people internationally, while Lewis Hamilton decided to wear a BLM t-shirt. Interesting! A small example within a sport dominated not by colour but wealth, raises a very interesting question ... where should our allegiance lie? Are we seeking to eradicate racism on all fronts or support an 'organisation' seeking to do so?

It has been very interesting as a black person in Northern Ireland, to listen to the national debate about BLM. Since the rise of this movement, questions have also been asked about whether or not 'white lives matter' or whether or not 'all lives matter'. Fingers have also been pointed at the black community with regards to black on black killings and the rise of gangs among non-white communities. Questions have also been asked about whether or not it is fair to solely focus on the 'current emancipation' of blacks — to the detriment and omission of other ethnic minorities. Why so much focus on the black community only? Why is it that the death of Mr Floyd has brought to the fore, yet again, feelings about racism and in particular ... slavery?

It is a fact of life that black and non-white minorities around the world have played second fiddle to whites historically. Now, how do I explain this without causing offense to my white brothers and sisters, which includes my wife? What slavery has done is that it has allowed the acceptability of one man's dominance over the other — whether it is white over black, white American dominating the native American people, white Australian over the Maori people, etc. Irrespective of the legal abolition of slavery by people like William Wilberforce, the attitudes of some remain to this very day and it is these attitudes of superiority by the few, which have been communicated from father to son over many a generation ... evident in areas of racial conflict throughout our planet. These attitudes are taught and what it develops within the listener is a mind-set of superiority and when fuelled, finds its way into every area of life. So in business, we don't have too many blacks in management, or we don't employ too many Roman Catholics in a Protestant-owned business or vice-versa in Northern Ireland, or Palestinians in a Jewish-owned business, etc. This mind-set of superiority, questions whether or not those inferior 'could actually do the job' let alone work alongside the 'rest of us'. The 'rules' of dominance are never overt — except in the case of historical Apartheid in South Africa or 1960s America, nor is it evident in law, but it's there, like the unseen gas in petrol poured over a fire ... destructive and dangerous with the potential to bring harm to all in its way. Sadly, I have often been the recipient of this mind-set over the years. Maybe as black people we have become sensitive to it and we must daily use the filter of discernment to decide whether an individual's ignorance is simply just a character flaw on their part or whether or not their ignorance towards you stems from an attitude of superiority. In my current role of school principal, I have seen it all ... from being called a monkey by a parent on the telephone, to being told to "go back to Africa" by another. It seems for a small minority, the attitude of superiority to say and do as they please to another human being, is hard to resist. It is this type of attitude that BLM seeks to protest against and seeks to overcome.

Now let us talk about the historical practical outworking of this attitude of superiority. You may have noticed that black people and ethnic minorities across our planet, often make up the work or labour force. In most cases they struggle financially from generation to generation. Why is this? The simple answer is that generations ago, land was forcibly taken or legally bought for next to nothing by those who had both the power and the means to do so. From generation to generation, this wealth was passed on. Now, how do I practically explain this? Let's use the simple example of a newly married couple purchasing a house. Let's take land owned by families. In many cases, a father very naturally gives his son or daughter a piece of land to build his/her new house upon when married. This allows for the possibility therefore of a larger size house. A much smaller mortgage is therefore required from the bank which leads to less monthly payments which leads to a better standard of living. Compare that to a couple (whether they be white or black) who is not privileged enough to have a piece of land valued at fifty thousand pounds given to them by their family. This would mean a smaller house with less grounds around it within the confines of a town or village. The maximum amount of funds is therefore borrowed from the bank, which means a higher mortgage rate, which means a higher interest rate, which means a slightly poorer way of life and which most likely will mean that both of them would be working for many a year to repay the mortgage. The ownership of land in any country brings along with it the prospect of wealth! Is it no wonder there is a call from some around the world, especially in South Africa, to reclaim the land from those who took it from its historical inhabitants? The current problem is, who has the rights to the land? If Dutch settlers to South Africa years ago, bought acres of land from the British who colonised it, paid the going rate for the land at the time, settled on it, worked it, farmed it ... do they not therefore legally and rightfully own it?

Now let us think about those who have been brought to another country through slavery or those who arrived in countries like the United Kingdom to assist with the post-war reconstruction of cities and so on. Where do they settle? They are housed in very tight working class areas. They work possibly six days a week and yet earn minimum wage if they're lucky. They struggle financially and pass on this financial struggle to their sons and daughters and so it goes on through the generations. They live a completely different life to those who come from families who own land or own businesses and so on and they are treated differently, often with disdain because of their plight. In their working class and often poverty-ridden communities, arise those who have visions of not accepting their lot. They seek escape via any means, be it wrong or illegal ... through crime, gang-activity and so on and often victimise the very same community from which they come. And so these communities go on and on, struggling to survive through no fault of their own, but simply because of a historical event years ago which they now, are the product of.

Now what about the black labourer with no education, who leaves his family and travels to the city in order to find employment, who now finds himself in a dormitory with like-minded individuals run by the local mining company, who spends his day underground and breathes in the dust which will inevitably shorten his life but who understands that without this job, he cannot feed his family? What about the historical white farmer in South Africa, who paid his black farm labourer the bare minimum and handed him a bottle of cheap liquor with his pay cheque in order to numb the pain of exploitation? You see, this is the historical experience of black people and ethnic minorities around the world. Due to white domination of blacks hundreds of years ago, we continue to reap this very vicious cycle of racism fuelled by finance over generations.

You see, I am of the opinion that all lives do matter ... for each of us need emancipation — some of us from the racism perpetuated against us within our modern world and others of us from the prejudice which encompasses our very being. Once we all view each other as equals, our world will be a better place. However, if I could advise the BLM on one or two issues, I would suggest that they do the following. Firstly, encourage all black and ethnic minority young people, to see the value of education and the need to be educated. Educational qualifications will allow them to not only shape the world in business, policy and leadership ... but also to demand respect as leaders within their given fields of study. Destroying institutions of learning as was done in Cape Town recently, is pure madness! Secondly, communicate the fact that absent fathers are damaging the self-worth of young black men and women, for if they have no fathers to role-model, gang leaders and people of crime will very naturally become 'fathers' to them. Black young men in particular need strong black role-models to look up to, to learn from, to discuss global issues with, to learn what true manhood is all about and this type of learning very naturally starts within the home. Thirdly, they are to communicate that black empowerment must never result in black exploitation of whites, as is currently the case in places like South Africa. If we do so, we become no better than those who once exploited us. In fact, we become ten times worse because we should know better ... as stated by Reverend Desmond Tutu in his warning to the ANC about their current governance of South Africa. In implementing these three key ideas, I do believe that leaders and supporters of BLM, will not just gain further support from all sides of the community, but will attain their objective a lot quicker.

Am I proud to be black? Would I be proud if I was born white? Do I wish that I was born white in order to have escaped the scourge of racism which has often been my experience? Does the voice of Black Lives Matter therefore appeal to me? Often I have to remind myself that I am who I am because God in His wisdom designated for me to be who I am. I have to remind myself that God has sought of me to fulfil a specific role within history. In doing so, He has placed me within a politically defined ethnic group, although the horrors which has stemmed from it is not of His making. He gave me a mind to think, a desire to know, the resilience to endure the difficulties that He knew I would face, the boldness to address the weaknesses within me and the humility to acknowledge that I need Him. Each of us are born within a particular context and we pursue life from within this context! We define our worldviews and opinions about race, politics, marriage, God, life, etc., from within this given context. We also seek to be the best individuals we could be irrespective of the difficulties which that particular context brings us and we desire to be a positive influence within our individual communities. So whatever our context, whether we are black or white, our goal remains the same — to bring justice and healing to our communities and to create change within the world at this very point in history.

I am of the opinion that all lives matter to God. Change in our world comes, when we have the welfare of others as the focus of who we are, irrespective of their colour! Our love for others will motivate us to pursue change in government policy, to work toward the eradication of racism and to strive toward a world which no longer uses race as a weapon, nor as an excuse to play the victim! Jesus championed the cause of the poor, the oppressed, the outcast, the ethnic minority (the Samaritans) and in particular the role of women in his community. Our role therefore is to look at His example as a blueprint for loving our fellow man and championing their cause, where and when required. Regardless of our generational privilege or hardship, regardless of whether we are white or black, regardless as to whether or not we are indigenous to the land in which we live or whether we arrived here as immigrants ... our goal is one and the same. We are to love our neighbour and seek their best in all we do.

To this end I strive! It is my hope that it is your goal too!

Conclusion: 'Mirror, mirror on the wall ...'

Without reflection, we go blindly on our way, creating more unintended consequences and failing to achieve anything useful.

(Margaret J. Wheatley)

It is particularly hard looking into the mirror of one's own life, for what we often see looking back at us, can only be described as an individual with a 'split-personality', especially if we claim to be people of faith. We encounter three people in the mirror each day — the one looking into the mirror and the two looking back at us! The two are interesting people; the first is a person of faith — the one who recognises that life is but a product of the goodness and blessing of God and the other, the 'dark side' — fighting to control our thoughts, our emotions and our wills. The latter seems to be the powerful one, so powerful that he has the ability and the potential to destroy us! These two look back at us each morning! They remain and travel with us to every encounter we face that day until we close our eyes to sleep. All day they compete, at logger-heads with each other — fighting to get the better of one another — two soldiers in combat seeking to outdo and outsmart one another and inevitably seeking to overpower the will of the other. We awake the next morning and the same process begins, over and over again, day after day, month after month, year after year!

Then there are times when the demons come — the areas in our lives which consistently haunt us, like a scab scratched and re-opened time after time when the healing is nearly complete. It's the heartache of personal struggle, those issues and temptations or addictions we are so susceptible to and more than often, likely to give in to. These are our areas of madness, our areas of weakness … our demons! These areas bring us heartache, for like a dog going back to its own vomit we so often return to those things that we know will only result in mess and yet, we return to it nonetheless! It is who we are when we are alone, those moments of silence and aloneness, when we are most susceptible to them. We then encounter them … and having given into them, we hear their laughter — the laughter of the demons in our own head and the implementation of the demon's joy, our personal guilt! However, the demons have a second poker with which to torment us, our moments of 'what ifs' and 'if only I had not!" These feelings of regret plague us, for often we have not taken the opportunities given to us in order to make things right or reconcile ourselves to those we have wronged, solely due to our pride. It is the one thing that the demons relish — our pride, for they don't even have to assist us with it … for by its very nature pride is self-destructive! Finally, they relish in the one thing we find most difficult to control, the one thing that communicates our thoughts, which speaks of the evil and negative desires within us and the damage we can cause with it, namely our tongues! Our demons are ever before us and once it has had its way with us, we do the inevitable — we raise our eyes to the mirror and there we see it — disappointment, hurt, powerlessness, anger, shame! Then we hear it — the inevitable laughter of our demons taking pleasure at our demise, taking joy in the fact that once again we failed, once again our wills have succumbed to theirs. Defeat! Yes, so it goes on, the inevitable battle of life ... good versus evil, the daily struggle for domination!

I have spent my lifetime in the midst of two cultures — one social and the other the culture of the Universal Church. In its ideal, our Church culture should be vastly different to that which we encounter in society but the sad reality is that the daily overlap is ever so stark! In society, we expect there to be a lesser standard, where immorality, wrongdoings, greed, lust for power and so on hold no surprise, but we don't expect it in the Church now, do we? However, the reality is that we see the same thing within church culture too ... every single day! Are we surprised at the fact that Christians too cheat the tax man, or struggle with issues of morality, or beat their wives and kids, or struggle with pride and self-righteousness, or are filled with hatred for their fellow man, or discriminate against others or are filled with sectarian hatred or struggle with porn? Are we surprised at this? I often have a personal giggle at Christians who are so 'appalled' at young people who find themselves pregnant — some after a single encounter and yet there are 'Christians' who spend years of their Christian life hating people 'on the other side' of the community! What hypocrisy! Have we all not had situations where after a service rendered, the Christian businessman or woman requests us to pay in cash rather than by cheque, knowing full well that here is a way to cheat the tax man? The lines between the cultures overlap and blur every single day! Let's not mention those of us who are so self-righteous, that if we were living in Jesus' day ... the locals would mistake us for being Pharisees — those who portrayed a life which says that we have it all together, yet in the meantime if people only knew what we were really like! What about the sexual thoughts we continually fight against, the innuendos and slightly-off comments we make or send on our phones? What about the craving for and lust for someone other than our spouses? What do we do when the demons come? Often the Church is no different from the world ... and yet, it should be!

There has been many a time when I have had to look into the mirror of my own life and ask myself a question — am I intrinsically a 'good' person? If I say 'yes' to that question, what am I measuring my goodness against? Is there some sort of measuring stick by which I could measure how good I currently am? Is there a point where I inevitably achieve a 'state of goodness'? If 'yes', have I reached it? Am I nearly there? Am I far off? When society refers to me as a 'good guy', what do they actually mean? Is it because I display an outward nature which is positive, caring, energetic, respectful — coupled with an element of faith? What if they could see my thoughts, my opinion about others, my desires, etc., would they still consider me to be 'good' or would they be aghast at the state of my mind? What if they were aware of my demons — would their perspective of me change? Would they excuse my 'lack of goodness' as mere 'characteristics of being human?' Which part of me do I actually allow them to see?

The reality is that God sees it all! He alone knows that there is nothing good about me! He alone has the x-ray vision to scan the entirety of my being and He alone is in the position of making a judgement on my state of 'goodness'! Sadly, from His perspective, there is nothing good within me. All that I am within my character, is due to His goodness and blessing. There remains within me many a bad thought, attitude and motivation which He needs to deal with before I reach eternity — and I am fast running out of 'earth years'!

I deal with people every single day! I see anger and hatred in some; pride and self-righteousness in others, etc. However, we all have two things in common. Firstly, each of us are trying to make our way in the world and secondly, we are all affected by the badness within us, in some way. We are messed-up people, living in a messed-up world and daily dealing with messed-up people. It is as simple as that! Everyone has their own agendas — even though in some cases it may sound 'spiritual', but how many times have personal agendas been disguised in spiritual language? We are selfish individuals at the very core of who we are. That's who we are! No wonder the Bible strongly suggests that we need rescued from a nature within us that results in all these selfish and wrong behaviours.

This belief system of 'nothing beyond the grave', held by so many in our world ... simply makes no intellectual sense to me at all. From the moment we are born, we do things to provide a better future for ourselves! We learn, study, work hard, invest, pension-plan, seek medical cover, financially prepare for our burial, etc., We do everything for a better future because intrinsically we are 'future people'! If planning for a better future is at the core of who we are as 'earthlings', how is it that we never plan for that which is beyond the grave? If 'future planners' are who we are, how come we never think about preparing for a future after the termination of our bodies?

When looking at ourselves as individuals we see two things that make us ... us; the body and inner spirit! There are 'stuff' within us which are non-material — personality, emotions, etc. We cannot see them, but we know they exist because we see the outworking of those things in our everyday lives. Why is it therefore so hard for us as humanity to consider the possibility of a spiritual world — which we cannot see but of which we see its outworking in everyday life? When we see barbaric acts in our world or humanity's capacity for evil, are we not encountering the spiritual world? When we sit at the bedside of a dying individual who passes from this life with a look of contentment, peace and expectation ... are we not encountering the spiritual world? When we witness the birth of our firstborn and encounter the realities of life right before our eyes and as we feel the lump in the back of our throats which progresses to the tear of joy which freely runs down our cheek ... are we not encountering the spiritual world? When we see an alcoholic who lost everything due to his addiction, approach a church altar and cry to God to be rescued from this compulsion ... are we not encountering the spiritual world? When we sit on the beach at sunset and observe the sun disappearing from the horizon and our emotions are stirred ... are we not encountering the spiritual world?

When Jesus informed His listeners that He was leaving to prepare eternity for us, why is that such a hard concept to swallow? Historically we cannot deny that Jesus lived — for our history books affirms His existence. However, the key question is whether or not Jesus is whom He claimed to be — that is, divine. If we agree that our bodies have non-material stuff which is driven by an intellect within us called the brain, why can we not conceive of a spirit world driven by an Intellect who has provided us with the non-material stuff we just mentioned earlier? These two ... physical body and spiritual reality combine within our beings every single day! What happens to us when we attend a funeral? We weep as we encounter the physical loss of that person! However, we also start thinking about our own death — the spiritual encounter! There are no atheists in fox holes — and all that! We are made to be spiritual. The reality of spirituality exists within us! It exists because a Creative individual gave us this capacity and placed into our psyche the trail of bread crumbs to reconnect the spiritual part of us to Himself! I guess we kick against this idea, because we would have to implement something which do not come naturally to us ... faith! To believe that God loves me, wants to be involved in my life and is currently investing in my earthly and non-material future ... is going to require an element of faith and implementing faith means that we hand the controls of who we are over to someone else — namely God! The problem for many of us is this — faith is simply a step into the unknown or something which we are not prepared to implement! Handing the controls of our lives over to someone else may be considered to be personal suicide but herein lies the problem — how can we control our eternal destiny when we are finite beings? How can we personally control our eternal destiny when we cannot even control what happens to us or our loved ones the minute we leave the front door in the morning? The truth is, we cannot! We have no control over today, let alone the next day, let alone the next year, let alone the future.

Our bodies are finite — they have a 'sell by date'. However, the part of us which makes us individuals — the non-material emotions, our personality, our souls — whatever term we give to it, is not! God has placed within our bodies, a blueprint which seeks love, care, companionship, feeling, the ability to be different to the animal, the capacity to desire, the ability to worship and so on. These intrinsic qualities do not come easy to us, for our base instinct is not to love or do good but completely the opposite! We do not desire to worship or give credit for who we are to someone else ... for our gut instinct is self-promotion, selfishness, me, what I want, etc. However, this Godly blue print gives us the capacity to find another meaning in life other than selfishness or simply making our way from the cradle to the grave! He builds within us a desire to reflect upon who we are as people. We therefore encounter moments when the blue-print is activated by loss, or by observing something which affects our emotion and when activated, it shouts loudly within us — "THERE

IS SOMETHING MORE TO THIS LIFE!" In that moment when our physical eyes observe the beauty around us, the blue-print activates our 'spiritual eyes' and reminds us that there is so much more to life than living and dying ... and everything in between. The spiritual part inside us reminds us that we are simply on a journey to somewhere else, something else, to someone else ... to the individual who placed us as individuals into this very moment in history ... God!

What does He want from us? What is His desire for us? The answer to that question is found in the mirror! When we look into the mirror of our lives, are we brave enough to recognise that our lives are not our own? Are we brave enough to admit that we are not in control of today, let alone the future? Are we brave enough to admit that as people we are innately self-ish? If there is a recognition of these traits within us — if we recognise the 'dark side' in the eyes looking back at us, then I guarantee you that very slowly another pair of eyes will start looking back at you — your spiritual self, your true self! Those eyes will initiate within you a sense of shame, a sense of guilt, a sense of emotion which will develop into a cry — a cry for help, a craving so deep that it will drive you to the realisation that God exists, that He sent us Jesus to show us the true meaning to life, to show us that we really need Him!

I am what I am today because God has bestowed upon me grace upon grace, goodness upon goodness, blessing upon blessing ... and some of you who know me can testify that I deserve none of these things! In the eyes of my contemporaries I have 'achieved' personally and professionally, but have I really? You see at some stage I will lose all I currently have — house, cars, friends, family, health, status, etc. At some stage death will rob me of all of these! Why then am I working so hard to accumulate material things which I am going to lose anyway? Inevitably therefore I am experiencing a 'temporary achievement' of sorts, a temporary arrangement which pretty soon I am destined to lose. Fact! No wonder the Apostle Paul speaks about the 'crown', the 'prize', an inheritance which is 'incorruptible', that which is not temporary, namely eternity! You see at the end of the day I am simply a transient member of the human race — I arrive and I will leave seventy plus years later if I'm blessed to live that long. I come from and go back to the creative source who gave me the potential to be like Himself — God! Soon, I will just be a memory to some, a grave-stone to others and a lost loved-one to my family. I will pass from this life pretty soon and what do I have to show for it — a house, cars, money, status? Is that it?

I have no issue as to what you choose to call this deity to whom we must one day all give account. In English we call him "God" but you may call Him something else. It doesn't matter to me and I don't think it matters to Him either. Some Christians state that there is a prescribed way of getting to know this deity. However, God is non-prescriptive in His being, for He deals with us as communities but also as individuals. What is prescribed in the Scriptures are the standards and values He wants us to adhere to and for the majority of those laws they are there for our own good. However, God alone sees into people's hearts and He alone knows if we have acknowledged his authority over us individually. I love the phrase 'status changer' when we talk about God, for this is exactly what He comes to do when He rescues us — He changes our status from being outcasts to being His sons and daughters!

Eternity is what my life is all about as I look at myself in the mirror. I have long stopped caring about what people think and how they think I should live as a Jesus-follower. I am responsible for my own life and I alone must answer the question as to my own destiny. Within that mirror, I must look beyond the façade of life and ask myself the questions concerning the status of my own soul and be brave enough to listen to the answers which follow.

What about you? Hopefully my life's journey gives you some idea that from the day I was born, God was preparing me for life after this planet — the people I met, the opportunities I received, the lessons learnt, the spiritual realities encountered, the mistakes I made, the sin I embarked upon with open eyes, etc. This too is you! God's claim on my life is also the story of your life. You see, try as you may, you cannot escape the reality of who God is — you simply cannot. There were times in my life — particularly the three years after dad's death that I did everything I could to silence the spiritual voice within me. My friend, I could not and neither can you. God has a plan to call you to Himself! He will pursue you for one reason only — because He loves you! Take note, I have very rarely mentioned church in these pages because eternity is not about church! Eternity is about relationship — a relationship with the divine! My own life is a testimony to that! Every single day I have to fight the filth within me, the filth within my head, the desires to want my own way, the drive for selfishness — and every single day driving to school I have no choice but to call upon God for the strength to live right — to bite my tongue when a pupil is being rude to me, the ability to be patient with my colleagues, to see the best in others when they display behaviour to the contrary — I seek God, daily! You have no need to point the finger of blame, shame and guilt at me — you have no need to remind me of my past and the things I have done wrong, because I see those things in the memory of my being every single day. I still too deal with personal struggles on a daily basis. Each day I am not only reminded of my own weaknesses but also of God's goodness to me. I am a fifty-two-year old